Auténtico

LEVELED VOCABULARY AND GRAMMAR WORKBOOK

3

GUIDED PRACTICE

SAVVAS

LEARNING COMPANY

Table of Contents

Dear Parents and Guardians:

Learning a second language can be both exciting and fun. As your child studies Spanish, he or she will not only learn to communicate with Spanish speakers, but will also learn about their cultures and daily lives. Language learning is a building process that requires considerable time and practice, but it is one of the most rewarding things your child can learn in school.

Language learning calls on all of the senses and on many skills that are not necessarily used in other kinds of learning. Students will find their Spanish class different from other classes in a variety of ways. For instance, lectures generally play only a small role in the language classroom. Because the goal is to learn to communicate, students interact with each other and with their teacher as they learn to express themselves about things they like to do (and things they don't), their personalities, the world around them, foods, celebrations, pastimes, technology, and much more. Rather than primarily listening to the teacher, reading the text, and memorizing information as they might in a social studies class, language learners will share ideas; discuss similarities and differences between cultures; ask and answer questions; and work with others to practice new words, sounds, and sentence structures. Your child will be given a variety of tasks to do in preparation for such an interactive class. He or she will complete written activities, perform listening tasks, watch and listen to videos, and go on the Internet. In addition, to help solidify command of words and structures, time will need to be spent on learning vocabulary and practicing the language until it starts to become second nature. Many students will find that using flash cards and doing written practice will help them become confident using the building blocks of language.

To help you help your child in this endeavor, we offer the following insights into the textbook your child will be using, along with suggestions for ways that you can help build your child's motivation and confidence—and as a result, their success with learning Spanish.

Textbook Organization

Your child will be learning Spanish using *Auténtico*, which means "authentic." The emphasis throughout the text is on learning to use the language in authentic, real ways. Chapters are organized by themes such as school and non-school activities; art and artists; health, physical fitness, and nutrition, etc. Each chapter begins with **Vocabulario en contexto**, which gives an initial presentation of new grammar and vocabulary in the form of pictures, short dialogues, and audio recordings. Students then watch the new vocabulary and grammar used in an authentic context in an engaging video in the **Videohistoria**. Once students have been exposed to the new language, the **Vocabulario en uso** and **Gramática y vocabulario en uso** sections offer lots of practice with the language as well as explanations of how the language works. The **Lectura, Puente a la cultura, Presentación oral**, and **Presentación escrita** sections provide activities for your child to use the language by understanding readings, giving oral or written presentations, and learning more about the cultural perspectives of Spanish speakers. The **Auténtico** section offers your child a chance to see how the language they have learned is used by native speakers in an authentic context such as a news report, talk show, or podcast. Finally, all chapters conclude with an at-a-glance review of the chapter material called **Repaso del capítulo** (*Chapter Review*), with summary lists and charts, and practice activities like those on the chapter test. If students have trouble with a given task, the **Repaso del capítulo** tells them where in the chapter they can go to review.

Here are some suggestions that will help your child become a successful language learner.

Routine:
Provide a special, quiet place for study, equipped with a Spanish-English dictionary, pens or pencils, paper, computer, and any other items your child's teacher suggests.

- Encourage your child to study Spanish at a regular time every day. A study routine will greatly facilitate the learning process.

Strategy:

- Remind your child that class participation and memorization are very important in a foreign language course.
- Tell your child that in reading or listening activities, as well as in the classroom, it is not necessary to understand every word. Suggest that they listen or look for key words to get the gist of what's being communicated.
- Encourage your child to ask questions in class if he or she is confused. Remind the child that other students may have the same question. This will minimize frustration and help your child succeed.

Real-life connection:

- Outside of the regular study time, encourage your child to review words in their proper context as they relate to the chapter themes. For example, when studying the chapter about art and artists, your child can create a short biography about a favorite singer or actor/actress using the vocabulary in Chapter 2.
- Motivate your child with praise for small jobs well done, not just for big exams and final grades. A memorized vocabulary list is something to be proud of!

Review:

- Encourage your child to review previously learned material frequently, and not just before a test. Remember, learning a language is a building process, and it is important to keep using what you've already learned.
- To aid vocabulary memorization, suggest that your child try several different methods, such as saying words aloud while looking at a picture of the items, writing the words, acting them out while saying them, and so on.
- Suggest that your child organize new material using charts, graphs, pictures with labels, or other visuals that can be posted in the study area. A daily review of those visuals will help keep the material fresh.
- Help your child drill new vocabulary and grammar by using the charts and lists in the textbook.

Resources:

- Offer to help frequently! Your child may have great ideas for how you can facilitate his or her learning experience.
- Ask your child's teacher, or encourage your child to ask, about how to best prepare for and what to expect on tests and quizzes.
- Ask your child's teacher about access to the eText and the digital course on Savvas Realize. These digital tools provide access to audio recordings and videos that support the text. The more your child sees and hears the language, the greater the retention.

Above all, help your child understand that a language is not acquired overnight. Just as for a first language, there is a gradual process for learning a second one. It takes time and patience, and it is important to know that mistakes are a completely natural part of the process. Remind your child that it took years to become proficient in his or her first language, and that the second one will also take time. Praise your child for even small progress in the ability to communicate in Spanish, and provide opportunities for your child to hear and use the language.

Don't hesitate to ask your child's teacher for ideas. You will find the teacher eager to help you. You may also be able to help the teacher understand special needs that your child may have, and work together with him or her to find the best techniques for helping your child learn.

Learning to speak another language is one of the most gratifying experiences a person can have. We know that your child will benefit from the effort, and will acquire a skill that will serve to enrich his or her life.

Copy the word or phrase in the space provided.

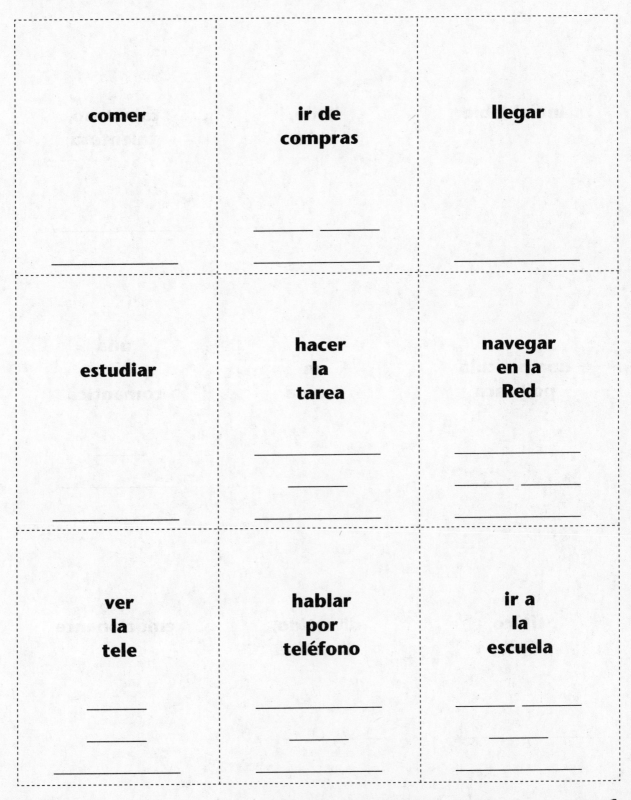

comer	ir de compras	llegar
_____	_____ _____ _____	_____

estudiar	hacer la tarea	navegar en la Red
_____	_____ _____	_____ _____ _____

ver la tele	hablar por teléfono	ir a la escuela
_____ _____	_____ _____	_____ _____ _____

Copy the word or phrase in the space provided.

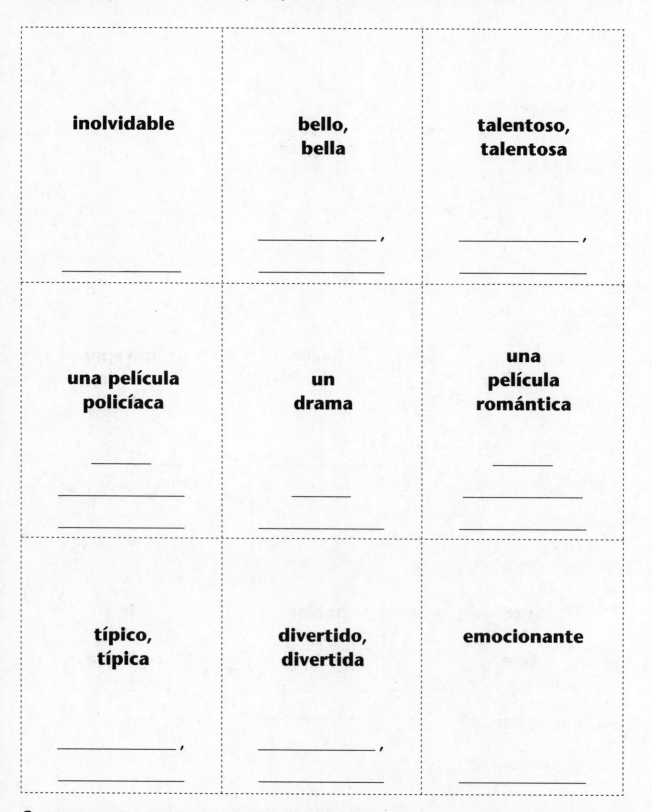

inolvidable

_____

bello,
bella

_____,

_____

talentoso,
talentosa

_____,

_____

una película
policíaca

_____

_____

un
drama

_____

una
película
romántica

_____

_____

típico,
típica

_____,

_____

divertido,
divertida

_____,

_____

emocionante

_____

Tear out this page. Write the English words on the lines. Fold the paper along the dotted line to see the correct answers so you can check your work.

comer _____

estudiar _____

hablar por teléfono _____

hacer la tarea _____

ir de compras _____

llegar _____

navegar en la Red _____

practicar deportes _____

tener una cita _____

ver la tele _____

típico, típica _____

divertido, divertida _____

emocionante _____

exagerado, exagerada _____

inolvidable _____

un drama _____

una película de horror _____

una película policíaca _____

una película romántica _____

Fold In ←

Tear out this page. Write the Spanish words on the lines. Fold the paper along the dotted line to see the correct answers so you can check your work.

to eat _____

to study _____

to talk on the phone _____

to do homework _____

to go shopping _____

to arrive _____

to surf the Web _____

to play sports _____

to have a date _____

to watch TV _____

typical _____

fun _____

touching _____

exaggerated _____

unforgettable _____

a drama _____

a horror movie _____

a police movie _____

a romance (movie) _____

Fold In

Para empezar

Verbos irregulares (p. 3)

- Remember that some verbs in Spanish have irregular **yo** forms. Look at the following list of common verbs that are irregular in the **yo** form only—the other forms of these verbs follow the regular conjugation rules.

dar: **doy**	poner: pon**go**	saber: **sé**
salir: sal**go**	caer: cai**go**	conocer: cono**zco**
traer: trai**go**	hacer: ha**go**	ver: **veo**

- Other verbs you have learned with irregular **yo** forms include **obedecer**, **ofrecer** and **parecer**, which are conjugated like **conocer**.

A. Answer each question by writing the irregular **yo** form of the verb given.

Modelo   ¿Sabes esquiar? Sí, (yo) _____*sé*_____ esquiar muy bien.

1. ¿Haces la tarea siempre? Sí, _____ la tarea todos los días.

2. ¿Dónde pones tus libros? _____ mis libros en mi mochila.

3. ¿Le das la tarea a la maestra? Sí, le _____ la tarea siempre.

4. ¿Traes tu libro de texto a casa? Sí, _____ mi libro a casa para estudiar.

5. ¿Ves la foto de José y María? Sí, _____ la foto. Es muy bonita.

6. ¿Obedeces a tus padres? Sí, siempre _____ a mis padres.

7. ¿Conoces a alguna persona famosa? Sí, (yo) _____ a Enrique Iglesias.

- Other verbs are irregular not only in the **yo** form but in all the forms. Look at the following list of important verbs that are irregular in all forms of the present tense.

ser		ir		decir	
soy	somos	voy	vamos	digo	decimos
eres	sois	vas	vais	dices	decís
es	son	va	van	dice	dicen

estar		oír		tener		venir	
estoy	estamos	oigo	oímos	tengo	tenemos	vengo	venimos
estás	estáis	oyes	oís	tienes	tenéis	vienes	venís
está	están	oye	oyen	tiene	tienen	viene	vienen

Verbos irregulares (continued)

B. Complete the following sentences with the correct forms of the verbs in parentheses. Follow the model.

Modelo (**salir**) María _____*sale*_____ a las 7.30 pero yo _____*salgo*_____ a las 8.

1. (**ir**)   Yo _____ a mi casa después de mis clases pero mis amigos _____ al gimnasio.

2. (**tener**) Mi padre _____ cuarenta y cinco años, pero yo _____ diecisiete.

3. (**saber**) Nosotros _____ que hay un examen mañana, pero yo no _____ si va a ser difícil.

4. (**decir**) José _____ que la clase de química es aburrida, pero yo _____ que es muy interesante.

5. (**traer**) Yo _____ mis libros de texto a casa cada noche, pero mi mamá _____ muchos papeles de su trabajo.

C. Write complete sentences to describe what happens in a Spanish class. Follow the model.

Modelo   Los estudiantes / tener / un examen / el viernes
            *Los estudiantes tienen un examen el viernes*.

1. Yo / saber / todas las respuestas del examen

    _____

2. Javier / ser / un estudiante muy serio

    _____

3. Nosotros / salir / de la clase / a las once

    _____

4. Yo / oír / una canción / en español

    _____

5. Ellas / conocer / a unos estudiantes de Puerto Rico

    _____

Presente de los verbos con cambio de raíz (p. 5)

- Remember that, in the present tense, stem-changing verbs have stem changes in all forms <u>except</u> the **nosotros/nosotras** and **vosotros/vosotras** forms.

- The types of stem changes are: O➡UE, U➡UE, E➡IE, and E➡I. Look at the chart below to see how **volver** (*ue*), **pensar** (*ie*), and **servir** (*i*) are conjugated. Their stem changes have been underlined:

volver		pensar		servir	
v<u>ue</u>lvo	volvemos	p<u>ie</u>nso	pensamos	s<u>i</u>rvo	servimos
v<u>ue</u>lves	volvéis	p<u>ie</u>nsas	pensáis	s<u>i</u>rves	servís
v<u>ue</u>lve	v<u>ue</u>lven	p<u>ie</u>nsa	p<u>ie</u>nsan	s<u>i</u>rve	s<u>i</u>rven

- Here is a list of common verbs with each type of stem change:

  O➡UE   poder, dormir, morir, volver, devolver, almorzar, recordar, encontrar, contar, costar, acostarse

  U➡UE   jugar

  E➡IE   perder, empezar, querer, preferir, pensar, divertirse, despertarse, sentirse, mentir, cerrar, comenzar, entender

  E➡I   pedir, servir, repetir, reír, sonreír, seguir, vestirse

A. Complete the sentences about Santiago's activities using the verbs in parentheses. Follow the model.

Modelo   (**despertarse**) Santiago *se despierta* muy temprano porque es un chico activo.

1. (**querer**)   Santiago _____ leer el periódico antes de salir para la escuela.

2. (**recordar**)   Santiago _____ su tarea y sus libros cuando sale.

3. (**comenzar**)   Santiago _____ su clase de francés a las ocho de la mañana.

4. (**sentarse**)   Santiago _____ cerca de la maestra para escuchar bien lo que ella dice.

5. (**pedir**)   Santiago _____ una ensalada y pollo.

6. (**volver**)   Santiago _____ a casa a las tres de la tarde.

7. (**jugar**)   y _____ un poco de fútbol con su hermano.

B. Ana is writing a letter to her pen pal. Look at the lines from her letter and underline the subject for each verb in the sentence. Then, complete the sentence with the correct forms of the verb given.

Modelo (preferir) <u>Yo</u> ___*prefiero*___ pasar tiempo con mi amiga Tere. Y <u>tú</u>, ¿con quién ___*prefieres*___ pasar tiempo?

1. **(contar)** Mis amigos y yo siempre _____ chistes. Y Uds., ¿_____ chistes?

2. **(poder)** Yo _____ hablar un poco de francés. Y tú, ¿_____ hablar otras lenguas?

3. **(almorzar)** Los otros estudiantes y yo _____ en la cafetería. Y Uds., ¿_____ en casa o en la escuela?

4. **(reír)** Mis amigos y yo _____ mucho cuando vemos películas cómicas. Y tú, ¿_____ mucho cuando vas al cine?

5. **(pensar)** Yo _____ estudiar biología en la universidad. Y tú y tus amigos, ¿qué _____ estudiar?

6. **(dormir)** Mis hermanos y yo _____ ocho horas todas las noches. Y tú, ¿_____ más de ocho horas o menos?

C. Write complete sentences to describe what the people in the sentences do for activities. Follow the model.

Modelo Este fin de semana / mis amigos y yo / querer / jugar al vóleibol.
    Este fin de semana, mis amigos y yo queremos jugar al vóleibol.

1. Nadia y Bárbara / siempre / perder / las llaves

   _____

2. La cafetería de la escuela / servir / comida saludable

   _____

3. Tú / poder / hablar ruso y jugar al ajedrez / ¿no?

   _____

4. La primera clase del día / empezar / a las ocho de la mañana

   _____

5. Yo / no entender / la tarea de matemáticas

   _____

Los verbos reflexivos (p. 7)

- Remember that reflexive verbs are usually used to talk about things people do to or for themselves. Each verb has two parts: a reflexive pronoun and a conjugated verb form.

  Look at the example of the reflexive verb **despertarse:**

despertarse	
me despierto	**nos** despertamos
te despiertas	**os** despertáis
se despierta	**se** despiertan

- Notice that the reflexive pronoun *se* is used for both the **él/ella/Ud.** and **ellos/ellas/Uds.** forms.

A. Underline the reflexive pronoun in each of the following sentences.

Modelo   Rafaela y Silvia <u>se</u> lavan el pelo por la mañana.

1. Yo <u>me</u> levanto a las nueve y media los sábados.

2. Mis amigos y yo <u>nos</u> ponemos las chaquetas cuando hace frío.

3. ¿Tú <u>te</u> cepillas los dientes después de almorzar?

4. Mi madre <u>se</u> viste con ropa elegante para la cena formal.

5. Los jugadores de béisbol van a acostar<u>se</u> temprano porque tienen un partido importante mañana.

B. Write the reflexive pronoun in each sentence to finish the descriptions of the Navarro household's daily preparations.

Modelo   El Sr. Navarro __se__ afeita antes de bañarse.

1. Laurena _se_ ducha por media hora.

2. Ramón y Nomar _se_ arreglan juntos.

3. Tú _te_ cepillas los dientes dos veces cada día.

4. La Sra. Navarro _se_ pinta las uñas por la noche.

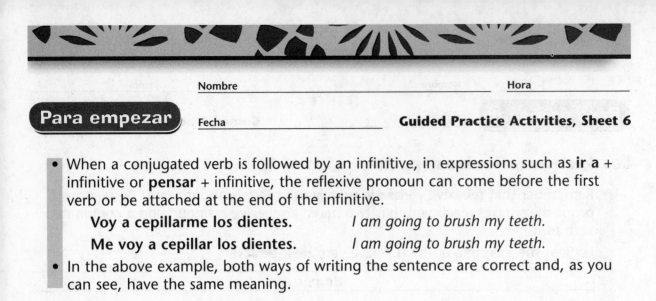

- When a conjugated verb is followed by an infinitive, in expressions such as **ir a** + infinitive or **pensar** + infinitive, the reflexive pronoun can come before the first verb or be attached at the end of the infinitive.

  Voy a cepillarme los dientes.   *I am going to brush my teeth.*

  Me voy a cepillar los dientes.   *I am going to brush my teeth.*

- In the above example, both ways of writing the sentence are correct and, as you can see, have the same meaning.

C. Complete each sentence using both ways to write the infinitive of the reflexive verbs in the box below. **¡Recuerda!** You will need to change the reflexive pronouns to fit the subject. Follow the model.

acostarse   lavarse   cepillarse   ~~secarse~~   afeitarse   ponerse

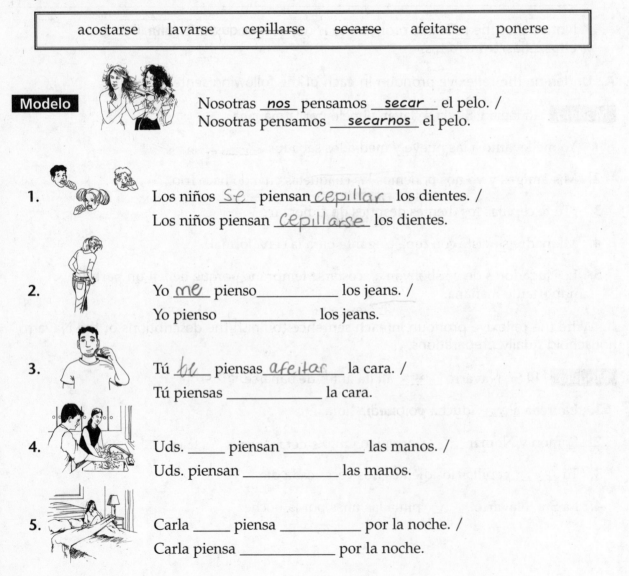

Modelo   Nosotras _*nos*_ pensamos _*secar*_ el pelo. /
Nosotras pensamos _*secarnos*_ el pelo.

1. Los niños _se_ piensan _cepillar_ los dientes. /
   Los niños piensan _cepillarse_ los dientes.

2. Yo _me_ pienso_____ los jeans. /
   Yo pienso _____ los jeans.

3. Tú _te_ piensas _afeitar_ la cara. /
   Tú piensas _____ la cara.

4. Uds. _____ piensan _____ las manos. /
   Uds. piensan _____ las manos.

5. Carla _____ piensa _____ por la noche. /
   Carla piensa _____ por la noche.

Verbos que se conjugan como gustar (p. 11)

- Remember that the verb **gustar** is conjugated a bit differently from most other verbs in Spanish. In sentences with **gustar**, the subject of the sentence is the thing or things that are liked. In the present tense, we use **gusta** before the thing that is liked (singular noun or infinitive) and **gustan** before the things that are liked (plural noun). For example:

    Me gusta el vóleibol.   *I like volleyball.*
    Me gustan los deportes.   *I like sports.*

  To show *who* likes the thing or things mentioned you place an *indirect object pronoun* before the form of **gustar**:

me gusta(n)	*I like*	**nos** gusta(n)	*we like*
te gusta(n)	*you like*	**os** gusta(n)	*you all (informal) like*
le gusta(n)	*he/she/you (formal) likes*	**les** gusta(n)	*they/you all like*

A. Complete the following sentences with the correct indirect object pronoun.

Modelo A mis padres ___*les*___ gustan las notas buenas en la escuela.

1. A mí __me__ gusta el fútbol americano.

2. A nosotros __nos__ gustan las ciencias, como la biología y la física.

3. A Manuel __le__ gusta el chocolate; ¡es delicioso!

4. A ella __le__ gusta la familia y por eso visita a su abuela con frecuencia.

5. ¿A ti __te__ gustan los animales como los perros y los gatos?

6. A Uds. __les__ gusta el programa nuevo en la televisión.

B. Now look back at the sentences in exercise A. Each verb ends in **-a** or **-an**. Draw a box around these endings. Then, circle the noun in the sentence that determines whether the verb is singular or plural.

Modelo A mis padres ___*les*___ gustan las notas buenas en la escuela.

Verbos que se conjugan como *gustar* (*continued*)

- There are several other verbs that work like **gustar**. Some important ones are:

  importar *to matter*   **encantar** *to love*   **interesar** *to interest*

  Al director le importan las reglas.   *The rules are important to the principal.*
  A mí me encanta comer helado.   *I love to eat ice cream.*
  A Jennifer le interesa la música.   *Jennifer is interested in music.*

C. Find the subject in each of the following sentences and underline it. Then, use the subject you underlined to help you determine the correct form of the verb. Circle your choice. Follow the model.

Modelo   A mí me ((encantan) / encanta) <u>las telenovelas</u>.

1. A Carolina Herrera le (interesan / (interesa)) <u>la ropa</u>.

2. A ti te ((importan) / importa) reunirte con amigos.

3. A Pablo le ((encantan) / encanta) <u>las fiestas de verano</u>.

4. A Uds. les (importan / (importa)) el béisbol.

D. Complete each sentence with the correct indirect object pronoun on the first line and the correct form of the verb in parentheses on the second line.

Modelo   A ti __te__ __encanta__ (encantar) la música folklórica.

1. A nosotros _nos_ _interesan_ (interesar) los artículos del periódico.

2. A ellas _les_ _importa_ (importar) la política.

3. A mí _me_ _gustan_ (gustar) los refrescos de frutas.

4. A Joaquín _le_ _interesa_ (interesar) la historia europea.

5. A nosotras _nos_ _encanta_ (encantar) la nueva canción de Shakira.

6. A los estudiantes _les_ _importan_ (importar) las tareas para sus clases.

7. ¿A ti _te_ _gusta_ (gustar) la comida de la cafetería?

8. A mi hermano _les_ _encantan_ (encantar) los deportes.

9. A nosotros _nos_ _interesa_ (interesar) ir al cine.

10. A Uds. _les_ _encanta_ (encantar) hablar por teléfono.

Para empezar   Fecha _____

Adjetivos posesivos (p. 12)

- Possessive adjectives describe an object by indicating who owns it. Remember that in Spanish, the possessive adjectives agree in number with the object being possessed, not with the person who owns it. For example:

    Mis clase de español es divertida.   *My Spanish class is fun.*
    Mis clases de español son divertidas.   *My Spanish classes are fun.*

- The following possessive adjectives are used in Spanish. Note that the **nosotros** and **vosotros** adjectives must also agree in gender (feminine or masculine) with the item possessed.

mi/mis *my*	**nuestro/nuestra/nuestros/nuestras** *our*
tu/tus *your (informal)*	**vuestro/vuestra/vuestros/vuestras** *your (group-informal)*
su/sus *his/her/your (formal)*	**su/sus** *their/your (group)*

A. In the following sentences a line is drawn under the item possessed to help you determine the correct possessive adjective. Circle one of the two options. Follow the model.

Modelo   Quiero ir al partido de básquetbol con (mi /(mis)) amigos esta noche.

1. Consuelo necesita traer ((su)/ sus) libro de texto a clase.

2. Nosotros vamos a (nuestra /(nuestras)) casas después de la escuela.

3. Enrique y Sara van a preparar ((su)/ sus) cena ahora.

4. ¿Tú tienes ((tu)/ tus) sombrero y (tu /(tus)) guantes?

5. Mi papá prefiere leer (su /(sus)) revistas en el sofá.

6. ¿Cuándo es ((nuestro)/ nuestros) examen de español?

7. (Mi /(Mis)) clases comienzan a las ocho y media de la mañana.

B. Read each possessive statement below. Then, write the corresponding possessive adjective in the second sentence. Follow the model.

Modelo   Es la mochila de Alicia. Es ___su___ mochila.

1. Son las tijeras de nosotros. Son __nuestras__ tijeras.

2. Son los gatos de la Sra. Barbosa. Son ____sus____ gatos.

3. Es el televisor de Pilar. Es ____su____ televisor.

4. Son los libros de nosotras. Son __nuestros__ libros.

Para empezar

C. Complete the following conversation between two people at a party with the correct possessive adjectives from the box. You will use each possessive adjective only once.

nuestros	~~mi~~	~~mis~~	~~tu~~	~~su~~	~~sus~~

Modelo **Teresa:** Las botas de Luisa son bonitas, ¿no?

Sonia: Sí, _____*sus*_____ botas son muy elegantes.

Teresa: Esta fiesta es fantástica. La mamá de Raúl prepara unas comidas muy sabrosas, ¿no?

Sonia: Sí, me encanta ___*mi*___ tortilla española. ¿Tus padres saben cocinar algo especial?

Teresa: Sí, ___*mis*___ padre sabe preparar unas enchiladas fenomenales, pero siempre tiene que preparar muchas porque tengo cinco hermanos y ___*su*___ hermanos pueden comerse un millón de enchiladas.

Sonia: ¡___*tu*___ familia es muy grande! Sólo tengo una hermana. En nuestra casa, mi hermana y yo preparamos la comida los fines de semana y ___*nuestros*___ padres la preparan durante la semana. Es una buena costumbre.

D. You need to answer some questions from an exchange student at your school. In the first blank, fill in the appropriate possessive adjective. In the second blank, finish the sentence so that it is true for you.

Modelo ¿A qué hora empieza tu clase de español?

_____*Mi*_____ clase de español empieza a _____*las dos*_____.

1. ¿Cuáles son tus clases favoritas?

_____*Mis*_____ clases favoritas son ___*español*___.

2. ¿Cuál es el nombre de tu profesor(a) de español?

_____*Su*_____ nombre es ___*Sra. Smith*___.

3. Tú y tus amigos escuchan música interesante. ¿Cuál es su grupo favorito?

___*Nuestra*___ grupo favorito es ___*backstreet boys*___.

4. ¿En qué ciudad vive tu familia?

_____*Mi*_____ familia vive en ___*Jacksonville*___.

5. ¿Cuáles son las comidas favoritas de tu mejor amigo/a?

_____*Su*_____ comidas favoritas son ___*pizza*___.

6. Tú y tus amigos hacen muchas actividades divertidas. ¿Cuál es su actividad favorita?

_____*Su*_____ actividad favorita es ___*fútbol*___.

El pretérito de los verbos (p. 17)

• Remember that the preterite is used to talk about past events. To conjugate regular **-ar**, **-er**, and **-ir** verbs in the preterite, use the following endings:

cantar		beber		salir	
canté	cantamos	bebí	bebimos	salí	salimos
cantaste	cantasteis	bebiste	bebisteis	saliste	salisteis
cantó	cantaron	bebió	bebieron	salió	salieron

A. Complete the sentences about what students did last summer with the correct preterite endings of each **-ar** verb. Pay attention to the regular endings in the chart above and to the accent marks.

Modelo   (**nadar**) Marcos y Raúl nad _aron_ ___ en el lago.

1. (**caminar**)   Yo camin _é_ ___ por la playa.

2. (**montar**)   Tú mont _aste_ ___ a caballo en las montañas.

3. (**pasear**)   Mis primos pase _aron_ ___ en bicicleta.

4. (**tomar**)   Nosotros tom _amos_ ___ el sol en la playa.

5. (**usar**)   Esteban us _ó_ ___ la computadora.

B. Complete the sentences by writing the correct preterite form of each **-er** or **-ir** verb. Follow the model. Pay attention to the regular endings and accent marks in the chart above.

Modelo   (**aprender**) Marta __aprendió__ un poco de francés antes de ir a París.

1. (**comer**)   Nosotros _comimos_ helado de fresa.

2. (**decidir**)   Ellos _decidieron_ visitar Puerto Rico.

3. (**correr**)   Yo _corrí_ ___ por el río con mi padre.

4. (**escribir**)   Tú me _escribiste_ una carta el mes pasado.

5. (**abrir**)   Mamá _abrió_ ___ la ventana.

- Some verbs have irregular conjugations in the preterite. Three of them, **hacer, dar,** and **ver**, are conjugated below:

hacer		**dar**		**ver**	
hice	hicimos	di	dimos	vi	vimos
hiciste	hicisteis	diste	disteis	viste	visteis
hizo	hicieron	dio	dieron	vio	vieron

- Note that unlike the regular preterite conjugations, these conjugations do <u>not</u> have written accent marks.

C. Complete each sentence with the correct form of the irregular preterite verb. Remember that these verb forms do not use written accent marks.

> **Modelo**   (dar)   Nosotros ____*dimos*____ una caminata por las montañas.

1. **(ver)**   Yo _vi_____ unos animales exóticos en el bosque.
2. **(hacer)**   Mis hermanos _hicieron_ camping una noche.
3. **(ver)**   ¿Tú _viste_____ unas flores bonitas?
4. **(dar)**   Mi hermana y yo _dimos____ un paseo por la playa.
5. **(hacer)**   La familia _hizo_____ muchas cosas divertidas.

D. First, circle the verb. If it is regular in the preterite tense, write **R**. If it is irregular in the preterite tense, write **I**. Then, use the preterite to write complete sentences about activities people did in the past. Follow the model.

> **Modelo**   __I__ Mis primos / (hacer) surf de vela / el verano pasado
> _Mis primos hicieron surf de vela el verano pasado._

1. __R__ Yo / (montar) en bicicleta / el fin de semana pasado
   Yo monté en bicicleta el fin de semana pasado

2. __I__ Nosotros / (dar) una caminata por el parque / anoche
   Nosotros dimos una caminata por el parque anoche

3. __R__ Mis amigos / (comer) en un restaurante / el martes pasado
   Mis amigos comieron en un resturante el martes pasado

4. __I__ Tú / (ver) una película / hace dos semanas
   Tú viste una película hace dos semanas

5. __I__ Mi mejor amigo y yo / (hacer) una parrillada / el mes pasado
   Mi mejor amigo y yo hicimos una parrillada el mes pasado

El pretérito de los verbos *ir* y *ser* (p. 19)

- The verbs **ir** and **ser** have the same conjugations in the preterite. You need to use context to determine whether the verb means *went* (**ir**) or *was/were* (**ser**). Look at the conjugations below:

ir		ser	
fui	fuimos	fui	fuimos
fuiste	fuisteis	fuiste	fuisteis
fue	fueron	fue	fueron

A. Determine whether **ir** or **ser** is used in the following sentences by indicating the meaning of the underlined preterite verb.

Modelo   Nosotras <u>fuimos</u> a la biblioteca para estudiar.

☑ went (**ir**)   ☐ were (**ser**)

1. La clase <u>fue</u> muy interesante.

    ☐ went (**ir**)   ☑ was (**ser**)

2. Las jugadoras <u>fueron</u> al estadio para competir.

    ☑ went (**ir**)   ☐ were (**ser**)

3. Los equipos de fútbol <u>fueron</u> excelentes.

    ☐ went (**ir**)   ☑ were (**ser**)

4. Yo <u>fui</u> al parque ayer para montar en monopatín.

    ☑ went (**ir**)   ☐ was (**ser**)

B. Read each sentence and decide if **ir** or **ser** is needed. Underline the correct infinitive. Then, write the correct preterite form in the blank.

Modelo   (<u>ir</u> / ser) Pablo ____*fue*____ a la playa con sus amigos.

1. (<u>ir</u> / ser)   Nosotros __*fuimos*__ al gimnasio para hacer ejercicio.

2. (ir / <u>ser</u>)   Los partidos de béisbol __*fueron*__ muy divertidos.

3. (<u>ir</u> / ser)   Yo __*fui*__ al centro comercial el fin de semana pasado.

4. (ir / <u>ser</u>)   Ellos __*fueron*__ los estudiantes más serios de la clase.

5. (ir / <u>ser</u>)   Benito se rompió el brazo. __*fue*__ un accidente terrible.

6. (<u>ir</u> / ser)   ¿Adónde __*fuiste*__ (tú) ayer?

El pretérito de los verbos que terminan in -car, -gar y -zar (p. 19)

- Remember that some verbs have spelling changes in the **yo** forms of the preterite to preserve the correct pronunciation. Look at the chart below to see how verbs that end in **-car**, **-gar**, and **-zar** change spelling in the preterite.
- Note that the other forms of the verb are conjugated normally:

tocar		llegar		empezar	
to**qué**	tocaste	lle**gué**	llegamos	empe**cé**	empezamos
tocaste	tocasteis	llegaste	llegasteis	empezaste	empezasteis
tocó	tocaron	llegó	llegaron	empezó	empezaron

C. First, look at the infinitives below and underline the ending (**-car**, **-gar**, or **-zar**) in each. Then, conjugate each verb in the preterite tense for the forms provided. Notice that the first column has the **yo** form. Remember that only the **yo** forms have a spelling change!

Modelo   bus<u>car</u>   yo bus_qué_   él bus_có_

1. jugar   yo ju_gué_   nosotros ju_gamos_

2. navegar   yo nave_gué_   él nave_gó_

3. sacar   yo sa_qué_   Uds. sa_caron_

4. almorzar   yo almor_cé_   nosotros almor_zamos_

5. investigar   yo investi_gué_   ella investi_egó_

6. cruzar   yo cru_cé_   los niños cru_zaron_

D. Complete the following paragraph about Carmen's activities last week by conjugating the verbs in the preterite. The first one has been done for you.

La semana pasada, mis amigas, Julia y Cristina, y yo ____fuimos____ (ir) al gimnasio.

Nosotras _hicimos_ (hacer) mucho ejercicio. Yo _corrí_ (correr) y mis amigas

nadaron (nadar) en la piscina. Después yo _practiqué_ (practicar) baloncesto

y ellas _dieron_ (dar) una caminata por un parque que está cerca del gimnasio.

Yo _llegué_ (llegar) a mi casa a las cinco y media y _comencé_ (comenzar) a

hacer mi tarea. Mi papá _preparó_ (preparar) la cena y después mis padres

vieron (ver) una película y yo _jugamos_ (jugar) unos videojuegos. Y tú,

¿qué _hiciste_ (hacer)?

Write the Spanish vocabulary word or phrase below each picture. Be sure to include the article for each noun.

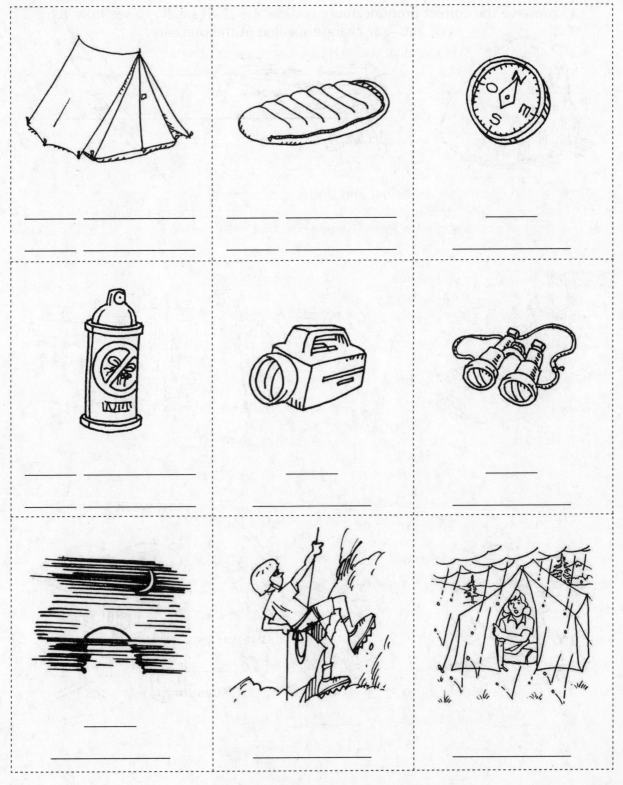

Write the Spanish vocabulary word or phrase below each picture. Be sure to include the article for each noun.

Copy the word or phrase in the space provided. Be sure to include the article for each noun.

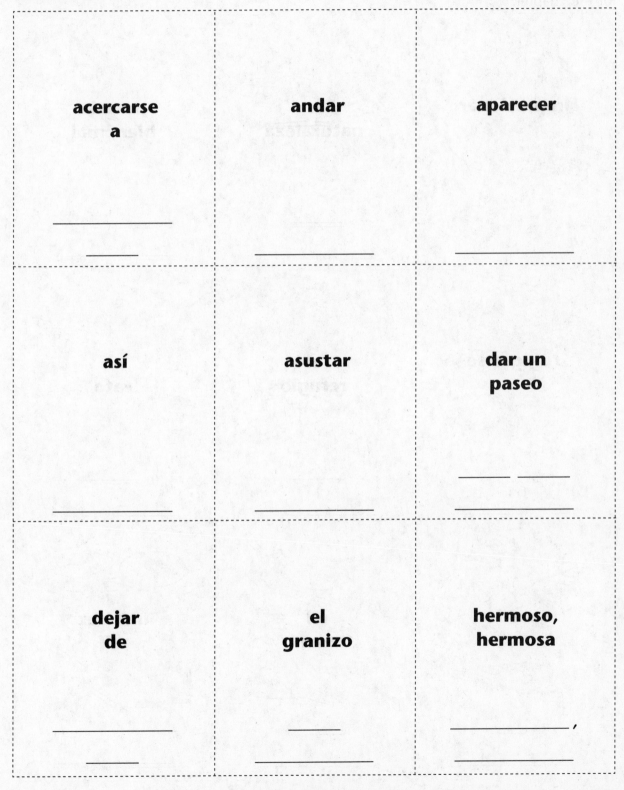

acercarse a	**andar**	**aparecer**
así	**asustar**	**dar un paseo**
dejar de	**el granizo**	**hermoso, hermosa**

Copy the word or phrase in the space provided. Be sure to include the article for each noun. The blank cards can be used to write and practice other Spanish vocabulary for the chapter.

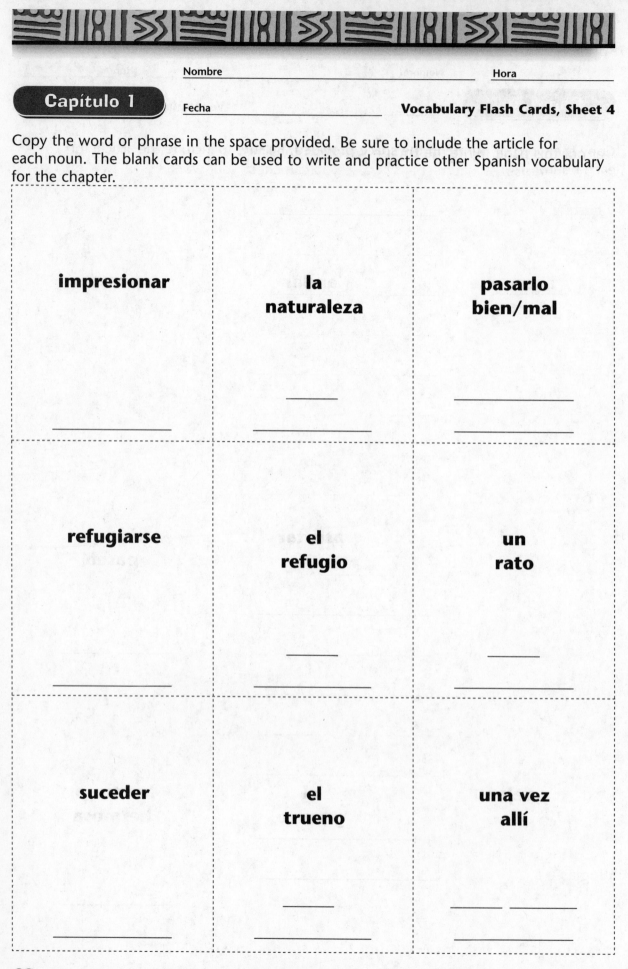

impresionar	la naturaleza	pasarlo bien/mal
refugiarse	el refugio	un rato
suceder	el trueno	una vez allí

Tear out this page. Write the English words on the lines. Fold the paper along the dotted line to see the correct answers so you can check your work.

el bosque _____

el desierto _____

hermoso, hermosa _____

la naturaleza _____

el paisaje _____

el refugio _____

la roca _____

la sierra _____

el valle _____

acercarse (a) _____

andar _____

asustar _____

dar un paseo _____

dejar de _____

escalar _____

perderse _____

refugiarse _____

Fold In

Tear out this page. Write the Spanish words on the lines. Fold the paper along the dotted line to see the correct answers so you can check your work.

wood, forest _____

desert _____

beautiful _____

nature _____

landscape _____

refuge, shelter _____

rock _____

sierra, mountain range _____

valley _____

to approach _____

to walk, to move _____

to scare _____

to take a walk, to stroll _____

to stop (doing something) _____

to climb (a rock or mountain) _____

to get lost _____

to take shelter _____

Fold In →

Tear out this page. Write the English words on the lines. Fold the paper along the dotted line to see the correct answers so you can check your work.

los binoculares   _____

la brújula   _____

la linterna   _____

el repelente de insectos _____

el saco de dormir   _____

la tienda de acampar   _____

caer granizo   _____

el granizo   _____

el relámpago   _____

el trueno   _____

suceder   _____

tener lugar   _____

al amanecer   _____

al anochecer   _____

Fold In →

Tear out this page. Write the Spanish words on the lines. Fold the paper along the dotted line to see the correct answers so you can check your work.

binoculars _____

compass _____

flashlight _____

insect repellent _____

sleeping bag _____

tent _____

to hail _____

hail _____

lightning _____

thunder _____

to occur _____

to take place _____

at dawn _____

at dusk _____

Fold In ←

El pretérito de los verbos con el cambio ortográfico i→y (p. 30)

- Remember that verbs ending in **-uir**, such as the verb **construir**, have a spelling change in the preterite. The **i** from the **él/ella/Ud.** and the **ellos/ellas/Uds.** forms becomes a **y**. Other verbs, such as **oír** and **creer**, also have this change. Look at the verbs **creer** and **construir** below as examples:

creer		construir	
creí	creímos	construí	construimos
creíste	creísteis	construiste	construisteis
creyó	cre**yeron**	construyó	constru**yeron**

A. The events below took place in the past. Circle the correct preterite form to complete each sentence.

Modelo   La semana pasada, Ernesto (lee /(leyó)) un libro sobre los bosques tropicales.

1. Recientemente unas tormentas violentas (**destruyeron** / **destruyen**) gran parte de un bosque.

2. ¿Tú (**oyes** /(**oíste**))algo sobre ese evento desastroso?

3. Ernesto y sus amigos ((**leyeron**)/ **leen**) algo sobre el paisaje hermoso del bosque.

4. Nosotros ((**creímos** / **creemos**) que esa parte del mundo era interesante.

5. Rafael ((**oyó**)/ **oye**) un anuncio sobre un viaje a los bosques de Chile.

6. Cuando nosotros fuimos al bosque, yo (**me caigo** /(**me caí**)) pero no me lastimé.

B. Complete the preterite verb forms by adding the correct endings.

Modelo   (creer) Mari y Toni cre_**yeron**_

1. (**destruir**) el oso destru_yeron_   5. (**caerse**)   ellos se ca_yeron_

2. (**leer**)   yo le_í_   6. (**leer**)   mi madre le_yó_

3. (**creer**)   nosotros cre_ímos_   7. (**oír**)   el oso o_yó_

4. (**oír**)   tú o_íste_   8. (**caerse**) nosotros nos ca_ímos_

El pretérito de los verbos con el cambio ortográfico i→y (*continued*)

C. Complete each sentence with the preterite forms of the verb in parentheses. Each sentence has two different forms of the same verb.

Modelo (destruir) El granizo ___destruyó___ las flores y los relámpagos ___destruyeron___ varios árboles.

1. (leer) Nosotros ___leímos___ el mismo mapa que ustedes ___leyeron___ cuando pasaron por aquí hace diez años.

2. (oír) Mis padres ___oyeron___ el trueno. Luego, yo lo ___oí___ también.

3. (caerse) Andrés ___se cayó___ cuando bajó del coche y sus amigos ___se caeyeron___ cuando salieron de la tienda de acampar.

4. (construir) Ayer, yo ___construí___ un edificio de bloques para mi sobrino y después, él ___construyo___ su propio edificio de bloques.

D. Write complete sentences using the preterite of the indicated verbs. Follow the model.

Modelo Los vecinos / no / **oír** / nada / sobre el accidente
___Los vecinos no oyeron nada sobre el accidente.___

1. Ellos / **leer** / las instrucciones para usar la brújula

   ___Ellos leyeron las instrucciones para usar la brújula___

2. Tú / **creer** / que / la tormenta / fue muy peligrosa

   ___Tú creíste que la tormenta fue muy peligrosa___

3. Los relámpagos / **destruir** / los árboles del bosque

   ___Los relámpagos destruyeron los árboles del bosque___

4. Nosotros / **oír** / el sonido del granizo cayendo

   ___Nosotros oímos el sonido del granizo cayendo___

5. Yo / **leer** / una novela al anochecer

   ___Yo leí una novela al anochecer___

Capítulo 1

Fecha _____

El pretérito de los verbos irregulares (p. 31)

- Several verbs have irregular stems in the preterite. Look at the chart below.

Verb	Stem	Verb	Stem
tener	tuv...	poner	pus...
estar	estuv...	saber	sup...
andar	anduv...	venir	vin...
poder	pud...		

- The irregular verbs share the same endings. The verbs **tener** and **saber** have been conjugated for you as examples.

tener		**saber**	
tuve	tuv**imos**	supe	sup**imos**
tuv**iste**	tuv**isteis**	sup**iste**	sup**isteis**
tuv**o**	tuv**ieron**	sup**o**	sup**ieron**

- Notice that none of these irregular forms has a written accent mark.
- The verbs **decir** and **traer** also have irregular stems and have different endings in the **ellos/ellas/Uds.** form. Look at the conjugations below:

  decir: dije, dijiste, dijo, dijimos, dijisteis, dij**eron**;
  traer: traje, trajiste, trajo, trajimos, trajisteis, traj**eron**

A. Underline the correct form of the irregular preterite verb in each sentence.

Modelo   María (**dije** / <u>**dijo**</u>) que se perdió en el bosque.

1. Nosotros (**trajiste** / ⟨**trajimos**⟩) los binoculares y la brújula.

2. Yo no (⟨**pude**⟩ / **pudo**) encontrar mi saco de dormir.

3. Los muchachos (**anduvo** / ⟨**anduvieron**⟩) por el bosque.

4. ¿Tú (⟨**viniste**⟩ / **vino**) al bosque para hacer camping?

B. Complete Paco's story of his day with the correct irregular preterite **yo** form of each verb.

Modelo   (poner) Yo _____*puse*_____ mis libros y tarea en mi mochila.

1. (decir) Yo le _*dije*_____ "Buenos días" a mi maestra de español.

2. (tener) Yo _*tuve*_____ un examen de física.

3. (estar) Yo _*estuve*_ en la escuela por 6 horas más.

4. (venir) Yo _*vine*_____ a mi casa a las cuatro y media.

C. A teacher asks her students about their weekend activities. Complete her questions with the **Uds.** form of the verb and the students' answers with the **nosotros** form. Follow the model.

Modelo (andar) Uds. ___anduvieron___ por el bosque, ¿no?
Sí, ___anduvimos___ por el bosque.

1. (poder) Uds. _pudieron_ jugar unos deportes, ¿no?
Sí, _pudimos_ jugar al bésibol y al hockey.

2. (tener) Uds. _tuvieron_ que limpiar sus cuartos, ¿no?
Sí, _tuvimos_ que limpiarlos.

3. (venir) Uds. _vinieron_ a ver la obra de teatro estudiantil, ¿no?
Sí, _vimos_ a verla.

4. (saber) Uds. _supieron_ lo que le pasó a Jorge ayer, ¿no?
Sí, lo _supimos_.

5. (decir) Uds. me _dijieron_ todo lo que hicieron, ¿no?
Sí, se le _dijimos_ todo.

D. First, identify the pictures. Then, use the pictures and verbs in the preterite to create complete sentences about what people did in the past. Follow the model.

Modelo Mario / estar / _____ / por tres horas
Mario estuvo en la tienda de acampar por tres horas.

1. mis amigos y yo / poder ver / _____ / impresionante / anoche
Mis amigos y yo pudimos vimos impresionante anoche

2. Ana y Felipe / andar por / _____ / durante todo el día
Ana y Felipe dieron por durante todo el día

3. tú / poner / _____ / en la mochila
Tú pusiste en la mochila

4. Yo / traer / _____ / para ver el sendero
Yo traje para vi el sendero

El pretérito de los verbos con los cambios e→i, o→u en la raíz (p. 33)

- Stem changing -**ar** and -**er** verbs, such as **pensar**, have <u>no stem changes</u> in the preterite. However, -**ir** verbs that have a stem change in the present tense also have a stem change in the preterite.
- If the -**ir** verb has an **e→ie** or **e→i** stem change in the present tense, such as **servir**, in the preterite the **e** will change to an **i** in the **él/ella/Ud.** and **ellos/ellas/Uds.** forms.
- If the -**ir** verb has an **o→ue** stem change in the present tense, such as **dormir**, in the preterite the **o** will change to a **u** in the **él/ella/Ud.** and **ellos/ellas/Uds.** forms.

servir	(e→i)	dormir	(o→u)
serví	servimos	dormí	dormimos
serviste	servisteis	dormiste	dormisteis
sirvió	sirvieron	durmió	durmieron

A. The following sentences are all in either the **él/ella/Ud.** or **ellos/ellas/Uds.** form. Fill in the missing vowel to tell what happened on a recent camping trip. Follow the model.

Modelo   (sentirse) Ana y Sofía se s _i_ ntieron muy cansadas después de escalar las rocas.

1. (dormir)   Francisco d _u_ rmió todo el día en su saco de dormir.

2. (servir)   El restaurante s _i_ rvió hamburguesas y perros calientes.

3. (divertirse) Mis amigos se div _i_ rtieron mucho en el viaje.

4. (morirse)   Un animal se m _u_ rió en el bosque. ¡Qué triste!

B. What Sara did last weekend was different from what her best friends did. Complete the sentences with the correct preterite forms of the verbs in parentheses. Be sure to include the stem change when describing what Sara's friends did. Follow the model.

Modelo   (sugerir) Yo ___sugerí___ un fin de semana tranquilo; mis amigas ___sugirieron___ un viaje al bosque.

1. (preferir) Yo _preferí_ ir al cine; mis amigas _prefieron_ ir a un café.

2. (dormir)   Yo _dormí_ en mi casa; mis amigas _durmieron_ en un hotel.

3. (vestirse) Yo _me vestí_ con jeans y una camiseta; mis amigas _se vistirse_ con chaquetas, guantes, gorros y botas.

4. (pedir)   Yo _pidí_ pollo frito en un restaurante; mis amigos _pidieron_ perros calientes preparados en la fogata.

5. (divertirse) Yo no _me divertí_ mucho; mis amigas _se divirtieron_ bastante.

C. Complete each sentence with the correct preterite verb form to tell what people did on a recent nature hike. Remember that only the **él/ella/Ud.** and **ellos/ellas/Uds.** forms have stem changes.

Modelo (vestirse) Tere __se__ __vistió__ con botas para andar por la montañas.

1. (dormir) Yo _dormí_ varias horas la noche antes de salir.

2. (sugerir) Mis padres _sugirieron_ un paseo en canoa.

3. (pedir) Mi hermano _pidió_ usar los binoculares.

4. (sentirse) Nosotros _se_ _sintimos_ muy cansados por la caminata.

5. (preferir) Tú _prefiriste_ usar la linterna para ver mejor.

6. (divertirse) Los chicos _se_ _divirtieron_ mucho cuando vieron unos animales pequeños.

7. (morirse) ¡Casi _se_ _murió_ de hambre cuando perdimos la comida para el almuerzo!

D. Write complete sentences by conjugating each stem-changing -**ir** verb in the preterite tense. Follow the model.

Modelo al anochecer / los niños / divertirse / jugando con las linternas

Al anochecer los niños se divirtieron jugando con las linternas.

1. los insectos / morir / al principio del invierno

Los insectos murieron al principio del invierno

2. Ángel y Estela / vestirse / de ropa elegante / para salir anoche

Ángel y Estela se vistieron de ropa elegante para salieron anoche

3. el camarero / sugerir / la sopa del día

El camarero sugirió la ropa del día

4. nosotros / dormir / por tres semanas en el saco de dormir

Nosotros dormimos por tres semanas en el saco de dormimos

5. yo / sentirse triste / después de ver la película

Yo me sintí despues de vi la película

Capítulo 1   Fecha _____   **Vocabulary Flash Cards, Sheet 5**

Write the Spanish vocabulary word or phrase below each picture. Be sure to include the article for each noun.

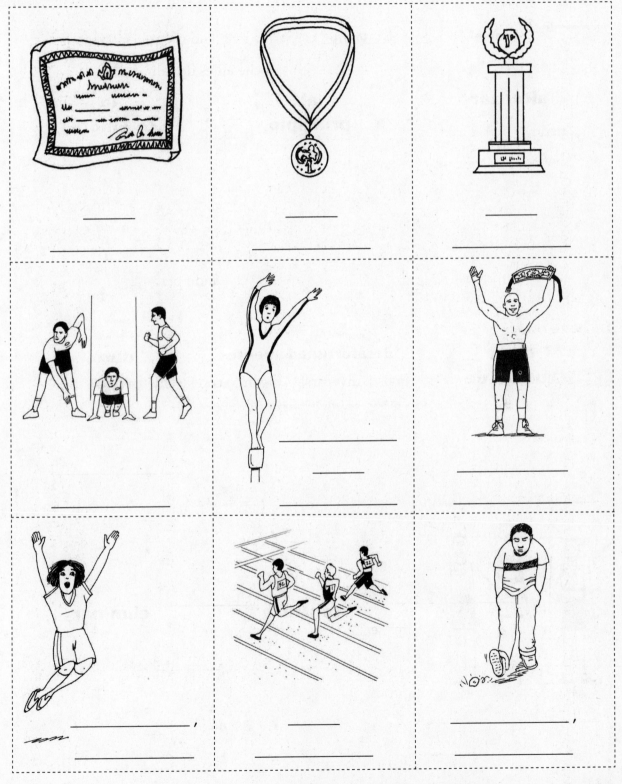

Write the Spanish vocabulary word or phrase below each picture. If there is a word or phrase, copy it in the space provided. Be sure to include the article for each noun.

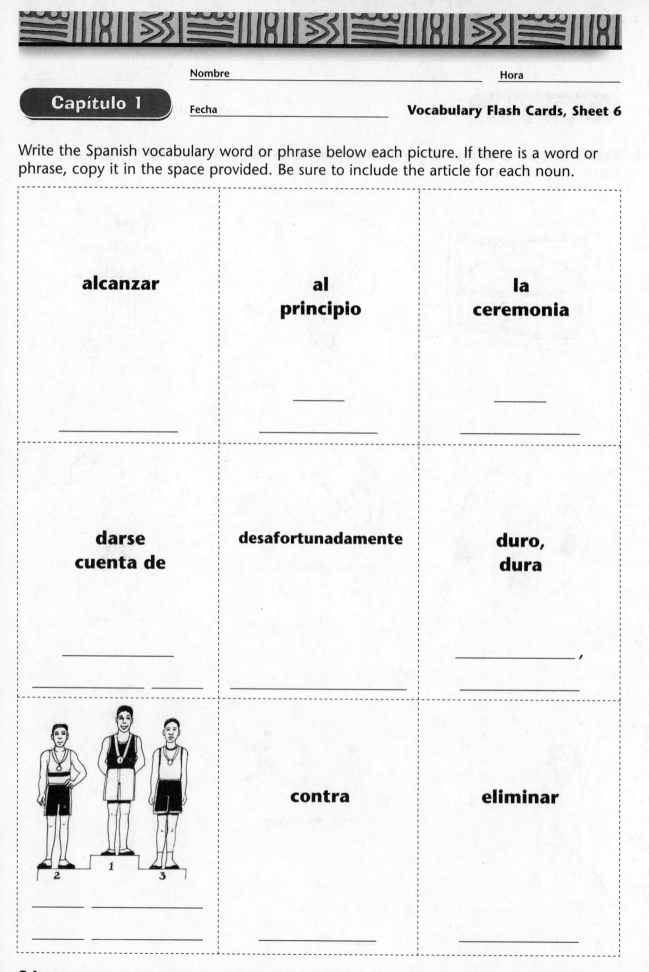

alcanzar

_____

al
principio

_____

la
ceremonia

_____

darse
cuenta de

_____

_____

desafortunadamente

_____

duro,
dura

_____,

_____

contra

_____

eliminar

_____

Copy the word or phrase in the space provided. Be sure to include the article for each noun.

emocionarse _____	**el entrenamiento** ___ _____	**estar orgulloso, orgullosa de** _____ _____, _____
¡Felicitaciones! _____	**hacer un esfuerzo** _____ _____	**hacia** _____
inscribirse _____	**la inscripción** ___ _____	**la meta** ___ _____

Copy the word or phrase in the space provided. Be sure to include the article for each noun. The blank cards can be used to write and practice other Spanish vocabulary for the chapter.

el/la participante

_____
_____

el/la representante

_____
_____

obtener

_____

sin embargo

_____
_____

tener lugar

_____
_____

vencer

_____

_____

_____

_____

Tear out this page. Write the English words on the lines. Fold the paper along the dotted line to see the correct answers so you can check your work.

el entrenamiento _____

entrenarse _____

hacer un esfuerzo _____

inscribirse _____

la inscripción _____

alcanzar _____

la carrera _____

el certificado _____

contra _____

eliminar _____

la entrega de premios _____

la medalla _____

la meta _____

obtener _____

el/la participante _____

el/la representante _____

Fold In

Tear out this page. Write the Spanish words on the lines. Fold the paper along the dotted line to see the correct answers so you can check your work.

training _____

to train _____

to make an effort _____

to register _____

registration _____

to reach _____

race _____

certificate, diploma _____

against _____

to eliminate _____

awards ceremony _____

medal _____

goal _____

to obtain, get _____

participant _____

representative _____

Fold In

Tear out this page. Write the English words on the lines. Fold the paper along the dotted line to see the correct answers so you can check your work.

salir campeón
(campeona)
_____
_____

el trofeo
_____

vencer
_____

animado,
animada
_____

desafortunadamente
_____

desanimado,
desanimada
_____

duro, dura
_____

emocionarse
_____

estar orgulloso(a) de
_____

impresionar
_____

hacia
_____

perder el equilibrio
_____

tener lugar
_____

al principio
_____

Fold In

Tear out this page. Write the Spanish words on the lines. Fold the paper along the dotted line to see the correct answers so you can check your work.

to become the
champion   _____

                         _____

trophy   _____

to beat   _____

excited   _____

                         _____

unfortunately   _____

discouraged   _____

                         _____

hard   _____

to be moved   _____

to be proud of   _____

to impress   _____

toward   _____

to lose one's balance   _____

to take place   _____

at the beginning   _____

Fold In ←

El imperfecto (p. 42)

- The imperfect tense is used to talk about habitual or repeated events in the past. Look at the conjugations of regular -**ar**, -**er**, and -**ir** verbs in the imperfect tense:

mont**ar**		com**er**		sal**ir**	
mont**aba**	mont**ábamos**	com**ía**	com**íamos**	sal**ía**	sal**íamos**
mont**abas**	mont**abais**	com**ías**	com**íais**	sal**ías**	sal**íais**
mont**aba**	mont**aban**	com**ía**	com**ían**	sal**ía**	sal**ían**

- Notice that the **yo** and **él/ella/Ud.** forms of each verb are the same.
- Notice that -**er** and -**ir** verbs have the same endings in the imperfect.

A. Write the imperfect endings of the -**ar** verbs in the first column, and the imperfect endings of the -**er** and -**ir** verbs in the second column.

Modelo ellos (**cantar**) cant _aban_   (**vivir**) viv _ían_

1. yo   (**entrenar**) entren _aba_   (**hacer**) hac _ía_
2. nosotros (**andar**)   and _ábamos_   (**correr**) corr _íamos_
3. tú   (**caminar**) camin _abas_   (**preferir**) prefer _ías_
4. él   (**jugar**)   jug _aba_   (**querer**) quer _ía_
5. Uds.   (**eliminar**) elimin _aban_   (**obtener**) obten _ían_

- There are only three irregular verbs in the imperfect: **ser**, **ir**, and **ver**. Look at the conjugations of these verbs below:

ser		ir		ver	
era	éramos	iba	íbamos	veía	veíamos
eras	erais	ibas	ibais	veías	veíais
era	eran	iba	iban	veía	veían

B. Complete each sentence with the correct form of the verb in parentheses.

Modelo Marisol _era_ (**ser**) una muchacha atlética.

1. Marisol y sus amigas ___iban___ (**ir**) al gimnasio para entrenarse todos los días.
2. Yo ___veía___ (**ver**) a Marisol y sus amigas en el gimnasio con frecuencia.
3. Nosotras ___éramos___ (**ser**) muy dedicadas y nuestra meta ___era___ (**ser**) participar en una carrera importante de la ciudad.
4. Mis padres siempre ___veían___ (**ver**) los partidos deportivos en la tele.

El imperfecto (*continued*)

C. A group of adults remembers their high school experiences. Complete each sentence with the correct imperfect verb form.

Modelo (**ganar**) Nuestros equipos siempre ___ganaban___ los campeonatos.

1. (**estar**)   Los estudiantes de nuestra escuela siempre _estaban_ muy animados por los partidos deportivos.

2. (**entrenarse**) Yo _me entrenaba_ en el gimnasio todos los días.

3. (**ir**)   Mi mamá _iba_ a todos los partidos de béisbol porque le encantaba ese deporte.

4. (**jugar**)   Tú _jugabas_ al béisbol cada primavera, ¿no?

5. (**hacer**)   Yo siempre _hacía_ un gran esfuerzo para alcanzar mis metas.

6. (**tener**)   Los partidos de fútbol americano _tenían_ lugar cerca de la escuela.

7. (**vencer**)   Nosotros siempre _vencíamos_ a nuestros rivales.

8. (**ser**)   Mi amigo Javier _era_ el muchacho más atlético de nuestra escuela.

D. Write sentences describing your childhood memories by conjugating the verbs in the imperfect tense and completing the sentences with information that applies to you. Follow the model.

Modelo Mis amigos y yo / siempre querer ir a...

Mis amigos y yo siempre queríamos ir a la piscina.

1. Yo / vivir en...

Yo vivía en mi casa

2. Mi mejor amigo(a) / jugar...

Mi mejor amigo jugaba futból

3. Mis amigos y yo / ver el programa...

Mis amigos y yo vía el programa comico

4. Mis padres / siempre decir...

Mis padres siempre decia

Usos del imperfecto (p. 44)

The imperfect is used:

- to describe events that happened regularly or habitually in the past
- to describe people and places in the past (for example: physical descriptions of what people or places looked like, or people's emotions)
- to describe past events that were ongoing or continuous (including things that "were happening" before being interrupted)
- to give the date, time, and someone's age in the past
- to talk about the weather in the past

A. Each sentence below provides a description in the past. Determine what is being described and write the corresponding letter next to the sentence. Then, underline the imperfect verb form in each sentence. Follow the model.

 a. person, place   **b. continuous action**   **c. date, time, age, weather**

Modelo   _c_ Eran las nueve y media de la noche.

1. _a_ Martín era alto, moreno y atlético.
2. _b_ Joaquín corría por las montañas.
3. _c_ Hacía mucho frío por la noche.
4. _C_ Los niños tenían cinco años.
5. _a_ La casa era roja y vieja.
6. _b_ La maestra enseñaba la lección.

B. Each statement below indicates what a situation was or how a person was when something happened. Based on the verbs in parentheses, write the correct imperfect verb form.

Modelo   (Llover) _Llovía_ mucho cuando los atletas salieron del estadio.

1. (estar)   Nosotros _estábamos_ en el gimnasio para ver la ceremonia de entrega de premios.

2. (Hacer)   _Hacía_ mucho frío cuando caminé a la escuela.

3. (entrenarse) Carlos _se entrenaba_ en el gimnasio cuando sus amigos llegaron.

4. (Ser)   _Eran_ las nueve cuando empezó el concurso.

5. (tener)   Nacho _tenía_ cinco años cuando empezó a jugar al fútbol.

6. (estar)   Las chicas _estaban_ desanimadas porque perdieron el partido.

- As you have just learned, the imperfect is used to talk about habitual events and to give descriptions in the past. The preterite, in contrast, is used to talk about events that happened once, or events that happened at a specific time in the past. Look at the examples below:

  I   Yo **me entrenaba** en el gimnasio todos los días.   *I trained in the gym every day (habitual).*

  P   Yo **me entrené** en el gimnasio ayer.   *I trained in the gym yesterday (once).*

  I   Yo **estaba** cansada porque eran las once de la noche.   *I was very tired (description) because it was 11pm (time in the past).*

  P   Yo **fui** al gimnasio el martes pasado.   *I went to the gym last Tuesday (once).*

C. Look at the following statements and circle the verb. Write **H** if the action is habitual (imperfect) and **O** if the action occurred one time (preterite). Follow the model.

Modelo   _O_   Yo (corrí) en la carrera ayer.

1. _O_   Nosotros (vencimos) al equipo de la escuela San Luis Obispo la semana pasada.

2. _O_   El verano pasado yo (participé) en una carrera muy dura.

3. _H_   Los estudiantes (practicaban) el vóleibol cada semana.

4. _H_   Los atletas (hacían) un esfuerzo increíble todos los días.

D. In the following sentences, a group of students remembers events that happened once (preterite) and how they felt or were when things took place (imperfect). Complete each sentence with the correct preterite or imperfect verb form.

Modelo   Federico _estaba_ (**estar**) orgulloso porque su equipo de fútbol americano _ganó_ (**ganar**) el campeonato.

1. Nosotros _perdimos_ (**perder**) el partido porque no _era_ (**ser**) muy atléticos.

2. Los jugadores _se sen___ (**sentirse**) muy felices cuando _recibía_ (**recibir**) el trofeo.

3. Todos los estudiantes _tenían_ (**tener**) mucho frío porque el partido de fútbol _tenía_ (**tener**) lugar en noviembre.

4. Martina _obtenía_ (**obtener**) un premio porque _tenía_ (**tener**) mucho talento.

5. Yo _participaba_ (**participar**) en un campeonato de básquetbol cuando _____ (**tener**) catorce años.

6. Nosotros _____ (**estar**) muy desanimados porque no _____ (**alcanzar**) nuestra meta.

Puente a la cultura (*pp. 48-49*)

A. The reading talks about **peregrinos**, or "pilgrims" who travel for days, even weeks to get to their destination. Imagine that, like the **peregrinos**, you had to plan a trip that would involve at least three days of traveling. Answer the questions below about such a journey.

1. What would you take with you to be prepared for your journey? _____

_____

2. Explain why you would bring each of the items above.

_____

_____

_____

3. How might you feel at the end of your journey? _____

_____

B. Read the following two passages from page 48 in your textbook. Look at the highlighted words and, using the sentence structure to guide you, decide whether the words are **personas** (people) or **lugares** (places). Mark your answer in the table below.

> *Hace más de mil años, en el extremo noroeste de España, se descubrió la* **tumba** *del* **apóstol** *Santiago, una figura fundamental de la religión católica.*
>
> *A lo largo de la* **ruta** *construyeron* **iglesias** *y* **albergues** *para recibir a los* **peregrinos**.

	personas	*lugares*
la tumba		
el apóstol		
la ruta		
las iglesias		
los albergues		
los peregrinos		

C. This article explains several possible reasons for visiting Santiago de Compostela. Put an **X** next to the reasons that are mentioned in the article.

1. _____ Puedes conocer a nuevas personas de todo el mundo.

2. _____ Puedes ver un sitio de importancia cultural e histórica.

3. _____ Puedes encontrar un buen trabajo allí.

4. _____ Puedes ver un lugar de importancia religiosa.

5. _____ Puedes comprar buena comida en los albergues.

Lectura (pp. 54–56)

A. Look at the title of the reading in your textbook. It contains two names in náhuatl (the language of the Aztecs). Based on this information, which subject do you think would best describe what the reading will be about?

    a. modern Mexicans   b. the Mexican landscape   c. a Native Mexican legend

B. Now, look at the captions on page 55 of your textbook. Answer the questions below.

  1. What do you think the words **príncipe** and **princesa** mean?

    _____

  2. What do you think is the relationship between the two people pictured?

    _____

C. This story focuses on a powerful king who seeks a suitable husband for his daughter, the princess. Read the following excerpt from the story. Circle the words or phrases that describe the characteristics the king is looking for.

> *Muchos príncipes ricos y famosos venían de todas partes de la región tolteca para ganar el amor de la princesa, pero ella no se enamoraba de ninguno. El rey, que quería para su hija un esposo rico de buena posición en la sociedad tolteca, ya estaba impaciente. A veces le preguntaba a la princesa qué esperaba.*

D. Now, read the excerpt that describes the different cultural backgorunds of the Chichimec prince and Toltec princess, who fall in love.

> *Los chichimecas no tenían una civilización tan espléndida como la de los toltecas. Vivían de la caza y la pesca en las montañas. Los toltecas pensaban que los chichimecas vivían como perros, y se reían de ellos.*

Does the Chichimec prince fit the description of what the Toltec king is looking for? Why or why not?

_____

_____

E. The love that the prince and princess have for each other causes a series of events to take place. Put in order the following details of the story in your textbook.

_____ La princesa tolteca y el príncipe chichimeca se casan.

_____ La princesa tolteca y el príncipe chichimeca sólo comen hierbas y frutas.

_____ La princesa tolteca es expulsada de Teotihuacán.

_____ La princesa tolteca y el príncipe chichimeca se duermen para siempre.

_____ El príncipe chichimeca es expulsado de su tribu.

F. This reading, like many legends, ends with what happened to the protagonists of the tale. Read the excerpt below and answer the questions that follow.

> *La princesa subió la montaña Iztaccíhuatl y el príncipe subió la montaña Popocatépetl. Cuando la princesa llegó a la cumbre (summit) de su montaña, se durmió y la nieve la cubrió (covered). El príncipe se puso de rodillas, mirando hacia la princesa y la nieve también lo cubrió.*

1. Does this story have a happy or tragic ending? _____

2. How does this resemble fairy tales that you are used to? How is this story similar or different?

   _____

   _____

3. How does nature figure into the end of this tale? Is it a hostile environment or gentle? Explain.

   _____

   _____

   _____

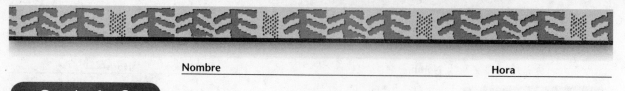

Concordancia y comparación de adjetivos (p. 65)

Remember that, in Spanish, adjectives must agree in gender (masculine or feminine) and number (singular or plural) with the nouns they describe. Look at the following rules for types of adjectives:

- For most adjectives, the masculine form ends in **-o** and the feminine form ends in **-a**.

    *el hombre viej**o***   *la mujer viej**a***

- Adjectives that end in **-e** or in a consonant (such as **-s** or **-l**), as well as those that end in **-ista**, may be either masculine or feminine.

    *el palacio **real***   *la ciudad **real***

    *el hombre depor**tista***   *la mujer depor**tista***

- If the masculine form of an adjective ends in **-or**, add an **-a** at the end to make the feminine form.

    *el hijo trabajad**or**   la hija trabajad**ora***

- Remember that if you have a group of both masculine and feminine nouns, you will use the plural, masculine form of the adjective.

    *el hombre y la mujer alt**os***

A. Circle the correct form of the adjective given, depending on the gender and number of what is being described.

Modelo   Prefiero el cuadro (**moderno** / moderna).

1. El arte de Picasso es muy (**interesante** / **interesantes**).

2. Salvador Dalí fue un artista (**surrealista** / **surrealistas**).

3. La profesora de arte de nuestra escuela es muy (**trabajador** / **trabajadora**).

4. Las pinturas de Frida Kahlo son muy (**personal** / **personales**).

5. Los colores de ese dibujo son muy (**vivas** / **vivos**).

B. Complete each sentence with the correct form of the adjective in parentheses. Some adjectives will not require changes!

Modelo   (sencillo)   Las flores de esa pintura de Picasso son ____*sencillas*____.

1. (realista)   Esos cuadros de Frida Kahlo no son muy _____.

2. (divertido)   El museo del Prado en Madrid es un lugar muy _____ para visitar.

3. (exagerado)   Las figuras de Botero tienen unas características _____.

4. (oscuro)   Los cuadros de Goya muchas veces son muy _____.

- To compare two things that are the same, use **tan** + *adjective* + **como**.
  *Los cuadros de Picasso son **tan interesantes como** los cuadros de Dalí.*
- To compare two things that are different, use **más / menos** + *adjective* + **que**.
  *El retrato de Botero es **más cómico que** el retrato de Velázquez.*
  Remember that the adjective must agree in gender and number with the noun it describes.

C. Use the signs provided to complete each of Juan's opinions using either **más...que**, **menos...que**, or **tan...como**. Then, circle the correct form of the adjective in parentheses based on the corresponding noun. Follow the model.

Modelo (+) Creo que el arte de Picasso es ___más___ (interesantes / (interesante)) ___que___ el arte de Velázquez.

1. (–) El color rosado es _____ (**vivo / viva**) _____ el color rojo.

2. (=) Creo que los museos son _____ (**divertido / divertidos**) _____ los cines.

3. (+) Ese mural de Diego Rivera es _____ (**grande / grandes**) _____ aquel retrato de Frida Kahlo.

4. (=) El pintor es _____ (**trabajador / trabajadora**) _____ la pintora.

5. (–) El papel y el plástico son _____ (**caros / caro**) _____ el oro y la plata.

- With the adjectives **bueno(a)**, **malo(a)**, **viejo(a)** and **joven**, you do not use the **más** or **menos** + *adjective* structure. Instead, use one of the following irregular comparative forms:

bueno(a)	**mejor (que)**	(*pl.* **mejores**)	*better (than)*
malo(a)	**peor (que)**	(*pl.* **peores**)	*worse (than)*
viejo(a)	**mayor (que)**	(*pl.* **mayores**)	*older (than)*
joven	**menor (que)**	(*pl.* **menores**)	*younger (than)*

D. Use the irregular comparative adjectives to create accurate comparisons.

Modelo Susana tiene 16 años y Martina tiene 18 años. Martina es ___mayor___ que Susana.

1. Ana tiene 13 años y Luz tiene 17 años. Ana es _____ que Luz.

2. Pedro saca una "A" en la clase de inglés y Jorge saca una "C." La nota de Pedro es _____ que la nota de Jorge.

3. Paco tiene 16 años y su abuelo tiene 83. El abuelo es _____ que Paco.

4. Los cuadros de Carla no son muy buenos, pero los cuadros de Tomás son excelentes. Los cuadros de Carla son _____ que los cuadros de Tomás.

Comparación de sustantivos y el superlativo (p. 67)

- To make a comparison of quantity between two nouns that are equal in number, use **tanto (tanta/tantos/tantas)** + *noun* + **como**. Be sure to pay attention to gender and number agreement.

    *Hay **tantos** actores **como** actrices en la obra de teatro.*

- To make a comparison of quantity between two nouns that are not equal, use **más/menos** + *noun* + **que.**

    *Hay **más** actores **que** músicos en la obra de teatro.*

    *Hay **menos** personas en el teatro **que** anoche.*

A. Use **menos...que** or **más...que** to create logical sentences.

Modelo   Hay tres actores y dos actrices. Hay __*más*__ actores __*que*__ actrices.

1. Hay dos directores y diez actores. Hay _____ directores _____ actores.

2. Hay doce personas en el coro y veinte personas en la orquesta. Hay _____ personas en la orquesta _____ en el coro.

3. Este año se van a presentar veinticinco conciertos y diez obras de teatro en el Teatro Santiago. Se van a presentar _____ obras de teatro _____ conciertos.

4. La actriz principal tiene mucho talento pero los otros actores no tienen mucho talento. Ellos tienen _____ talento _____ la actriz principal.

5. En la ciudad hay cuatro cines y dos teatros. Hay _____ cines _____ teatros.

B. Use **tanto, tanta, tantos** or **tantas** to complete each sentence.

Modelo   Hay dos guitarras y dos pianos en la orquesta. Hay __*tantas*__ guitarras como pianos.

1. La actriz principal tiene mucho talento y el actor principal tiene mucho talento. El actor tiene _____ talento como la actriz.

2. Se presentan dos obras dramáticas y dos obras musicales en el teatro este fin de semana. Se presentan _____ obras dramáticas como obras musicales.

3. Ayer asistieron doscientas personas a la obra y hoy asisten doscientas. Hoy hay _____ gente como ayer.

4. Hay diez músicos y diez bailarines en la obra. Hay _____ músicos como bailarines.

5. Hoy las entradas cuestan $15 y anoche las entradas costaron $15. Las entradas cuestan _____ dinero hoy como ayer.

Comparación de sustantivos y el superlativo (*continued*)

- To say something is the "most" or the "least," you use a structure called the superlative. To form the superlative, use **el/la/los/las + noun + más/menos + adjective**.

   *Celia Cruz es **la cantante más talentosa**.*

   *Creo que Roger Ebert es **el crítico más inteligente**.*

- To compare one thing within a large group, use **de** + the group or category.

   *Marta es la más alta **de** todas las actrices.*

C. Complete the following superlatives with the missing elements. Follow the model.

> **Modelo** (+) La clase de español es la ____*más*____ divertida de mi escuela.

1. Andrés es el más alto _____ mi clase de español.

2. (+) El domingo es el día _____ tranquilo de la semana.

3. (+) Mariana tiene la voz _____ bella del coro.

4. (–) Ésa es la escena _____ emocionante del drama.

5. Las hermanas Cruz son las músicas más talentosas _____ la escuela.

- Use the adjectives **mejor(es)** and **peor(es)** + noun to express *best* and *worst*.

   *Plácido Domingo es **el mejor** cantante.*

   *Esos son **los peores** efectos especiales.*

D. Read the description of the following theater, art, and music students. Use the context of the sentence to decide whether to use **mejor / mejores** or **peor / peores**. Complete the sentences with your choice.

> **Modelo** Maricarmen tiene una voz muy bonita. Es la ___*mejor*___ cantante del coro.

1. Ramón no puede bailar muy bien. Es el _____ bailarín del grupo.

2. Sonia y Teresa actúan muy bien. Son las _____ actrices de su escuela.

3. El director de la obra es muy antipático y grita mucho. ¡Es el _____ director del mundo!

4. Nuestra orquesta toca perfectamente. Es la _____ orquesta de la ciudad.

5. Los argumentos de estas dos obras son muy aburridos. Son los _____ argumentos.

Write the Spanish vocabulary word or phrase below each picture. Be sure to include the article for each noun.

_____   _____   _____

_____   _____ ,   _____

_____   _____ ,   _____

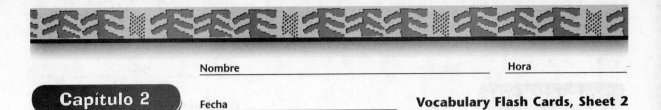

Nombre _____   Hora _____

Capítulo 2   Fecha _____   **Vocabulary Flash Cards, Sheet 2**

Write the Spanish vocabulary word below each picture. If there is a word or phrase, copy it in the space provided. Be sure to include the article for each noun.

_____   _____   _____

_____   _____   _____

_____   _____   _____

_____   _____   _____

a través   **abstracto,**
de   **abstracta**

_____   _____ ,

_____   _____

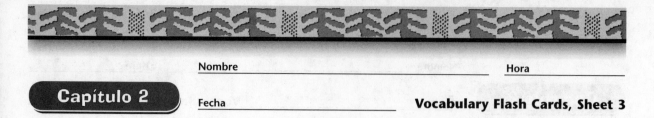

Copy the word or phrase in the space provided. Be sure to include the article for each noun.

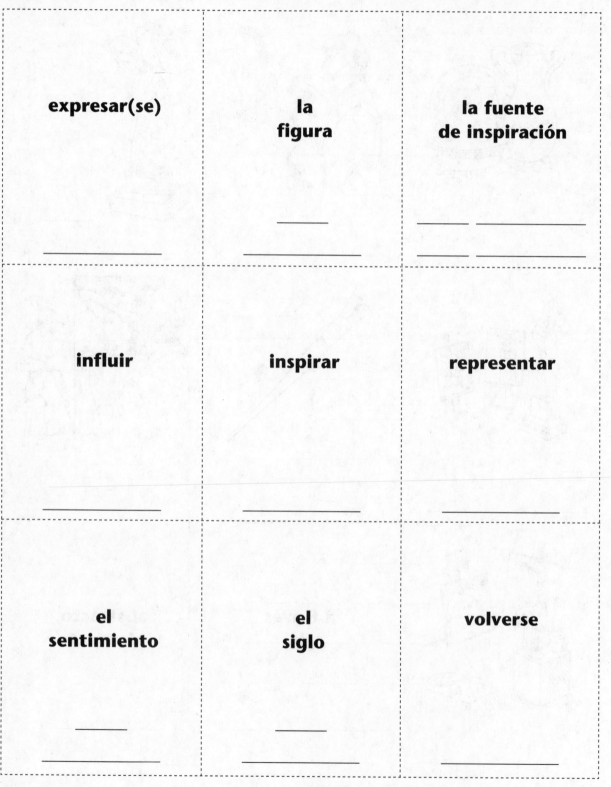

expresar(se)	**la figura**	**la fuente de inspiración**
_____	_____	_____
influir	**inspirar**	**representar**
_____	_____	_____
el sentimiento	**el siglo**	**volverse**
_____	_____	_____

Tear out this page. Write the English words on the lines. Fold the paper along the dotted line to see the correct answers so you can check your work.

abstracto, abstracta _____

a través de _____

el autorretrato _____

la cerámica _____

el escultor,
la escultora _____

la escultura _____

expresar(se) _____

famoso, famosa _____

la figura _____

el fondo _____

la fuente de
inspiración _____
_____

la imagen _____

influir (i→y) _____

inspirar _____

mostrar(ue) _____

el mural _____

Fold In ←

Tear out this page. Write the Spanish words on the lines. Fold the paper along the dotted line to see the correct answers so you can check your work.

abstract _____

through _____

self-portrait _____

pottery _____

sculptor _____

_____

sculpture _____

to express (oneself) _____

famous _____

figure _____

background _____

source of inspiration _____

_____

image _____

to influence _____

to inspire _____

to show _____

mural _____

Fold In ←

Tear out this page. Write the English words on the lines. Fold the paper along the dotted line to see the correct answers so you can check your work.

la naturaleza muerta _____

la obra de arte _____

la paleta _____

parado, parada _____

el pincel _____

la pintura _____

el primer plano _____

representar _____

el retrato _____

sentado, sentada _____

el sentimiento _____

el siglo _____

el taller _____

el tema _____

volverse (ue) _____

Fold In

Tear out this page. Write the Spanish words on the lines. Fold the paper along the dotted line to see the correct answers so you can check your work.

still life   _____

work of art   _____

palette   _____

standing   _____

brush   _____

painting   _____

foreground   _____

to represent   _____

portrait   _____

seated   _____

feeling   _____

century   _____

workshop   _____

subject   _____

to become   _____

Fold In ←

Pretérito vs. imperfecto (p. 78)

- Remember that you have learned two past tenses: the preterite and the imperfect. Look at the information below for a summary of when to use each tense:

Preterite
- actions that happened once or were completed in the past
- to relate a series of events that happened

Imperfect
- habitual or repeated actions in the past
- descriptions such as background information, physical appearance, emotions, time, date, age, and weather

When you have two verbs in one sentence, use the following rules:
- If two actions were going on simultaneously and did not interrupt each other, put both verbs in the imperfect:

  Yo *leía* mientras mi hermana *pintaba.*

- If one action that is in progress in the past is interrupted by another action, put the action in progress in the imperfect and the interrupting action in the preterite:

  Los estudiantes *pintaban* cuando su maestro *salió* de la clase.

A. Read each of the following statements about Picasso's life and career. Then decide if the statement is about something Picasso *used to do* or if it is something he *did once.* Place a checkmark in the box of your choice.

Modelo   Pablo Ruiz Picasso **nació** en Málaga el 25 de octubre de 1881.

    ☐ used to do   ☑ did once

1. **Hizo** un viaje a París en 1900.

    ☐ used to do   ☑ did once

2. **Pasaba** mucho tiempo con el artista André Breton y la escritora Gertrude Stein.

    ☑ used to do   ☐ did once

3. **Hacía** cuadros monocromáticos.

    ☑ used to do   ☐ did once

4. **Quería** expresar la violencia y la crueldad de la Guerra Civil Española.

    ☑ used to do   ☑ did once

5. **Pintó** el cuadro *Guernica* para ilustrar los horrores de la guerra.

    ☐ used to do   ☑ did once

B. Javier recently visited his friend Domingo's art studio. Read each part of the story and decide if it gives *description/background information* or if it tells *what happened* in the story. Circle your choice.

Modelo	Eran las tres y hacía buen tiempo.	What happened	**Description**

1. Llegué al taller de Domingo a las tres y media.   **What happened**   Description

2. Llamé a la puerta, pero nadie contestó.   **What happened**   Description

3. La puerta estaba abierta.   What happened   **Description**

4. Entré en el taller.   **What happened**   Description

5. Encontré a Domingo.   **What happened**   Description

6. No tenía ganas de trabajar más.   What happened   **Description**

C. Choose the correct form of each verb to complete these sentences about an artist.

1. Cuando (**era** / fui) niña, me (**gustaba** / gustó) mucho el arte.

2. Siempre (**tomaba** / tomé) clases de arte y (**dibujaba** / dibujé) en mi tiempo libre.

3. La semana pasada, (empezaba / **empecé**) una pintura nueva.

4. Primero, (pintaba / **pinté**) el fondo con colores oscuros y después, (incluía / **incluí**) unas figuras de animales.

D. Complete the following sentences with the preterite or the imperfect form of the verb.

Modelo	___Eran___ (ser) las dos cuando la clase de arte ___empezó___ (empezar).

1. Los estudiantes ya __trabajaban__ (**trabajar**) cuando su profesor __entró__ (**entrar**).

2. El profesor les ___dijo___ (**decir**), «Uds. son muy trabajadores».

3. Luego, el profesor ___hizo___ (**hacer**) una demostración de una técnica artística nueva.

4. Mientras los estudiantes __practicaban__ (**practicar**), el profesor __caminó__ (**caminar**) por la clase para observar sus avances.

5. El profesor __estaba__ (**estar**) contento porque sus estudiantes __aprendieron__ (**aprender**) la técnica muy bien.

Estar + participio (p. 81)

- To form the past participle of **-ar** verbs, add **-ado** to the root of the verb. For **-er** and **-ir** verbs, add **-ido** to the root. See the examples below.

| lavar   lav**ado** *(washed)* | comer   com**ido** *(eaten)* | servir   serv**ido** *(served)* |

A. Write the past participle form for each verb. Follow the model.

Modelo (crear) __*creado*__

1. (inspirar) _____

2. (vestir) _____

3. (representar) _____

4. (vender) _____

5. (influir) _____

6. (pintar) _____

7. (tomar) _____

8. (mover) _____

- It is common to use the past participle with the verb **estar** to give descriptions. Remember that since the past participle is being used as an adjective in these cases, it must agree in gender and number with the noun it describes:

  *El pintor **está cansado.*** *Las pintoras **están cansadas.***

B. Read the following descriptions of famous paintings. Underline the noun in the sentence. Then, circle which form of the past participle best completes each sentence.

Modelo Las dos <u>chicas</u> están (sentada /(sentadas)).

1. La ventana del fondo está (**cerrado / cerrada**).

2. El fondo está (**pintado / pintados**) con colores oscuros.

3. Dos gatos están (**dormidos / dormidas**) en el sofá.

4. La cena está (**preparada / preparado**).

5. La pintura está (**basado / basada**) en los sueños del artista.

6. El pintor está (**incluido / incluida**) en la pintura.

7. Unos temas importantes están (**representadas / representados**).

• Some verbs have irregular past participles. Look at the list below:

poner: **puesto**	decir: **dicho**	hacer: **hecho**	escribir: **escrito**	ver: **visto**
abrir: **abierto**	morir: **muerto**	romper: **roto**	volver: **vuelto**	resolver: **resuelto**

C. Read the following description of an artist's workshop. First, write the past participle of the verb in parentheses. Next, complete the sentences with the correct form of this past participle. Be careful to make its ending match the noun in the sentence in number and gender.

Modelo   (poner:_*puesto*_) Cuando entré en el taller, las luces no estaban _*puestas*_ .

1. (abrir:_____) La ventana estaba _____ y hacía frío.

2. (romper:_____) Una pintura grande estaba _____ en el suelo.

3. (poner:_____) Los pinceles y la paleta estaban _____ en la mesa.

4. (escribir:_____) Unas notas para pinturas futuras estaban _____ en el cuaderno del artista.

5. (hacer:_____) Una escultura de un animal estaba _____ .

6. (morir:_____) Un ratón estaba _____ en el taller. ¡Qué horror!

D. The classroom was a mess when the students arrived Monday morning. Use the verbs in parentheses to write a sentence using **estar** + *past participle*. Follow the model.

Modelo   Las ventanas ___*estaban*___ ___*abiertas*___ (**abrir**).

1. Unas palabras _____ _____ (**escribir**) en la pared.

2. Las paletas _____ _____ (**poner**) en el suelo.

3. Las botellas de agua de la maestra _____ _____ (**beber**).

4. La computadora _____ _____ (**romper**).

5. Los libros de texto _____ _____ (**perder**).

6. Unos insectos habían entrado por la ventana y _____ _____ (**morir**) en el suelo.

Capítulo 2

Write the Spanish vocabulary word or phrase below each picture. Be sure to include the article for each noun.

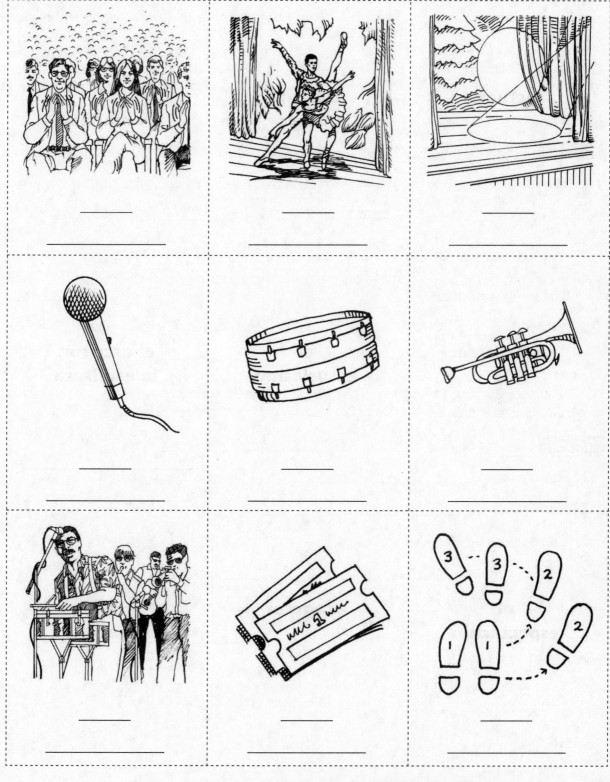

_____   _____   _____

_____   _____   _____

Copy the word or phrase in the space provided. Be sure to include the article for each noun.

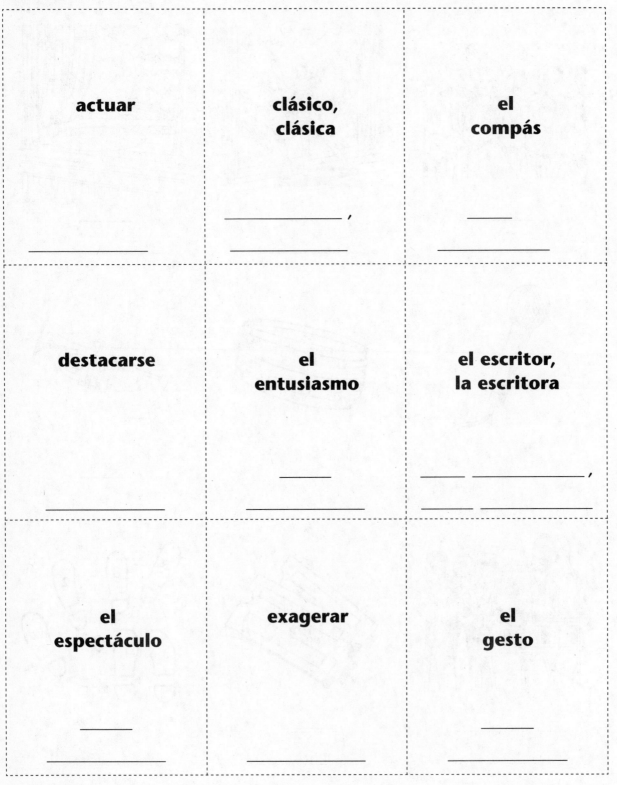

actuar

_____

clásico, clásica

_____ ,

_____

el compás

_____

_____

destacarse

_____

el entusiasmo

_____

_____

el escritor, la escritora

_____ ,

_____

el espectáculo

_____

_____

exagerar

_____

el gesto

_____

_____

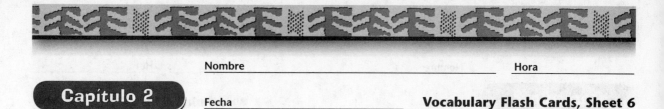

Copy the word or phrase in the space provided. Be sure to include the article for each noun.

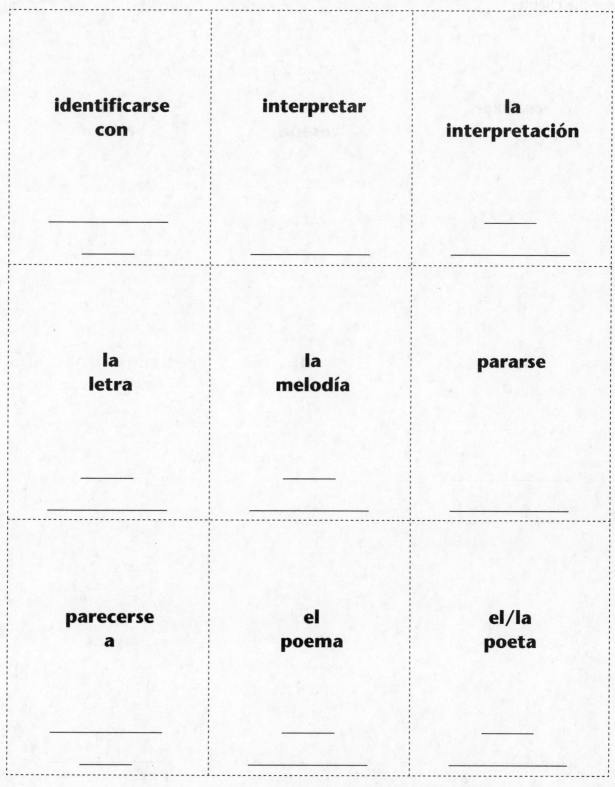

identificarse con	interpretar	la interpretación
_____ _____	_____	_____
la letra	**la melodía**	**pararse**
_____	_____	_____
parecerse a	**el poema**	**el/la poeta**
_____	_____	_____

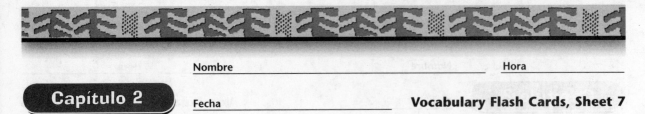

Copy the word or phrase in the space provided. Be sure to include the article for each noun. The blank cards can be used to write and practice other Spanish vocabulary for the chapter.

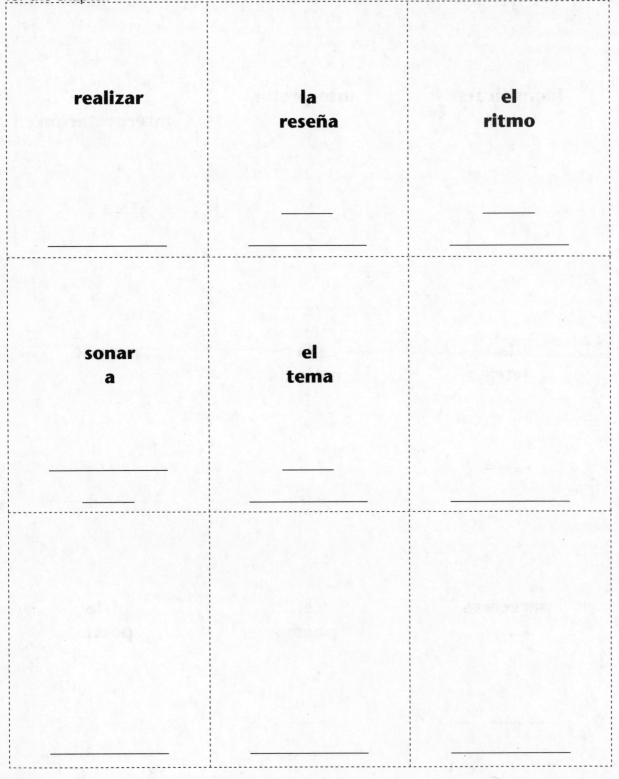

realizar

_____

la reseña

_____

el ritmo

_____

sonar a

_____

el tema

_____

_____

Tear out this page. Write the English words on the lines. Fold the paper along the dotted line to see the correct answers so you can check your work.

actuar
_____

el aplauso
_____

clásico, clásica
_____

el compás
_____

el conjunto
_____

la danza
_____

destacar(se)
_____

la entrada
_____

el entusiasmo
_____

el escenario
_____

el escritor,
la escritora
_____

el espectáculo
_____

exagerar
_____

el gesto
_____

identificarse con
_____

Fold In

Tear out this page. Write the Spanish words on the lines. Fold the paper along the dotted line to see the correct answers so you can check your work.

to perform   _____

applause   _____

classical   _____

rhythm   _____

band   _____

dance   _____

to stand out   _____

ticket   _____

enthusiasm   _____

stage   _____

writer   _____

                    _____

show   _____

to exaggerate   _____

gesture   _____

to identify oneself with _____

Fold In ←

Tear out this page. Write the English words on the lines. Fold the paper along the dotted line to see the correct answers so you can check your work.

la interpretación _____

interpretar _____

la letra _____

la melodía _____

el micrófono _____

el movimiento _____

pararse _____

el paso _____

el/la poeta _____

realizar _____

la reseña _____

el ritmo _____

sonar(ue) (a) _____

el tambor _____

la trompeta _____

Fold In →

Tear out this page. Write the Spanish words on the lines. Fold the paper along the dotted line to see the correct answers so you can check your work.

interpretation   _____

to interpret   _____

lyrics   _____

melody   _____

microphone   _____

movement   _____

to stand up   _____

step   _____

poet   _____

to perform, accomplish   _____

review   _____

rhythm   _____

to sound (like)   _____

drum   _____

trumpet   _____

Fold In ←

Ser y estar (p. 90)

- Remember that Spanish has two verbs that mean "to be": **ser** and **estar**. Look at the rules below to review the circumstances in which each verb should be used:

  Ser **is used . . .**
  - to describe permanent physical and personal characteristics
  - to describe nationality or origin
  - to describe someone's job or profession
  - to tell where and when an event will take place
  - to tell whom something belongs to

  Estar **is used . . .**
  - to describe temporary physical conditions or emotions
  - to give location
  - as part of the progressive tenses, such as *está escuchando* or *estaba escuchando*

A. Use **es** or **está** to describe the director of a show.

El director...

1. nació en Madrid. _____ español.

2. trabaja mucho todos los días. _____ muy serio.

3. cree que los actores están trabajando muy bien esta noche. _____ contento.

4. Tiene mucho dinero. _____ rico.

5. Lleva un traje elegante esta noche. _____ muy guapo.

6. _____ músico también.

B. Complete the paragraph with the appropriate present tense forms of **ser** or **estar**.

Nuestra escuela _____ preparando una presentación de la obra de teatro *Romeo y*

Julieta. *Romeo y Julieta* _____ la historia de dos jóvenes que _____ enamorados,

pero sus familias _____ enemigas. Marta Ramos _____ la actriz principal:

interpreta el papel de Julieta. Marta _____ una chica muy talentosa que _____ de

Puerto Rico. Ella _____ muy entusiasmada porque este viernes _____ la primera

representación de la obra. _____ en el teatro de la escuela a las siete de la noche. Todos

los actores _____ trabajando mucho esta semana para memorizar el guión. Los

acontecimientos de las vidas de Romeo y Julieta _____ muy trágicos, pero la obra

_____ magnífica.

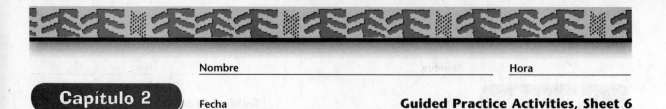

Nombre _____   Hora _____

Capítulo 2   Fecha _____   **Guided Practice Activities, Sheet 6**

Ser y estar (continued)

- Sometimes using **ser** or **estar** with the same adjective causes a change in meaning:

El café *es bueno*.	Coffee is good. (in general).
El café *está bueno*.	The coffee tastes good. (today).
El actor *es aburrido*.	The actor is boring. (in general)
El actor *está aburrido*.	The actor is bored. (today)
La directora *es bonita*.	The director is pretty. (in general)
La directora *está bonita*.	The director looks pretty. (today)
Los actores *son ricos*.	The actors are rich. (in general)
La comida *está rica*.	The food is tasty. (today)

C. Decide if the following statements refer to what the people in a show are like in general, or if they describe what they are like in today's show.

1. **La cantante...**

   a. es bonita.   **hoy   en general**

   b. está nerviosa.   **hoy   en general**

   c. es cómica.   **hoy   en general**

   d. es colombiana.   **hoy   en general**

2. **Los actores…**

   a. están elegantes.   **hoy   en general**

   b. son ricos.   **hoy   en general**

   c. están contentos.   **hoy   en general**

   d. son talentosos.   **hoy   en general**

D. You and a friend are commenting on a variety show. Read each statement and decide which response best states the situation. The first one has been done for you.

1. La actriz tiene un vestido especialmente bonito esta noche.

   a. Es guapa.   **b.** Está guapa.

2. Los músicos no tocan mucho y quieren irse.

   a. Son aburridos.   **b.** Están aburridos.

3. Esos hombres tienen mucho dinero y coches lujosos.

   a. Son ricos.   **b.** Están ricos.

4. Las cantantes se sienten bien porque cantaron muy bien la canción.

   a. Son orgullosos.   **b.** Están orgullosas.

5. El camarero nos preparó un café especialmente delicioso esta noche.

   a. El café es rico.   **b.** El café está rico.

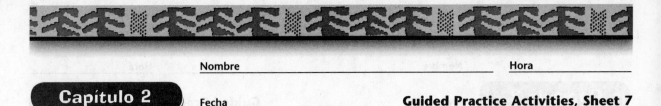

Verbos con distinto sentido en el pretérito y en el imperfecto (p. 92)

- Some verbs have different meanings in the preterite and the imperfect. Look at the following chart to understand these changes in meaning:

Verbo	Imperfecto	Pretérito
saber	knew a fact or how to do something	found out
conocer	knew a person or place	met for the first time
querer	wanted to	tried to
no querer	didn't want to	refused to
poder	could, was able to	tried and succeeded in doing

A. Choose which idea is being expressed by the underlined verb in each sentence.

Modelo   Los estudiantes <u>conocieron</u> al actor famoso.
      ☑ met   ☐ knew

1. Jorge <u>quería</u> ser el galán de la obra de teatro.

  ☐ tried to   ☐ wanted to

2. Lupe <u>quiso</u> sacar fotos del espectáculo.

  ☐ tried to   ☐ wanted to

3. Yo <u>sabía</u> el título del poema.

  ☐ found out   ☐ knew

4. Mi mamá <u>supo</u> que nuestro vecino es artista.

  ☐ found out   ☐ knew

5. <u>No quería</u> aprender la melodía de esta canción aburrida.

  ☐ refused to   ☐ didn't want to

6. <u>No quise</u> entrar al teatro.

  ☐ refused to   ☐ didn't want to

7. <u>Pudimos</u> realizar el baile sin problemas.

  ☐ managed to, succeeded in   ☐ were able to, could

8. <u>Podíamos</u> identificarnos con el protagonista.

  ☐ managed to, succeeded in   ☐ were able to, could

B. Ana tells the story of how she finally got to meet a famous salsa singer. Complete the following sentences with the correct preterite or imperfect form of the verb in parentheses.

Modelo   Yo _____conocí_____ (**conocer**) a Carlos, mi mejor amigo, hace dos años.

1. Hacía muchos años que Carlos _____ (**conocer**) a una cantante de salsa.

2. Yo _____ (**saber**) bailar salsa y me gustaba ir a los clubes de salsa.

3. Una noche Carlos y yo decidimos ir al club donde trabajaba la cantante pero luego yo _____ (**saber**) que tenía que trabajar y no pude ir.

4. Carlos _____ (**saber**) que yo quería conocer a su amiga y la invitó a mi casa al día siguiente.

5. Yo _____ (**conocer**) a la cantante y fue el día más fantástico de mi vida.

C. Complete the following sentences with the correct preterite or imperfect **yo** form of the verb in parentheses.

Modelo   Yo _____quise_____ (**querer**) aprender los pasos de la salsa, pero no sé bailar bien y la clase fue un desastre.

1. Yo _____ (**querer**) leer en un café. Por eso le pregunté al dueño del café si era posible.

2. Yo _____ (**querer**) leer la poesía en el café, pero me puse nerviosa y no pude terminar el poema.

3. Julia no _____ (**querer**) salir con Pepe, pero salieron porque él es el mejor amigo de su novio.

4. Julia no_____ (**querer**) salir con Pepe y por eso él tuvo que ir solo al cine.

5. El director nos dijo que nosotros _____ (**poder**) participar en la obra de teatro.

6. Nosotros no teníamos mucho dinero, pero _____ (**poder**) comprar las entradas porque sólo costaban $5. Las compramos ayer.

Puente a la cultura (pp. 96–97)

A. Look at the paintings by Francisco de Goya on the pages surrounding the article. Check off all words on the following list that could be used to describe one or more of the works you see.

☐ realistas   ☐ abstractos

☐ retratos   ☐ surrealistas

☐ oscuros   ☐ monocromáticos

B. This reading contains many *cognates*, or Spanish words that look and sound like English words. Can you determine the meanings of the following words? Circle the option that you think represents the correct meaning.

1. la corte   **a.** curtain   **b.** court

2. los triunfos   **a.** triumphs   **b.** trumpets

3. la época   **a.** epoch, age   **b.** epicenter

4. las tropas   **a.** traps   **b.** troops

5. las imágenes   **a.** imaginations   **b.** images

6. los monstruos   **a.** monsters   **b.** monsoons

C. This reading talks about four important events in Goya's life and how each event affected the art he created. Match each event with the painting or type of paintings it led Goya to produce.

1. _____ Se enfermó

2. _____ Llegó a ser Pintor de la Cámara

3. _____ Hubo una guerra entre España y Francia

4. _____ Trabajó para la Real Fábrica de Tapices

a. *El 3 de mayo de 1808*

b. bocetos *(sketches)* de la vida diaria en Madrid

c. las "Pinturas negras"

d. retratos de los reyes y la familia real

Lectura (pp. 102–105)

A. The reading in your book, *Cuando era puertorriqueña*, is an excerpt from an autobiography. From what you know of autobiographies, check off the items you might find in this reading.

□ important events in one's life

□ first person narration

□ talking animals

□ real-world settings

□ analysis of scientific data

B. Read the following excerpt from the story. Based on what you read, write the letter of the teacher who would most likely discuss each topic below with his or her students.

> —Mister Gatti, el maestro de gramática, te dirigirá … Y Missis Johnson te hablará acerca de lo que te debes de poner y esas cosas.

1. ____ la ropa   **a.** Mr. Gatti

2. ____ la pronunciación   **b.** Mrs. Johnson

3. ____ la fonética

4. ____ el inglés

C. The girl in the story, Esmeralda, has her first audition to get into the Performing Arts High School. Circle the best choice below to complete the statements about the events leading up to and including the audition.

1. Esmeralda quería salir muy bien en su audición porque (**quería salir de Brooklyn / quería ser una actriz famosa**).

2. Cuando Esmeralda se enfrentó con el jurado (**se le salió un inglés natural / se le olvidó el inglés**).

3. Antes de presentar su soliloquio, Esmeralda estaba (**tranquila / nerviosa**).

4. Cuando presentó su soliloquio, (**habló con mucha expresión / habló muy rápido**).

5. Las mujeres del jurado sabían que Esmeralda (**estaba nerviosa / tenía talento**).

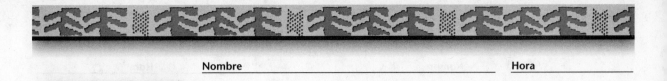

D. Now, read the statements about the events following the audition, and circle whether they are true (**cierto**) or false (**falso**).

1. La mamá de Esmeralda fue con ella a la audición. **cierto** **falso**

2. Esmeralda tuvo la oportunidad de pronunciar su soliloquio
una segunda vez. **cierto** **falso**

3. Bonnie y Esmeralda hicieron el papel de hermanas. **cierto** **falso**

4. En la segunda actuación, Esmeralda imaginó que estaba
decorando un árbol de Navidad. **cierto** **falso**

5. Esmeralda no fue admitida a la Performing Arts High School. **cierto** **falso**

E. The end of this autobiography occurs years after the audition of Esmeralda, although it recalls the events as if they had just happened. Read the excerpt and answer the questions that follow.

> *Me dijo que el jurado tuvo que pedirme que esperara afuera para poderse reír, ya que les parecía tan cómico ver a aquella chica puertorriqueña de catorce años chapurreando (babbling) un soliloquio acerca de una suegra posesiva durante el cambio de siglo, las palabras incomprensibles porque pasaban tan rápidas.*

1. Why, does it turn out, that the jury panel asked Esmeralda to wait outside?

   _____

2. What did the jury find funny about Esmeralda?

   _____

   _____

Pronombres de complemento directo (p. 113)

- In Spanish, as in English, direct objects describe who or what directly receives the action of a verb. Direct object pronouns are often used to avoid repeating words in conversation.

    ¿Comes frijoles todos los días?

    *Sí, **los** como todos los días.*

    The direct object pronouns in Spanish are:

me	nos
te	os
lo/la	los/las

- Direct object pronouns are usually placed in front of a conjugated verb.

    ¿Quieres el pan tostado?   *Sí, **lo** quiero.*

- If a conjugated verb is followed by an infinitive or present participle, the direct object pronoun can also be attached to the end of the infinitive or participle.

    *Sí, **los** voy a comer.*   *Sí, voy a comer**los**.*
    ***Lo** estoy comiendo.*   *Estoy comiéndo**lo**.*

A. Everyone is doing different things before dinner. First, underline the direct object pronoun in each sentence. Then, match each statement with the food to which it refers.

1. _a_ ᵇ José María l̲a̲ quiere.

2. _d_ La tía de Margarita está comiéndol̲a̲s̲.

3. _C_ Mis amigos l̲o̲s̲ prueban.

4. _b_ ᵃ Luisa va a prepararl̲o̲.

a. el pan tostado

b. la carne de res

c. los espaguetis

d. las salchichas

B. Read the following sentences about who is making what for the family picnic. Underline the direct object in first sentence. Then, write the direct object pronoun that should replace it in the second sentence. Follow the model.

Modelo   Mi tía Anita prepara l̲a̲ ̲e̲n̲s̲a̲l̲a̲d̲a̲.   _La_ prepara.

1. Mi tía Donna trae l̲a̲s̲ ̲p̲a̲p̲a̲s̲. _las_ trae.

2. Mi tío Bill arregla e̲l̲ ̲p̲l̲a̲t̲o̲ ̲d̲e̲ ̲f̲r̲u̲t̲a̲s̲. _l̶a̶s̶ lo_ arregla.

3. Mi prima Laura prepara u̲n̲o̲s̲ ̲p̲o̲s̲t̲r̲e̲s̲ ̲d̲e̲l̲i̲c̲i̲o̲s̲o̲s̲. _los_ prepara.

4. Mamá pone l̲a̲ ̲m̲e̲s̲a̲. _la_ pone.

C. You are helping a friend prepare for a dinner party. Respond to each of her questions using direct object pronouns. Remember that you will need to change the verbs to the **yo** form to answer the questions. Follow the model.

Modelo   ¿Serviste la ensalada?   Sí, _la   serví_ .

1. ¿Cortaste la sandía?   Sí, _la corté_ .

2. ¿Probaste los camarones?   Sí, _los probé_ .

3. ¿Compraste los dulces?   No, no _los compré_ .

4. ¿Preparaste el postre?   No, no _lo preparé_ .

5. ¿Cocinaste las galletas?   Sí, _las cociné_ .

D. Look at the picture of Pablo and his parents eating breakfast. Then, answer the questions below using **sí** or **no**. Write the correct direct object pronoun in your answer. Follow the model.

Modelo   ¿Come Pablo yogur?   _Sí, lo come._

1. ¿Come salchichas?   _no, las come_

2. ¿Bebe leche?   _sí, la bebe_

3. ¿Come cereal?   _sí, lo come_

4. ¿Comen tocino los padres de Pablo?   _Sí, los comen tocino los padres de pablo_

5. ¿Comen huevos?   _no, los comen_

6. ¿Beben café?   _no, llo beben_

7. ¿Comen frutas?   _sí, las comen_

8. ¿Beben jugo de piña?   _no, lo beben jugo de piña_

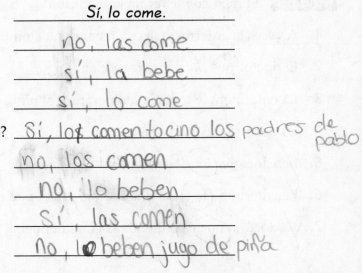

A ver si recuerdas — 3-2   **79**

Pronombres de complemento indirecto (p. 115)

- To indicate *to whom* or *for whom* an action is performed, you use indirect object pronouns in Spanish. The indirect object pronouns are:

me	nos
te	os
le	les

- Indirect object pronouns follow the same rules for placement as direct object pronouns. They usually go before a conjugated verb, but can also be attached to the end of an infinitive or a present participle.

    *María **me** prepara el desayuno.*

    *María **te** va a preparar el desayuno. / María va a preparar**te** el desayuno.*

- To clarify who the indirect object pronoun refers to, you can add **a** + a noun or the corresponding subject pronoun.

    *El doctor **le** da las pastillas **a José**.*

    *La enfermera **les** pone una inyección **a ellas**.*

- Remember that one common use of the indirect object pronouns is with verbs like **gustar, encantar,** and **doler.**

A. Doctors and nurses do a lot of things for their patients. First, read the following statements and circle the direct object pronoun. Then, indicate for whom the action is done by choosing a letter from the box below.

a. for me	**c.** for one other person
b. for us	**d.** for a group of other people

Modelo   El médico (me) receta la medicina. ___a___

1. A veces (la) enfermera les da regalos a los niños. __d__

2. El doctor (nos) pone una inyección. __b__

3. La enfermera le toma la temperatura al niño. __a__

4. La doctora (me) examina. __a__

5. (Los) doctores (les) dan recetas a sus pacientes. __d__

6. (La) enfermera (le) toma una radiografía al paciente. __c__

7. (La) doctora (nos) recomienda la comida buena. __c__

Pronombres de complemento indirecto (*continued*)

B. Write the correct indirect object pronouns to complete the sentences about what an assistant does for others in his office.

| Modelo | El asistente siempre ___*le*___ prepara café al jefe. |

1. El asistente ___nos___ sirve café a nosotros también.

2. El asistente ___me___ manda (a mí) documentos por correo electrónico.

3. El asistente ___les___ trae fotocopias a <u>los trabajadores</u>.

4. ¿El asistente ___te___ prepara los materiales para la reunión (a ti)?

5. El asistente ___le___ dice la verdad a su jefe.

C. Help the school nurse understand what's wrong with each student. Using the information provided, write a sentence about each picture. Be sure to include an indirect object pronoun in each sentence.

| Modelo | (Ronaldo / doler / el brazo) |
| | *A Ronaldo le duele el brazo.* |

1. (Catrina / no gustar / medicina) (tomar)
   a Catrina le no gustó el medicina
   la

2. (A mí / doler / la espalda)
   a mí me doler la espalda
   duele

3. (Las chicas / doler / la cabeza)
   a las chicas les doter la cabeza
   duele

4. (Nosotros / doler / el estómago)
   a nosotros nos doter el estómago
   duele

5. (Enrique / no gustar / la inyección)
   a enrique le no gustar la inyección

Capítulo 3

Fecha _____ **Vocabulary Flash Cards, Sheet 1**

Write the Spanish vocabulary word or phrase below each picture. Be sure to include the article for each noun.

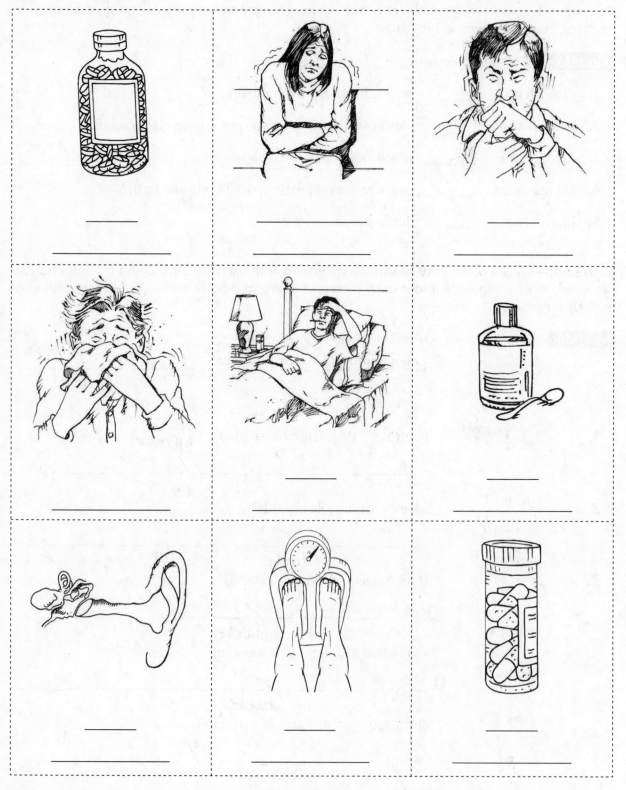

Write the Spanish vocabulary word below each picture. If there is a word or phrase, copy it in the space provided. Be sure to include the article for each noun.

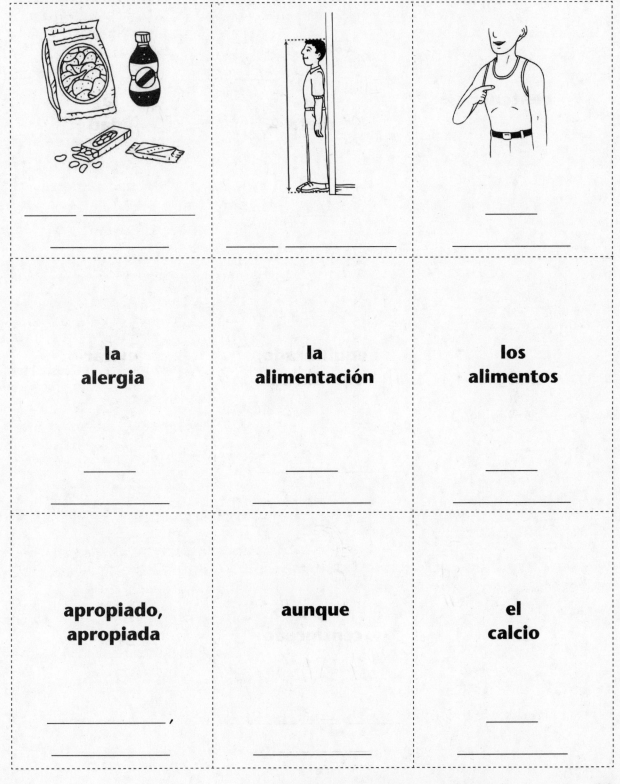

_____ _____	_____ _____	_____ _____
la alergia _____	**la alimentación** _____	**los alimentos** _____
apropiado, apropiada _____ , _____	**aunque** _____	**el calcio** _____

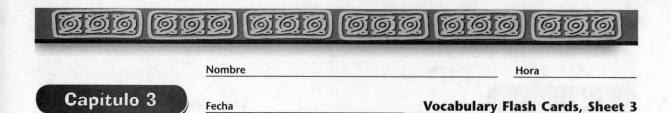

Copy the word or phrase in the space provided. Be sure to include the article for each noun.

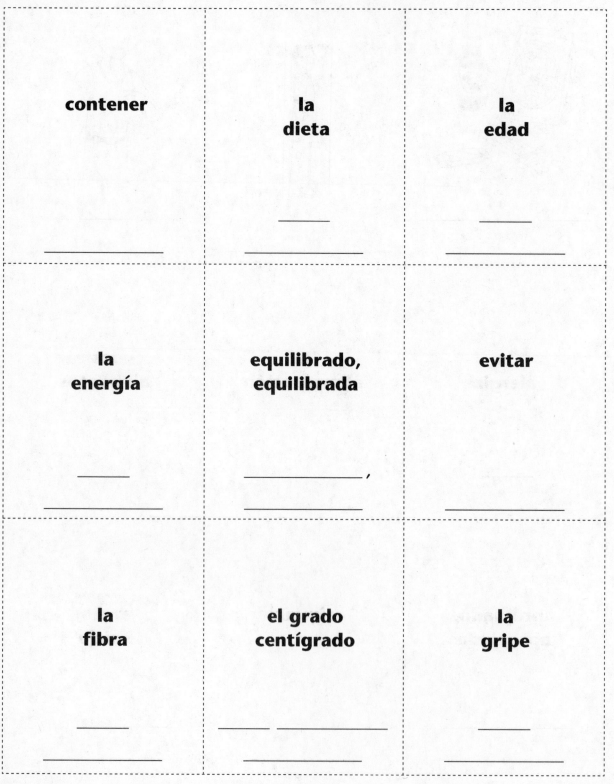

contener	**la dieta**	**la edad**
_____	_____	_____
_____	_____	_____
la energía	**equilibrado, equilibrada**	**evitar**
_____	_____,	
_____	_____	_____
la fibra	**el grado centígrado**	**la gripe**
_____	_____	_____

Copy the word or phrase in the space provided. Be sure to include the article for each noun.

el hábito alimenticio	el hierro	lleno, llena
la merienda	la proteína	nutritivo, nutritiva
saltar (una comida)	saludable	vacío, vacía

Capítulo 3

Copy the word or phrase in the space provided. Be sure to include the article for each noun. The blank cards can be used to write and practice other Spanish vocabulary for the chapter.

el carbohidrato	**tomar**	**la vitamina**
_____ _____	_____	_____ _____
_____	_____	_____
_____	_____	_____

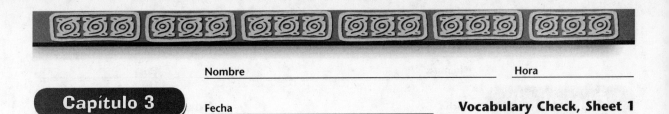

Tear out this page. Write the English words on the lines. Fold the paper along the dotted line to see the correct answers so you can check your work.

la alergia _____

el antibiótico _____

los alimentos _____

apropiado, apropiada _____

aunque _____

el calcio _____

la comida basura _____

contener _____

la dieta _____

la edad _____

la energía _____

equilibrado, equilibrada _____

estar resfriado, resfriada _____

la estatura _____

estornudar _____

evitar _____

la fiebre _____

la fibra _____

Fold In

Tear out this page. Write the Spanish words on the lines. Fold the paper along the dotted line to see the correct answers so you can check your work.

allergy _____

antibiotic _____

food _____

appropriate _____

_____

despite, even when _____

calcium _____

junk food _____

to contain _____

diet _____

age _____

energy _____

balanced _____

_____

to have a cold _____

height _____

to sneeze _____

to avoid _____

fever _____

fiber _____

Fold In

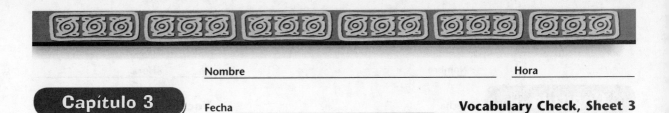

Tear out this page. Write the English words on the lines. Fold the paper along the dotted line to see the correct answers so you can check your work.

el grado centígrado _____

la gripe _____

el hábito alimenticio _____

el hierro _____

el jarabe _____

lleno, llena _____

la manera _____

la merienda _____

el nivel _____

nutritivo,
nutritiva _____

el oído _____

el pecho _____

la proteína _____

saltar (una comida) _____

saludable _____

tomar _____

la tos _____

vacío, vacía _____

Fold In ←

Tear out this page. Write the Spanish words on the lines. Fold the paper along the dotted line to see the correct answers so you can check your work.

centigrade degree _____

flu _____

eating habit _____

iron _____

syrup _____

full _____

way _____

snack _____

level _____

nutritious _____

_____

ear _____

chest _____

protein _____

to skip (a meal) _____

healthy _____

to take, to drink _____

cough _____

empty _____

Fold In ←

Nombre _Christina Nguyen_   Hora __6__

Mandatos afirmativos con *tú* (p. 125)

- Affirmative **tú** commands are informal commands telling one person to do something. To form them, you use the present indicative **él/ella/Ud.** form of the verb. Note that this also applies to stem-changing verbs.

   Toma vitaminas.   *Take vitamins*

   Pide una ensalada.   *Order a salad.*

A. Decide if each of the following statements is an observation the doctor has made about what you normally do, or if it is something the doctor is telling you to do (command).

Modelo	Caminas en el parque.	☑ observación	☐ orden del médico
1.	Practica deportes.	☑ observación	☐ orden del médico
2.	Descansas después de clases.	☑ observación	☐ orden del médico
3.	Levanta pesas.	☐ observación	☑ orden del médico
4.	Saltas el desayuno.	☐ observación	☑ orden del médico
5.	Bebe leche.	☑ observación	☐ orden del médico

B. Write the affirmative **tú** commands of the verbs in parentheses.

Modelo   ___Duerme___ (**Dormir**)

1. _desayuna_ (**Desayunar**)   **4.** ___bebe___ (**Beber**)

2. _come_ (**Comer**)   **5.** ___pide___ (**Pedir**)

3. _evita_ (**Evitar**)   **6.** _compra_ (**Comprar**)

- Some verbs have irregular affirmative **tú** command forms. Look at the list below.

hacer: **haz**	tener: **ten**	salir: **sal**	venir: **ven**	decir: **di**
ir: **ve**	ser: **sé**	poner: **pon**	mantener: **mantén**	

C. Change the sentences to affirmative **tú** commands to give a friend health advice.

Modelo   Necesitas hacer ejercicio. ___Haz___ ejercicio.

1. Necesitas salir a correr. _Sal_ a correr.

2. Necesitas ser atlético. _Sé_ atlético.

3. Necesitas ir al gimnasio tres veces por semana. _Ve_ al gimnasio.

4. Necesitas venir al parque conmigo para jugar fútbol. _ven_ al parque conmigo.

5. Necesitas mantener una buena salud. _mantén_ una buena salud.

Mandatos afirmativos con *tú* (*continued*)

- With affirmative commands, any reflexive, direct object, or indirect object pronouns are attached to the end of the verb.

   Cóme*lo*.   *Eat it.*

   Láva*te* las manos.   *Wash your hands.*

- When you attach a pronoun to a verb with two or more syllables, you will need to add a written accent mark to maintain the stress. The accent mark will usually go on the third-to-last vowel of the command.

D. Give the students advice to encourage better eating habits. Write the command form of the verb with the appropriate direct object pronoun for the underlined noun. Don't forget to add the accent mark to the stressed syllable.

Modelo   Ana no come <u>las verduras</u>.   _Cómelas._

1. José no bebe <u>leche</u>. _bébelo_

2. Andrés no toma <u>las vitaminas</u>. _tómalas_

3. Luci no compra <u>el jugo de naranja</u>. _Cómprala_

4. Beatriz no evita <u>la comida basura</u>. _evítala_

E. Write the command form of the verb with the reflexive pronoun to give your brother advice about his daily routine. Don't forget to add the accent mark to the stressed syllable as needed.

Modelo   (cepillarse) ___Cepíllate___ los dientes dos veces al día.

1. (lavarse) ___lávate___ las manos antes de comer.

2. (despertarse) ___despertate___ temprano por la mañana.

3. (acostarse) ___acostate___ antes de las nueve de la noche.

4. (ducharse) ___duchate___ todos los días.

5. (ponerse) ___ponete___ un sombrero y una chaqueta cuando hace frío.

6. (cortarse) ___cortate___ las uñas una vez por semana.

Mandatos negativos con *tú* (p. 126)

- Negative **tú** commands, used to informally tell one person not to do something, are formed differently from affirmative **tú** commands. Use the following rules to form negative **tú** commands:

  1) Put the verb in the **yo** form of the present tense.
  2) Get rid of the **-o** at the end of the verb.
  3) For **-ar** verbs, add the ending **-es**.

     For **-er** and **-ir** verbs, add the ending **-as**.

     caminar: *no camines*   beber: *no bebas*   escribir: *no escribas*

- Following these rules, verbs that have irregular **yo** forms or stem changes in the present tense will have the same stem changes in the negative **tú** commands.

  poner: no pon**gas**   obedecer: no obede**zcas**
  servir: no s**irv**as   contar: c**uent**es

A. Decide if each of the following statements is an observation the doctor has made about what you normally do, or if it is a suggestion about what you shouldn't do. Check off your choice.

1. No comes frutas.   ☑ observación   ☐ orden del médico

2. No comas comida basura.   ☐ observación   ☑ orden del médico

3. No descansas mucho.   ☑ observación   ☐ orden del médico

4. No tienes energía.   ☑ observación   ☐ orden del médico

5. No saltes comidas.   ☐ observación   ☑ orden del médico

B. Some students have confessed their bad habits. Tell them not to do it anymore! Be careful to use the correct ending: **-as** or **-es**.

Modelo   Como muchos dulces. __No__ __comas__ muchos dulces.

1. Bebo refrescos con mucho azúcar. __No__ __bebas__ esos refrescos.

— 2. Tomo mucho café todos los días. __No__ __tomes__ tanto café.

3. Pido comida basura en los restaurantes. __No__ __pidas__ esa comida.

— 4. Cocino muchas comidas fritas. __No__ __cocines__ tantas comidas fritas.

C. José is a student with study habits that need to change. Complete his part with the present tense **yo** form. Then, complete his friend's advice with a negative **tú** command, using the same verb. Follow the model.

Modelo (hacer) —Siempre ____hago____ las tareas después de medianoche.

—José, no ____hagas____ las tareas tan tarde en la noche.

1. (poner) —Siempre ____pone____ mi tarea debajo de la cama.

—José, no ____pongas____ la tarea allí.

2. (escoger) —Siempre ____escoge____ las clases más fáciles.

—José, no ____escogas____ sólo las clases fáciles.

3. (salir) —Siempre ____salie____ temprano de mis clases.

—José, no ____salias____ temprano de tus clases.

4. (destruir) —Siempre ____destrue____ mis exámenes cuando saco malas notas.

—José, no ____destruas____ los exámenes. Estúdialos para entender tus errores.

• When including a direct object, indirect object, or reflexive pronoun with a negative command, the pronoun must be placed *in front of* the verb.

  No **te** acuestes muy tarde.

  No comas mucha grasa. No **la** comas.

D. Rewrite the following commands using direct object pronouns. Follow the model.

Modelo No comas muchos dulces. *No los comas*.

1. No compres esas comidas. No las compres   3. No tomes tanto café. No lo tomes

2. No bebas esos refrescos. No los bebas   4. No pidas esa comida. No la pidas

• Some verbs have irregular negative **tú** command forms. Look at the list below.

| dar: **no des** | ir: **no vayas** | estar: **no estés** | ser: **no seas** | saber: **no sepas** |

E. Write the correct negative **tú** command for each sentence to help a mother give commands to her teenage daughter.

Modelo (ir) No __vayas__ a lugares desconocidos sin otra persona.

1. (dar) No le __des__ tu número de teléfono a nadie.

2. (ser) No __seas__ irresponsable.

3. (estar) No __estés__ enojada conmigo.

4. (ir) No __vayas__ a las fiestas de la universidad.

Mandatos afirmativos y negativos con *Ud.* y *Uds.* (p. 127)

- To give formal commands to one person, you need to use an **Ud.** command. To give commands to a group of people, you need to use an **Uds.** command. Both types of commands are formed in a similar manner to the negative **tú** commands.
- To make an **Ud.** command, remove the final **-s** from the negative **tú** command.

  Estudi**e** (Ud.)   No estudi**e** (Ud.)

- To make an **Uds.** command, replace the **-s** of the negative **tú** command with an **-n.**

  Estudi**en** (Uds.)   No estudi**en** (Uds.)

- As you can see from the examples above, the negative commands have the same verb forms as the affirmative commands. The only difference is that they are preceded by the word *no.*

A. Write the correct endings for commands that students and Sra. Méndez, their teacher, give each other. Pay attention to whether you are writing an **Ud.** or an **Uds.** command.

Modelo (**hablar**) Sra. Méndez, habl *e* (Ud.) más despacio, por favor.

1. (**tomar**)   Estudiantes, tom _en_ (Uds.) apuntes, por favor.

2. (**repetir**)   Sra. Méndez, repit _a_ (Ud.) la frase otra vez, por favor.

3. (**escribir**) Sra. Méndez, escrib _a_ (Ud.) las palabras nuevas en la pizarra, por favor.

4. (**hacer**)   Estudiantes, no hag _an_ (Uds.) tanto ruido, por favor.

5. (**decir**)   Sra. Méndez, no dig _a_ (Ud.) que hay más tarea, por favor.

- Verbs that end in **-car, -gar,** and **-zar** have spelling changes in the **Ud.** and **Uds.** commands. See the examples below.

  Bus**que** (Ud.)   No bus**quen** (Uds.)

  Jue**gue** (Ud.)   No jue**guen** (Uds.)

  No almuer**ce** (Ud.)   Almuer**cen** (Uds.)

B. Write the correct **Ud.** command form for each verb below. Pay attention to verb endings to determine the spelling change. Follow the model.

Modelo (**Practicar**) _Practique_ la pronunciación con frecuencia.

1. (**llegar**)   No _llegue_ tarde a la clase.

2. (**Empezar**)   _empiece_ a escribir ahora. stem changing

3. (**Cruzar**)   _cruce_ la calle aquí.

4. (**sacar**)   No _saque_ la comida en este momento.

5. (**tocar**)   No _toque_ la mesa sucia.

Capítulo 3   Fecha 3/31/23   **Guided Practice Activities, Sheet 6**

- The same verbs that are irregular in the negative **tú** commands are also irregular in the **Ud.** and **Uds.** commands. See the list below for a reminder.

> dar: **dé/den**   ir: **vaya/vayan**   ser: **sea/sean**   estar: **esté/estén**   saber: **sepa/sepan**

C. Provide the correct **Uds.** commands for a group of student athletes.

Modelo   (Ser) _____ *Sean* _____ honrados y trabajadores.

1. (**Ir**) _____ vayan _____ al gimnasio a levantar pesas.

2. (**dar**)   No le _____ dén _____ la pelota a un jugador del otro equipo.

3. (**Saber**) _____ sepan _____ el horario de partidos.

4. (**ser**)   No _____ sean _____ descorteses con el otro equipo.

- The rules for placement of direct object, indirect object, and reflexive pronouns for **Ud.** and **Uds.** commands are the same as those for the **tú** commands.
- Pronouns are attached to affirmative commands.
  > Tome (Ud.) vitaminas. Tóme**las.**
  > Levánten**se** (Uds.) temprano.
- Pronouns go in front of negative commands.
  > No **se** acueste (Ud.) tarde.
  > No coman (Uds.) muchas hamburguesas. No **las** coman.
- Remember that with reflexive verbs the pronoun will be *se* for both **Ud.** and **Uds.** commands.

D. Provide the **Ud.** commands that Paco gives his father during the day. A "+" indicates you should write an affirmative command; a "−" indicates a negative command. Don't forget the reflexive pronoun!

reflexive
chop off
ending

Modelo   (+ levantarse) _____ *Levántese* _____ ahora.

1. (− afeitarse)   no se afeite hoy.

2. (+ ducharse)   dúcharse ahora.

3. (− lavarse)   no se lave el pelo con el champú de su mamá.

4. (+ cepillarse)   cépillese los dientes.

5. (+ ponerse)   póngase ese traje gris.

6. (− irse)   no se vaya ahora.

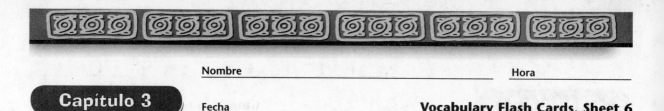

Capítulo 3 Fecha _____ **Vocabulary Flash Cards, Sheet 6**

Write the Spanish vocabulary word or phrase below each picture. Be sure to include the article for each noun.

Capítulo 3   Fecha _____   **Vocabulary Flash Cards, Sheet 7**

Write the Spanish vocabulary word below each picture. If there is a word or phrase, copy it in the space provided. Be sure to include the article for each noun.

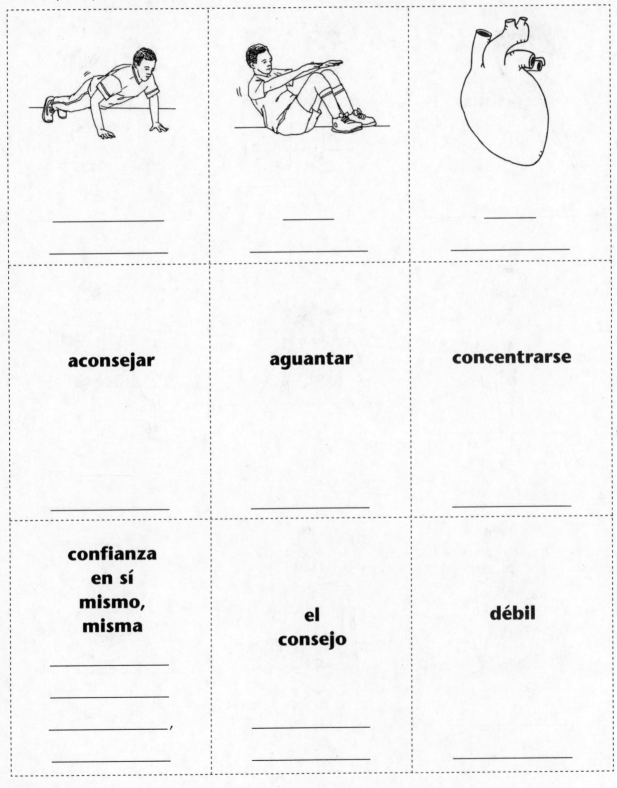

_____ _____	_____ _____	_____ _____
aconsejar _____	**aguantar** _____	**concentrarse** _____
confianza en sí mismo, misma _____ _____ _____ , _____	**el consejo** _____ _____	**débil** _____ _____

Copy the word or phrase in the space provided. Be sure to include the article for each noun.

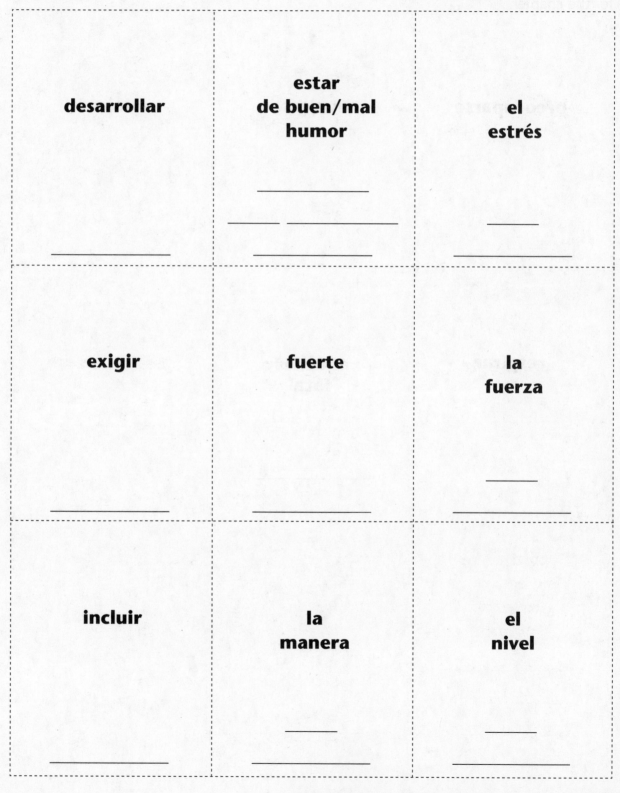

desarrollar

_____

**estar
de buen/mal
humor**

_____

_____ _____

**el
estrés**

_____

exigir

_____

fuerte

_____

**la
fuerza**

_____

incluir

_____

**la
manera**

_____

**el
nivel**

_____

Copy the word or phrase in the space provided. Be sure to include the article for each noun. The blank cards can be used to write and practice other Spanish vocabulary for the chapter.

preocuparse	**quejarse**	**relajarse**
_____	_____	_____
respirar	**sentirse fatal**	
_____	_____	_____
_____	_____	_____

Tear out this page. Write the English words on the lines. Fold the paper along the dotted line to see the correct answers so you can check your work.

abdominales _____

aconsejar _____

aguantar _____

caerse de sueño _____

el calambre _____

el consejo _____

concentrarse _____

confianza en sí mismo(a) _____

el corazón _____

débil _____

desarrollar _____

ejercicios aeróbicos _____

estar de buen/
mal humor _____
_____

estar en forma _____

estirar _____

Fold In

Tear out this page. Write the Spanish words on the lines. Fold the paper along the dotted line to see the correct answers so you can check your work.

crunches _____

to advise _____

to endure; to tolerate _____

to be exhausted, sleepy _____

cramp _____

advice _____

to concentrate _____

self-confidence _____

heart _____

weak _____

to develop _____

aerobics _____

to be in a good/
bad mood _____

to be fit _____

to stretch _____

Fold In →

Tear out this page. Write the English words on the lines. Fold the paper along the dotted line to see the correct answers so you can check your work.

el estrés _____

estresado, _____
estresada

exigir _____

flexionar _____

la fuerza _____

hacer bicicleta _____

hacer cinta _____

hacer flexiones _____

el músculo _____

preocuparse _____

quejarse _____

relajar(se) _____

respirar _____

sentirse fatal _____

el yoga _____

Fold In

Capítulo 3   Fecha _____   **Vocabulary Check, Sheet 8**

Tear out this page. Write the Spanish words on the lines. Fold the paper along the dotted line to see the correct answers so you can check your work.

stress   _____

stressed out   _____
                                _____

to demand   _____

to flex, to stretch   _____

strength   _____

to use a stationary bike   _____

to use a treadmill   _____

to do push-ups   _____

muscle   _____

to worry   _____

to complain   _____

to relax   _____

to breathe   _____

to feel awful   _____

yoga   _____

Fold In →

El subjuntivo: Verbos regulares (p. 136)

- When someone gives advice, recommendations, suggestions, or demands to another person, Spanish uses the *subjunctive mood*.

- A sentence that includes the subjunctive can be thought of as having two separate halves, which are connected by the word **que**.

    Yo recomiendo que tú *hagas* ejercicio.   *I recommend that you exercise.*

- Notice that the first half (**Yo recomiendo**) includes a verb in the regular present tense and introduces a suggestion, demand, etc. The second half (**tú hagas ejercicio**) includes a verb in the subjunctive and tells what the first person wants the second person to do.

- Verbs in the subjunctive form may look somewhat familiar to you because they follow the same conjugation rules as the **Ud./Uds.** commands. To form verbs in the subjunctive, follow the rules below:

    1) Put the verb in the **yo** form of the present indicative (regular present tense).
    2) Take off the **-o**.
    3) a. For **-ar** verbs, add the following endings: **-e, -es, -e, -emos, -éis, -en**
       b. For **-er** and **-ir** verbs, add the following endings: **-a, -as, -a, -amos, -áis, -an**

- Below are three examples of verbs conjugated in the present subjunctive.

entrenar		**correr**		**tener**	
entren**e**	entren**emos**	corr**a**	corr**amos**	teng**a**	teng**amos**
entren**es**	entren**éis**	corr**as**	corr**áis**	teng**as**	teng**áis**
entren**e**	entren**en**	corr**a**	corr**an**	teng**a**	teng**an**

A. Underline the verbs in the present subjunctive in the following sentences.

Modelo   Mis padres recomiendan que yo <u>haga</u> mi tarea.

1. El doctor quiere que los pacientes <u>coman</u> bien.

2. Los profesores exigen que los estudiantes <u>estudien</u>.

3. Yo no permito que tú <u>fumes</u>.

4. Tú prefieres que nosotros <u>tomemos</u> clases de yoga.

5. A nosotros no nos gusta que nuestro padre <u>salte</u> comidas.

6. Recomiendo que nosotros <u>evitemos</u> la comida basura.

B. Oprah Winfrey is known for her dedication to health and fitness. First, identify if each of the following activities is a custom **(C)** or a recommendation **(R)** of Oprah. Then, choose the correct verb to complete the sentence.

| Modelo | _R_ Oprah le aconseja a la chica que (**hace** /(**haga**)) cinta. |

she does

1. _C_ Oprah siempre ((**se estira**)/ **se estire**) antes de correr.

2. _R_ Oprah quiere que los jóvenes ((**evitan**) / **eviten**) la comida basura.

3. _R_ Oprah recomienda que nosotros (**nos relajamos** /(**nos relajemos**)) un poco.

4. _RC_ Oprah ((**come**)/ **coma**) alimentos nutritivos cada día.

- You can also use impersonal expressions to give recommendations, suggestions, and demands. These impersonal expressions are followed by **que** and then the subjunctive. Some common expressions are:

  Es importante...   **Es necesario...**   **Es bueno...**   **Es mejor...**

  Es importante que *los atletas* **cuiden** *su corazón.*

_4/13/23_

C. In each sentence, circle the impersonal expression that indicates a suggestion for healthy living. Then, use the correct present subjunctive form to complete the sentence.

| Modelo | (Es necesario) que yo ___*tome*___ (**tomar**) 8 vasos de agua al día. |

1. Es mejor que Miguel _elimine_ (**eliminar**) el estrés.

2. Es importante que Eva y Adán _coman_ (**comer**) frutas y verduras.

3. Es necesario que Gabriela _haga_ (**hacer**) ejercicio.

4. Es bueno que los niños _incluyan_ (**incluir**) carbohidratos en su dieta.

D. Complete the sentences about a coach's recommendations for his athletes by conjugating the verbs correctly. Remember that your first verb will be in the indicative and your second verb will be in the subjunctive. Follow the model.

| Modelo | el entrenador / recomendar / que / nosotros / practicar todos los días |
| | _El entrenador recomienda que nosotros practiquemos todos los días._ |

1. es importante / que / nosotros / entregar nuestra tarea

_____

2. el entrenador / no permitir / que / nosotros / llegar tarde al partido

_____

3. es bueno / que / nosotros / traer nuestros uniformes / a la escuela

_____

4. el entrenador / exigir / que / nosotros / tener una buena actitud

_____

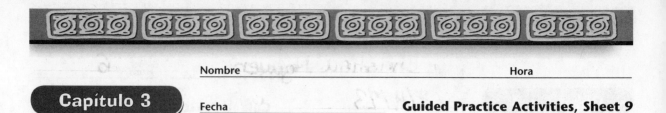

Capítulo 3   Fecha _____

El subjuntivo: Verbos irregulares (p. 139)

• There are six irregular verbs in the present subjunctive. See the chart below for the conjugations of these verbs.

ser	sea, seas, sea, seamos, seáis, sean
estar	esté, estés, esté, estemos, estéis, estén
dar	dé, des, dé, demos, deis, den
ir	vaya, vayas, vaya, vayamos, vayáis, vayan
saber	sepa, sepas, sepa, sepamos, sepáis, sepan
haber	haya, hayas, haya, hayamos, hayáis, hayan

A. Choose the correct form of the subjunctive verb to complete each of the following sentences about healthy living. Circle your choice.

Modelo   Te sugiero que tú no ((estés) / estén) tan estresado.

1. Es importante que nosotros (**mantengas / mantengamos**) una buena salud.

2. Quiero que ellos (**vayamos / vayan**) a la práctica de fútbol.

3. El doctor me recomienda que (**sepa / sepas**) tomar buenas decisiones.

4. Es muy bueno que (**haya / hayas**) una clase de yoga este viernes.

5. Los enfermeros no permiten que nosotras (**sean / seamos**) perezosas.

B. A group of students discusses the emphasis on health in their community. Complete the sentences with the correct present subjunctive form.

Modelo   (saber) Es importante que nosotros ____*sepamos*____ más sobre la buena salud.

1. (estar)   Todos recomiendan que nosotros _____ en forma.

2. (dar)   Si no te gusta correr, es importante que (tú) _____ un paseo por el parque.

3. (ser)   Los padres no deben permitir que sus hijos _____ perezosos.

4. (haber)   Es bueno que _____ dos parques en nuestra ciudad.

5. (saber)   Los líderes de la ciudad quieren que los jóvenes _____ llevar una vida sana.

6. (estar)   Nos gusta que la piscina _____ abierta hasta las diez durante el verano.

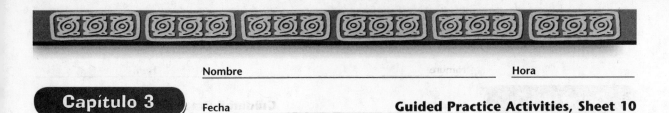

El subjuntivo: Verbos irregulares (*continued*)

C. Look at the list of recommendations given by a director of a health club. First, underline the verb that best completes the sentence. Then, write the correct form of the verb using the subjunctive mood. Follow the model.

Modelo   Los doctores prefieren que los jóvenes (**ser** / saber) _____*sean*_____ activos.

1. Quiero que la gente (**dar / estar**) _____ relajada.

2. Les recomiendo que Uds. (**ir / saber**) _____ al club atlético.

3. Exijo que todos nosotros (**estar / ir**) _____ al gimnasio juntos.

4. Es necesario que (**haber / dar**) _____ clubes atléticos disponibles.

5. Es importante que nosotros (**haber / saber**) _____ algo sobre el cuerpo humano.

D. Complete the following statements about exercise and healthy living.

Modelo   Mis padres / exigir / que / todos nosotros / dar una caminata / en las montañas

Mis padres exigen que todos nosotros demos una caminata en
las montañas.

1. Yo / recomendar / que / mis amigos / ser / activos

_____

2. Es necesario / que / la gente / saber / dónde está el gimnasio

_____

3. Es bueno / que / haber / clases de ejercicios aérobicos / en nuestra escuela

_____

4. El entrenador / sugerir / que / yo / ir / al lago para nadar

_____

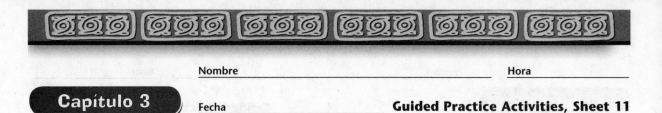

El subjuntivo: verbos con cambio de raíz (p. 141)

- Stem-changing verbs follow slightly different rules than other verbs in the subjunctive. Verbs ending in **-ar** and **-er** have stem changes in all forms except the **nosotros** and **vosotros** forms.

cont**ar**		perd**er**	.
c**ue**nte	contemos	p**ie**rda	perdamos
c**ue**ntes	contéis	p**ie**rdas	perdáis
c**ue**nte	c**ue**nten	p**ie**rda	p**ie**rdan

- The **-ir** stem-changing verbs have stem changes in *all* forms of the subjunctive, but the stem change for the **nosotros** and **vosotros** forms differs slightly.

- If the **-ir** verb has an **o→ue** stem change, such as **dormir**, the **o** will change to a **u** in the **nosotros** and **vosotros** forms. If the **-ir** verb has an **e→ie** stem change, such as **preferir**, the **e** will change to an **i** in the **nosotros** and **vosotros** forms. If the verb has an **e→i** stem change, such as **servir**, it has the same stem change in all forms. Look at the examples below.

dorm**ir**		prefer**ir**		serv**ir**	
d**ue**rma	d**u**rmamos	pref**ie**ra	pref**i**ramos	s**i**rva	s**i**rvamos
d**ue**rmas	d**u**rmáis	pref**ie**ras	pref**i**ráis	s**i**rvas	s**i**rváis
d**ue**rma	d**ue**rman	pref**ie**ra	pref**ie**ran	s**i**rva	s**i**rvan

A. Circle the correct verb form to complete each sentence. Pay attention to whether the statement is trying to persuade someone to do something (subjunctive) or if it is just an observation about someone's lifestyle (indicative).

Modelo   Siempre ((vuelves)/ **vuelvas**) a casa tarde.

1. Te enojas cuando (**pierdes / pierdas**) partidos.

2. Es importante que (**te diviertes / te diviertas**) cuando practicas deportes.

3. Siempre (**empiezas / empieces**) tu tarea muy tarde.

4. Exijo que (**comienzas / comiences**) a hacer la tarea más temprano.

5. Con frecuencia (**te despiertas / te despiertes**) tarde para tus clases.

6. Es mejor que (**te acuestas / te acuestes**) antes de las diez para poder dormir lo suficiente.

B. A talk show host tells her TV audience what she recommends for a healthly lifestyle. Complete each sentence with the **Uds.** form of the verb in the present subjunctive.

Modelo   (entender) Recomiendo que Uds. __entiendan__ cómo mantener la salud.

1. (volver)   Es mejor que Uds. ~~volver~~ *vuelren* temprano a casa para cenar.

2. (divertirse) Exijo que Uds. __se diviertan__ durante el día.

3. (despertarse) Es bueno que Uds. __se despierten__ temprano todos los días.

4. (repetir)   Es necesario que Uds. __repitan__ todas estas reglas.

C. Many people are giving health advice to you and your friends. Complete each sentence with the **nosotros** form of the verb in the present subjunctive. **¡Cuidado!** Remember that only -ir verbs have stem changes in the **nosotros** form of the subjunctive.

Modelo   (pedir) Julia nos recomienda que __pidamos__ una ensalada.

1. (dormir)   Pati nos recomienda que __durmamos__ más horas.

2. (probar)   Paco nos recomienda que __probemos__ esas comidas nuevas.

3. (empezar) Carmen nos recomienda que __empecemos__ lentamente.

4. (vestirse) Mateo nos recomienda que __nos vestamos__ con ropa cómoda.
              visitamos

D. Write complete sentences using the words provided. Each sentence should have one verb in the regular present tense and one in the present subjunctive. Don't forget to add the word **que**!

Modelo   Mis padres / querer / yo / seguir / sus consejos

          Mis padres quieren que yo siga sus consejos.

1. El entrenador / sugerir / los atletas / dormir / ocho horas cada noche

   _____

2. La profesora / recomendar / nosotros / pedir / ayuda

   _____

3. Mi amigo / recomendar / yo / empezar un programa de ejercicio

   _____

4. Él / querer / nosotros / divertirse / en nuestro trabajo

   _____

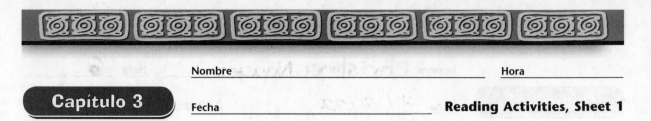

Puente a la cultura (pp. 144–145)

A. You are about to read about an ancient Mexican ball game somewhat similar to basketball. See if you can answer the following questions about the sport of basketball.

1. How many players from each team are on the court at once? _____

2. How many points can a person earn for a basket?

   _____

3. Which of the following _cannot_ be considered as a rule of basketball?

   a. no aggressive behavior toward other players

   b. you must dribble the ball using your hands

   c. you must attempt to score within a time limit

   d. you must pass the ball with your feet

B. Use the Venn diagram below to compare **ullamalitzi**, the ancient Aztec ball game with the modern game of basketball. Write the letters of each statement in the appropriate places: the left circle if they apply only to basketball, the right circle if they apply only to the Aztec ball game, or in the middle if they apply to both. The first one is done for you.

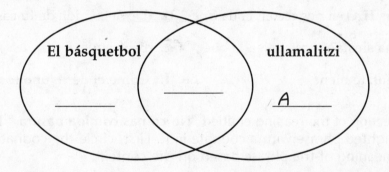

El básquetbol   ullamalitzi

_____   _____ /A/ _____

A. ~~Los nobles juegan~~.   F. Los jugadores usan las manos.
B. Los partidos aparecen en la tele.   G. Los jugadores no pueden usar las manos.
C. Hay una pelota bastante grande.   H. Muchas personas ven los partidos.
D. La pelota pesa ocho libras.   I. Los atletas llevan uniformes.
E. Hay un anillo.

C. Place a check mark next to the adjectives that correspond with the characteristics of Aztec society that the article describes.

☐ aburrida   ☐ desorganizada

☐ religiosa   ☐ atlética

☐ artística

Lectura (pp. 150–152)

A. Use the pictures on pages 150–151 of your textbook to help you determine what the reading will be about. Write two types of advice you think this article will give you, judging by the pictures.

1. _____

2. _____

B. This reading is divided up into six sections. Look at the different sections on pages 150–152 and read each subtitle. Try to anticipate what each section will be about by thinking about the meaning of the subtitle. You can also use the pictures in your textbook to help you. Then, write the letter of the command below that best relates to each subtitle in the reading. The first one has been done for you.

1. __f__ **Aliméntate bien**   **a.** Lávate las manos.

2. _____ **No comas comida basura**   **b.** Mantén la espalda derecha.

3. _____ **Muy limpias**   **c.** Duerme ocho horas al día.

4. _____ **Más H₂O**   **d.** Lleva comida de tu casa.

5. _____ **¿Una siesta?**   **e.** Bebe agua.

6. _____ **Siéntate bien.**   **f.** ~~Come el desayuno todos los días.~~

C. Look at the section of the reading entitled "**No comas comida basura.**" Each excerpt contains a highlighted phrase with a cognate in it. First, circle the cognate. Then, try to determine the meaning of the phrase based on the context.

«*Mejor escoge alimentos **que echen a andar tu motor**.*»

1. _____

«*Las palomitas de maíz y **las frutas deshidratadas** son una buena opción en lugar de comidas fritas.*»

2. _____

D. Each section of the reading is divided into goals, steps for reaching the goal, and pieces of advice. Look at the section titled **"Muy limpios"** on p. 151 and check off the answer that best summarizes the content of each part of this section.

1. **Meta**

   _____ tener dientes blancos

   _____ tener dientes y manos limpios

2. **¡Lógralo!**

   _____ cepillarse los dientes antes de comer y lavarse las manos después

   _____ lavarse las manos frecuentemente con un gel y cepillarse los dientes después de comer

3. **Nuestros consejos**

   _____ llevar siempre jabón en tu mochila junto con un hilo dental

   _____ usar mentas todos los días en lugar de cepillarse los dientes

E. Do not get frustrated if you cannot understand every word of the article. Read the sections **"Más H₂0"**, **"¿Una siesta?"**, and **"Siéntate bien"** and write the main point of each section in one sentence. The main point has been done for you for the section **"Más H₂0."**

1. **Más H$_2$O**

   It is important to drink water or juice instead of soda to maintain energy
   and good health.

2. **¿Una siesta?**

   _____

   _____

3. **Siéntate bien**

   _____

   _____

Otros usos de los verbos reflexivos (p. 161)

- Reflexive verbs in Spanish are often used to talk about actions one does to or for oneself, as opposed to other people. Note that, in the first example below, the woman wakes herself up, but in the second, she wakes her husband up.

  La mujer *se despierta*. (reflexive)   *The woman wakes (herself) up.*

  La mujer *despierta a su esposo*.   *The woman wakes her husband up.*
  (non-reflexive)

- Many reflexive verbs are associated with elements of one's daily routine:

  - **acostarse** (*to go to bed*)
  - **afeitarse** (*to shave*)
  - **bañarse** (*to bathe*)
  - **despertarse** (*to wake up*)
  - **divertirse** (*to have fun*)
  - **ducharse** (*to shower*)
  - **levantarse** (*to get up*)
  - **ponerse** (*to put on*)
  - **sentirse** (*to feel*)
  - **vestirse** (*to dress oneself*)
  - **lavarse el pelo, las manos**, etc. (*to wash one's own hair, hands, etc.*)
  - **cepillarse el pelo, los dientes**, etc. (*to brush one's own hair, teeth, etc.*)

A. Complete the following sentences by circling the correct reflexive or non-reflexive verb forms. For each sentence, determine who the object of the verb is. If it is the same person who is performing the action, the reflexive verb form is required.

Modelo   El perro siempre ((despierta)/ se despierta) a los niños.

1. Marta (**lava / se lava**) el pelo.

2. La mamá (**peina / se peina**) a su hija pequeña.

3. Los hermanos Sánchez (**cepillan / se cepillan**) los dientes.

4. Nosotros (**bañamos / nos bañamos**) el perro.

5. Tú (**levantas / te levantas**) a las seis de la mañana.

B. Write the correct reflexive or non-reflexive present-tense verb form in the space provided. Note: the first space will be left blank if the verb is not reflexive. Follow the model.

Modelo   (**vestir/vestirse**) Juanito ___se___ ___viste___ en el dormitorio.

1. (**cepillar/cepillarse**) Nosotros _____ _____ los dientes después de desayunar.

2. (**despertar/despertarse**) Tú _____ _____ a tu mamá a las seis.

3. (**poner/ponerse**) Carla y Alicia _____ _____ unas faldas cortas.

4. (**sentir/sentirse**) Yo _____ _____ mal, pero tengo que ir a la escuela.

- There are some reflexive verbs that are used to express a change in condition or emotion.

  enojarse (*to get angry*)　　**aburrirse** (*to get bored*)

  cansarse (*to get tired*)　　**ponerse** + *adjective* (*to become scared, nervous, etc.*)

- Other verbs change meaning depending on whether they are used reflexively.

  ir: to go　　　　　　　　　**irse**: to leave

  quedar: to be located　　　**quedarse**: to stay in a place

  quitar: to take away　　　　**quitarse**: to take off (clothing)

  perder: to lose　　　　　　**perderse**: to get lost

  dormir: to sleep　　　　　　**dormirse**: to fall asleep

  volver: to return　　　　　　**volverse** + **adjective (i.e. loco)**: to become (i.e. crazy)

- Some verbs and expressions are always reflexive:

  darse cuenta de: to realize　　**quejarse**: to complain

  portarse bien/mal: to behave well/badly

C. Write the correct reflexive or non-reflexive present-tense verb form in the spaces provided. Note: the first space will be left blank if the verb is not reflexive.

Modelo　(**enojar**) Antonio ___se___ ___enoja___ cuando su hermano usa sus cosas.

1. (**quejar**)　Los profesores _____ _____ de sus estudiantes perezosos.

2. (**quitar**)　El camarero _____ _____ la mesa después de la cena.

3. (**cansar**)　Yo _____ _____ cuando hago problemas matemáticos difíciles.

4. (**perder**)　Nosotros _____ _____ la tarea siempre.

- Reflexive pronouns can either go before the conjugated verb or on the end of a participle or infinitive. If the pronoun is attached to the present participle, add an accent mark.

  Me estoy lavando las manos.　　*Estoy lavándome las manos.*

  Te vas a duchar.　　　　　　*Vas a ducharte.*

D. Write the correct present participle or infinitive of the verbs in parentheses.

Modelo　(**cepillarse**) Estoy ___cepillándome___ los dientes.

1. (**irse**)　　　¿Quieres _____ ahora?

2. (**dormirse**)　Estamos _____ porque estamos muy aburridas.

3. (**enojarse**)　Mis padres van a _____ si no llego a casa a tiempo.

4. (**volverse**)　¡Estoy _____ loca de tanto trabajar!

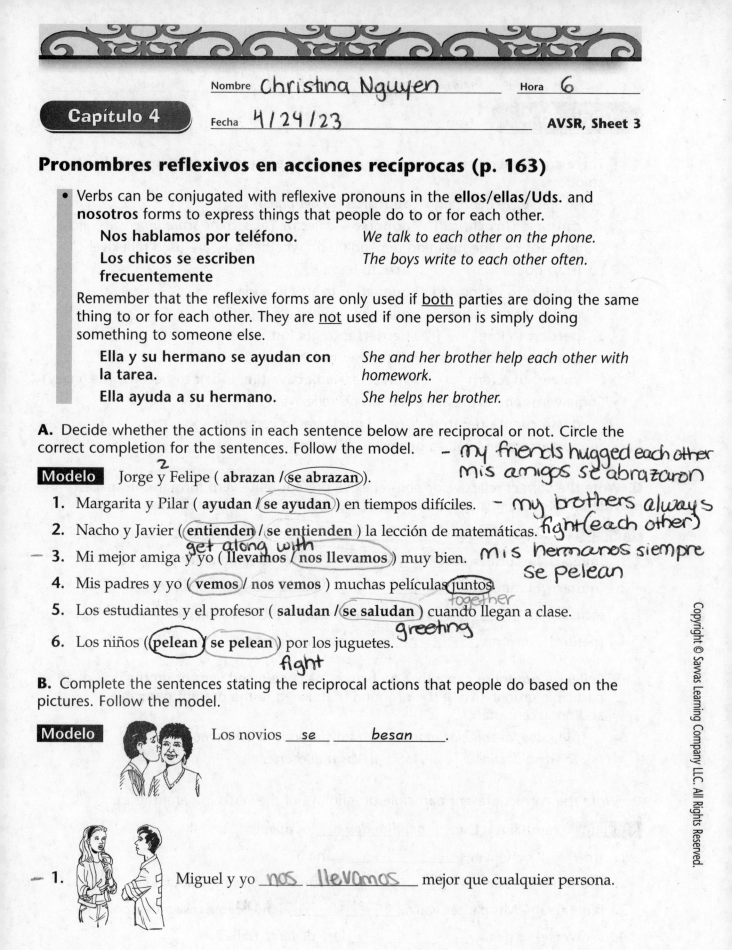

Pronombres reflexivos en acciones recíprocas (p. 163)

- Verbs can be conjugated with reflexive pronouns in the **ellos/ellas/Uds.** and **nosotros** forms to express things that people do to or for each other.

  Nos hablamos por teléfono.   *We talk to each other on the phone.*

  Los chicos se escriben frecuentemente   *The boys write to each other often.*

  Remember that the reflexive forms are only used if <u>both</u> parties are doing the same thing to or for each other. They are <u>not</u> used if one person is simply doing something to someone else.

  Ella y su hermano se ayudan con la tarea.   *She and her brother help each other with homework.*

  Ella ayuda a su hermano.   *She helps her brother.*

A. Decide whether the actions in each sentence below are reciprocal or not. Circle the correct completion for the sentences. Follow the model.

- my friends hugged each other
- mis amigos se abrazaron

Modelo   Jorge y Felipe (abrazan / (se abrazan)).

1. Margarita y Pilar (ayudan / (se ayudan)) en tiempos difíciles.
   - my brothers always fight (each other)
2. Nacho y Javier ((entienden) / se entienden) la lección de matemáticas.
3. Mi mejor amiga y yo (llevamos / (nos llevamos)) muy bien.   *get along with*   mis hermanos siempre se pelean
4. Mis padres y yo ((vemos) / nos vemos) muchas películas (juntos).   *together*
5. Los estudiantes y el profesor (saludan / (se saludan)) cuando llegan a clase.   *greeting*
6. Los niños ((pelean) / se pelean) por los juguetes.   *fight*

B. Complete the sentences stating the reciprocal actions that people do based on the pictures. Follow the model.

Modelo   Los novios ___se___ ___besan___.

1. Miguel y yo ___nos___ ___llevamos___ mejor que cualquier persona.

2. Elena y yo _nos_ _abrazamos_.

3. Oswaldo y Paco _se_ _saludan_.

4. Manolo y Ricardo _se_ _dan_ la mano.

C. Abuelita Cecilia is telling her grandchildren how the family was when she was little. Complete each sentence with the reciprocal verb form in the imperfect tense. Follow the model.

Modelo (abrazar) Mis primos y yo siempre _nos_ _abrazábamos_ en las reuniones familiares.

1. (pelear)   Mis hermanitos _se_ _peleaba_ frecuentemente cuando jugaban al béisbol.

2. (llevar)   Mis padres y yo _nos_ _llevaba_ muy bien generalmente.

3. (conocer)   Mis padres y los padres de mis amigos _se_ _conozcía_ bien.

4. (escribir) Mis amigos que vivían en otras ciudades y yo _nos_ _escribíamos_ cartas porque no había correo electrónico.

5. (comprender) Mi hermana mayor y yo _nos comprendíamos_ muy bien.

6. (leer)   Mis padres eran poetas y _se_ _leían_ la su poesía con frecuencia.

7. (parecer)   Mis hermanos _se_ _parecían_ mucho.

8. (contar)   Mis primos y yo _nos_ _contábamos_ chistes cómicos.

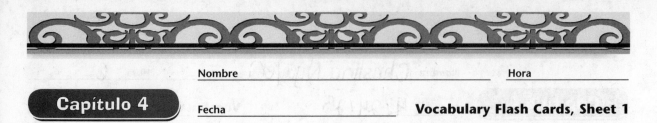

Write the Spanish vocabulary word below each picture. If there is a word or phrase, copy it in the space provided. Be sure to include the article for each noun.

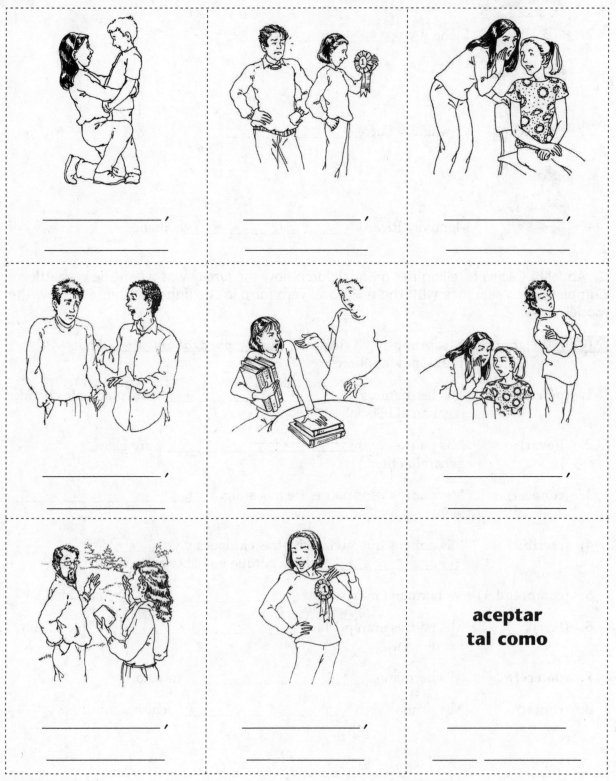

aceptar
tal como

Copy the word or phrase in the space provided. Be sure to include the article for each noun.

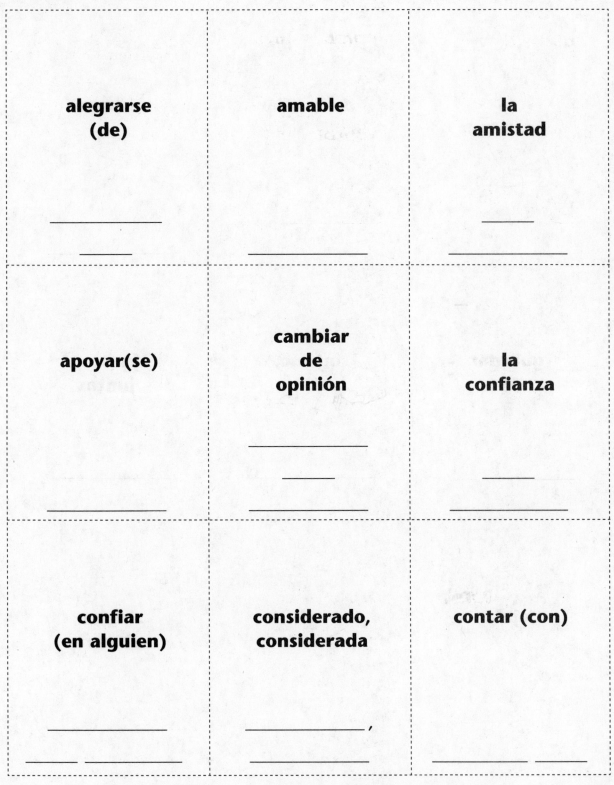

alegrarse (de)	amable	la amistad
apoyar(se)	cambiar de opinión	la confianza
confiar (en alguien)	considerado, considerada	contar (con)

Copy the word or phrase in the space provided. Be sure to include the article for each noun.

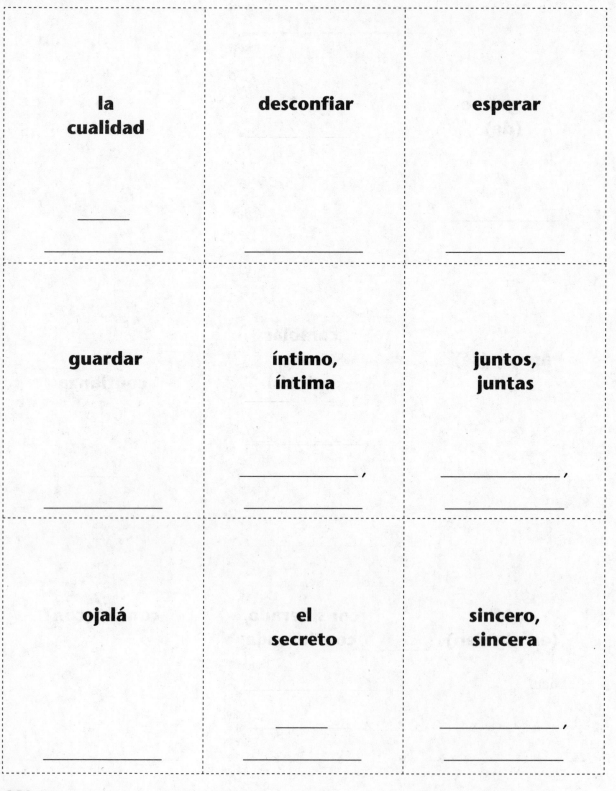

la cualidad	desconfiar	esperar
guardar	íntimo, íntima	juntos, juntas
ojalá	el secreto	sincero, sincera

Tear out this page. Write the English words on the lines. Fold the paper along the dotted line to see the correct answers so you can check your work.

aceptar tal como
(soy)

_____

_____

alegrarse

_____

amable

_____

la amistad

_____

apoyar(se)

_____

_____

cambiar de opinión

_____

cariñoso, cariñosa

_____

celoso, celosa

_____

chismoso, chismosa

_____

comprensivo,
comprensiva

_____

la confianza

_____

confiar ($i \rightarrow í$)

_____

considerado,
considerada

_____

contar con

_____

la cualidad

_____

desconfiar

_____

Fold In →

Tear out this page. Write the Spanish words on the lines. Fold the paper along the dotted line to see the correct answers so you can check your work.

to accept (me)
the way (I am)   _____
                                 _____

to be delighted   _____

kind   _____

friendship   _____

to support; to back   _____
(one another)

to change one's mind   _____

loving, affectionate   _____

jealous   _____

gossipy   _____

understanding   _____
                                 _____

trust   _____

to trust   _____

considerate   _____
                                 _____

to count on   _____

quality   _____

to mistrust   _____

Fold In

Tear out this page. Write the English words on the lines. Fold the paper along the dotted line to see the correct answers so you can check your work.

egoísta _____

entrometido, entrometida _____

_____

esperar _____

guardar (un secreto) _____

honesto, honesta _____

íntimo, íntima _____

juntos, juntas _____

ojalá _____

el secreto _____

sincero, sincera _____

sorprender(se) _____

temer _____

tener en común _____

tener celos _____

vanidoso, vanidosa _____

Fold In →

Tear out this page. Write the Spanish words on the lines. Fold the paper along the dotted line to see the correct answers so you can check your work.

selfish   _____

meddlesome,   _____
interfering   _____

to hope (for)   _____

to keep (a secret)   _____

honest   _____

intimate   _____

together   _____

I wish, I hope   _____

secret   _____

sincere   _____

to (be) surprised   _____

to fear   _____

to have in common   _____

to be jealous   _____

vain, conceited   _____

Fold In

El subjuntivo con verbos de emoción (p. 174)

- In Chapter 3, you learned to use the subjunctive in sentences in which someone expresses their desires, requests, or advice for someone else. Another instance in which the subjunctive is used is when one person expresses <u>emotion</u> about someone or something else. Look at the examples below.

Temo que mi amiga se enferme.	*I am afraid my friend will get sick.*
Nos sorprende que el maestro nos dé un examen.	*We are surprised that the teacher gives us an exam.*

The following list of verbs and expressions are used to indicate emotion:

temer: to be afraid

sentir: to regret / be sorry

alegrarse de: to be happy

esperar: to hope

me, te... gusta: I / you . . . like

me, te... enoja: it angers me, you . . .

ojalá: I hope or wish

es bueno: it is good

es malo: it is bad

es una lástima: it's a shame/pity

A. Each sentence describes a person's feeling about someone's actions. Circle the logical emotion for each sentence. Then underline the subjunctive verb in each sentence.

Modelo (**Me molesta** / **Me alegro de**) que no me <u>aceptes</u> tal como soy.

1. (**Es una lástima** / **Es bueno**) que no me <u>comprendas</u>.

2. (**Me gusta** / **Me enoja**) que siempre <u>cambies</u> de opinión.

3. (**Es malo** / **Espero**) que no <u>tengas</u> celos.

4. (**Es triste** / **Ojalá**) que no <u>seas</u> sincera.

5. (**Es bueno** / **Siento**) que tu novia y tú no <u>tengan</u> mucho en común.

B. Complete each sentence with the correct subjunctive form of the verb.

Modelo Espero que mis amigos siempre me ____comprendan____ (**comprender**)

1. Es una lástima que José _____ egoísta. (**ser**)

2. Me alegro de que Juana _____ conmigo. (**contar**)

3. Me sorprende que Carlos no _____ a su novia. (**apoyar**)

4. Es ridículo que mis padres _____ de mí. (**desconfiar**)

C. Now, go back to exercise B and circle the verb or expression of emotion in each sentence. Follow the model.

Modelo Espero que mis amigos siempre me comprendan.

- Note that **"que"** marks a change in subject, and thus the subjunctive mood. In impersonal expressions, the verb **es** counts as one subject.

  Es importante que tú seas honesto.   *It is important that you be honest.*

D. Combine the elements below to create a sentence using the subjunctive. Remember to use **que** after the first verb in each sentence. Follow the model.

Modelo   Mis padres / temer / yo / no / ser / sincero

Mis padres temen que yo no sea sincero.

1. Yo / alegrarse de / mis hermanos / ser / cariñosos

2. Es triste / mis amigos / no guardar / mis secretos.

3. Nosotros / sentir / tus padres / no / apoyar / tus decisiones

4. Es una lástima / tu mejor amiga / tener celos

- If there is only one subject in the sentence, **"que"** is omitted and the infinitive is used after the conjugated verb or expression of emotion.

  **(Yo) Me alegro de tener muchos   *I am happy to have (that I have)*
  amigos.**   *many friends.*

5/8/23

E. Read each sentence and determine whether to use the infinitive or the present subjunctive. Look for the "**que**" and a change in subject. Follow the model.

Modelo   (escuchar) Me molesta que mis hermanos ___*escuchen*___ mis conversaciones con mis amigos.

1. (poder)   Siento no _poder_ ir a la fiesta. Estoy enfermo.

2. (ser)   Es bueno que nosotros _seamos_ sinceros.

3. (aceptar)   Me alegro de que mis padres me _acepten_ tal como soy.

4. (guardar)   Esperamos _guardemos_ los secretos de nuestra familia.

5. (tener)   Es bueno _tener_ muchos amigos comprensivos.

Los usos de *por* y *para* (p. 177)

• The prepositions **por** and **para** have several distinct uses in Spanish.
Por is used to indicate:

  • an exchange, such as with money
  *Pago dos dólares **por** una taza de café.*

  • a substitution or replacement
  *Trabajo **por** mi mejor amigo cuando él está enfermo.*

  • the reason for doing something
  *La profesora se enojó **por** las malas notas de sus estudiantes.*

  • an approximate length of time
  *Mi amigo y yo nos hablamos **por** varias horas.*

  • a means of transportation / communication
  *Mi amigo y yo nos comunicamos **por** correo electrónico.*

  • where an action takes place
  *Mis padres corrieron **por** el río.*

  • The following expressions also use **por**:
  **por favor, por eso, por supuesto, por ejemplo, por lo general,
  por primera (segunda, etc.) vez, por la mañana (tarde, noche)**

Para is used to indicate:

  • deadlines or moments in time
  *Este reportaje es **para** el viernes.*

  • a destination
  *Salimos **para** Madrid a las nueve.*

  • a function or goal
  *Esta cámara digital sirve **para** sacar fotos.*

  • the recipient of an action
  *Este regalo de boda es **para** los novios.*

  • a purpose (in order to)
  *Llamé a mi amigo **para** contarle el secreto.*

  • an opinion
  ***Para** ti, la amistad es muy importante.*

A. Read each of the following statements using the preposition **por** and decide why **por** was used instead of **para**.

____D__ 1. Ella se casó **por** dinero.

____C__ 2. Pagué $15 **por** el disco compacto.

____B__ 3. Dio un paseo **por** el parque.

____E__ 4. Corté el césped **por** mi padre.

____A__ 5. Leyó el libro **por** muchas horas.

A. length of time

B. where an action takes place

C. an exchange

D. reason or motive

E. action on someone's behalf

B. Read each of the following statements using the preposition **para** and decide why **para** was used instead of **por**. The first one is done for you.

_C_ **1.** Necesito escribir un informe **para** mañana.

_D_ **2.** Las frutas son buenas **para** la salud.

_E_ **3.** **Para** mí, es muy importante guardar los secretos.

_A_ **4.** **Para** ser buen amigo necesitas ser paciente.

_F_ **5.** Tengo una carta **para** Isabel.

_B_ **6.** El tren sale **para** México a las siete.

A. purpose, in order to
B. destination
~~**C.** a point in time, deadline~~
D. function, goal
E. opinion
F. recipient of an action

C. Circle **por** or **para** for each of the following sentences. Follow the model.

Modelo   Esta carretera pasa ((**por**)/ **para**) Texas.

1. No sé si hay una piscina (**por** /(**para**)) aquí.

2. Vivimos en Puerto Rico ((**por**)/ **para**) mucho tiempo.

3. Cecilia pagó mucho ((**por**)/ **para**) su vestido de Prom.

4. ((**Por**)/ **Para**) mí, el deporte más divertido es el fútbol.

5. No puedo ir. ¿Puedes ir ((**por**)/ **para**) mí?

6. Compramos un regalo (**por** /(**para**)) Silvia. Es su cumpleaños.

7. Francisco tomó el avión (**por** /(**para**)) San Juan.

8. No pudimos acampar (**por** /(**para**)) la tormenta.

9. Los proyectos son (**por** /(**para**)) el lunes.

10. Siempre voy ((**por**)/ **para**) el gimnasio antes de ir a la piscina.

11. Quiero ir al parque ((**por**)/ **para**) jugar al fútbol.

12. Prefiero viajar (**por** /(**para**)) avión.

Capítulo 4

Copy the word or phrase in the space provided. Be sure to include the article for each noun.

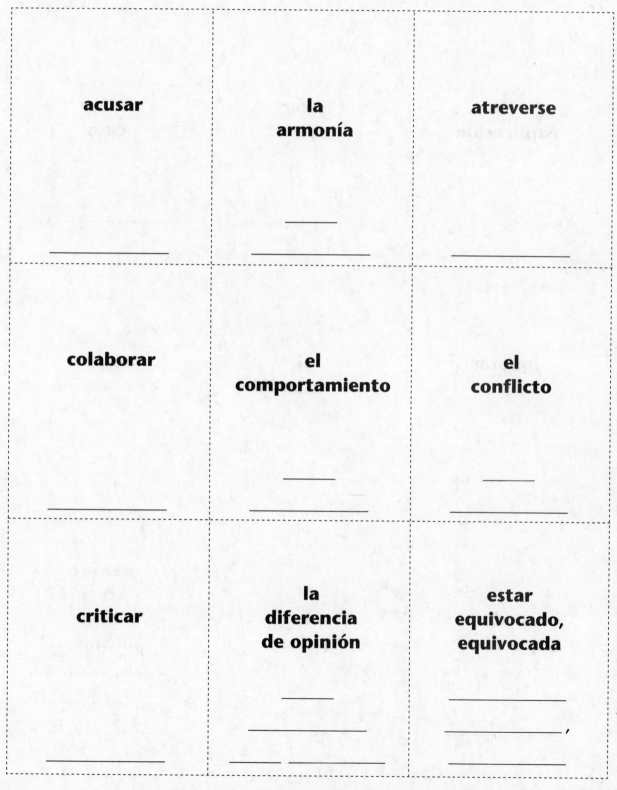

acusar	la armonía	atreverse
	___	
___	___	___

colaborar	el comportamiento	el conflicto
	___	___
___	___	___

criticar	la diferencia de opinión	estar equivocado, equivocada
	___	___
	___	___ ,
___	___	___

Copy the word or phrase in the space provided. Be sure to include the article for each noun.

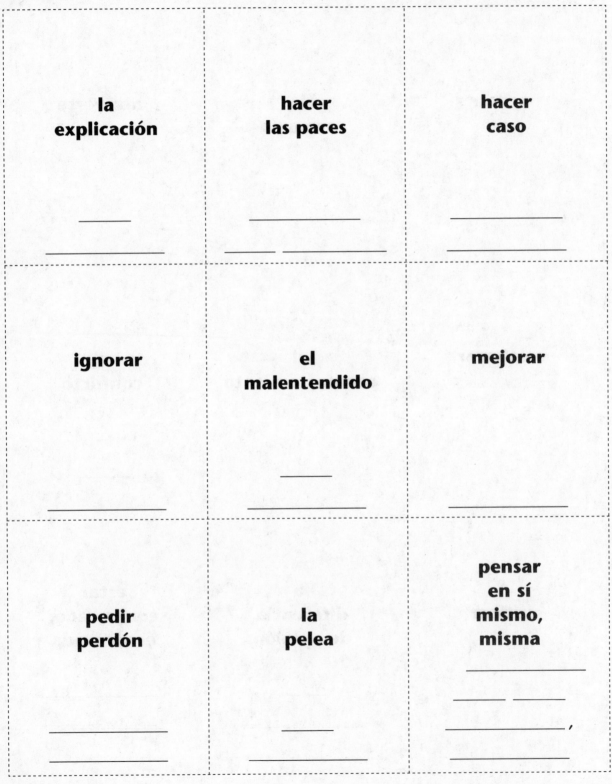

la
explicación

_____
_____

hacer
las paces

_____
_____

hacer
caso

_____
_____

ignorar

_____

el
malentendido

_____
_____

mejorar

_____

pedir
perdón

_____
_____

la
pelea

_____
_____

pensar
en sí
mismo,
misma

_____
_____
_____ ,
_____

Copy the word or phrase in the space provided. Be sure to include the article for each noun.

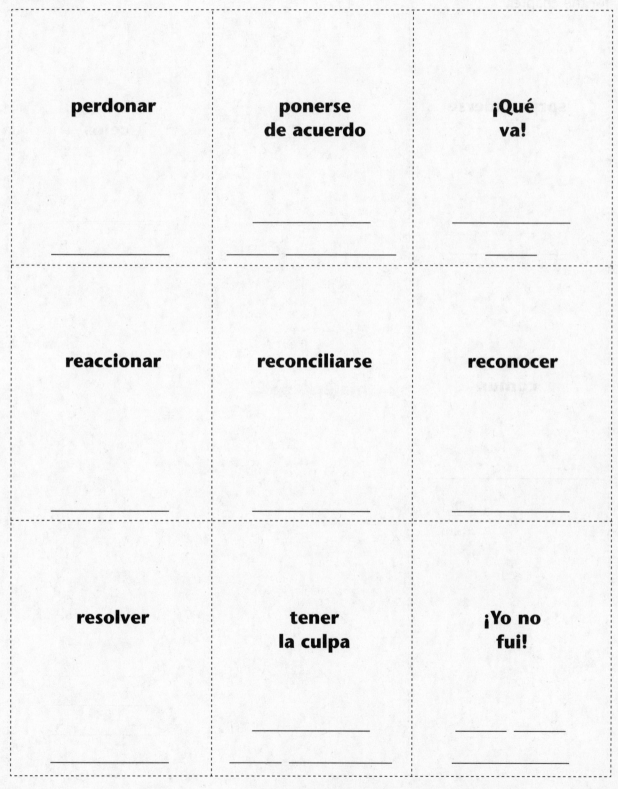

perdonar	**ponerse de acuerdo**	**¡Qué va!**
reaccionar	**reconciliarse**	**reconocer**
resolver	**tener la culpa**	**¡Yo no fui!**

Copy the word or phrase in the space provided. Be sure to include the article for each noun. The blank cards can be used to write and practice other Spanish vocabulary for the chapter.

sorprenderse _____	**temer** _____	**tener celos** _____ _____
tener en común _____ ___ ___ _____	 _____	 _____
    _____	 _____	 _____

Tear out this page. Write the English words on the lines. Fold the paper along the dotted line to see the correct answers so you can check your work.

acusar   _____

la armonía   _____

atreverse   _____

colaborar   _____

el comportamiento   _____

el conflicto   _____

criticar   _____

la diferencia
de opinión   _____

estar equivocado,
equivocada   _____

la explicación   _____

hacer caso   _____

hacer las paces   _____

ignorar   _____

el malentendido   _____

Fold In

Nombre ______ Hora ______

Capítulo 4

Fecha ______ **Vocabulary Check, Sheet 6**

Tear out this page. Write the Spanish words on the lines. Fold the paper along the dotted line to see the correct answers so you can check your work.

to accuse	______
harmony	______
to dare	______
to collaborate	______
behavior	______
conflict	______
to criticize	______
difference of opinion	______
to be mistaken	______
explanation	______
to pay attention; to obey	______
to make peace	______
to ignore	______
misunderstanding	______

Fold In

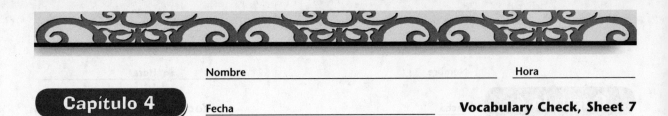

Tear out this page. Write the English words on the lines. Fold the paper along the dotted line to see the correct answers so you can check your work.

mejorar _____

pedir perdón _____

la pelea _____

pensar en sí
mismo, misma _____

perdonar _____

ponerse de acuerdo _____

_____

reaccionar _____

reconciliarse _____

_____

reconocer _____

resolver (o➔ue) _____

tener la culpa _____

¡Qué va! _____

¡Yo no fui! _____

Fold In ←

Tear out this page. Write the Spanish words on the lines. Fold the paper along the dotted line to see the correct answers so you can check your work.

to improve _____

to ask for forgiveness _____

fight _____

to think of oneself _____

_____

to forgive _____

to reach an
agreement _____

to react _____

to become friends
again _____

to admit; to recognize _____

to resolve _____

to be guilty _____

No way! _____

It was not me! _____

Fold In

Capítulo 4   Fecha 4/26/23

Mandatos con *nosotros* (p. 188)

· Subjunctive form

- You can express **nosotros** commands two different ways in Spanish. The English equivalent of a **nosotros** command is "*Let's . . .*"

  One way is to use **Vamos** + **a** + infinitive.

  Vamos a bailar.   *Let's dance.*

  Another way is to use to the **nosotros** form of the subjunctive.

  Bailemos.   *Let's dance.*

- Remember that **-ir** stem-changing verbs change **o→u** or **e→i** in the **nosotros** form.

  Durmamos aquí.   *Let's sleep here.*

- Remember that verbs ending in **-car**, **-gar**, and **-zar** change spelling in the subjunctive.

  Juguemos a las cartas.   *Let's play cards.*

A. Read each of the following statements about Juanita and her best friend. Decide if each statement tells what they normally do, or if it's a suggestion. Follow the model.

Modelo Guardemos los secretos.

☐ normalmente   ☑ sugerencia

1. Tenemos mucho en común.

   ☑ normalmente   ☐ sugerencia

2. Resolvamos los problemas.

   ☐ normalmente   ☑ sugerencia

3. Celebramos los días festivos juntos.

   ☑ normalmente   ☐ sugerencia

4. Seamos honestas.

   ☐ normalmente   ☑ sugerencia

llevar 5. Llevemos ropa parecida.

   ☐ normalmente   ☑ sugerencia

comer
6. Comamos en un restaurante.

   ☐ normalmente   ☑ sugerencia

7. No peleamos. *pelearse*

   ☑ normalmente   ☐ sugerencia

8. No mintamos a los profesores.

   ☐ normalmente   ☑ sugerencia

9. No critiquemos a los demás.

   ☐ normalmente   ☑ sugerencia

10. Hagamos las paces.

   ☐ normalmente   ☑ sugerencia

B. Write the **nosotros** commands for each verb given. Follow the model.

Modelo (salir) ___*salgamos*___

1. (pedir) ___pidamos___
2. (mentir) ___mintamos___
3. (almorzar) ___almuecemos___

4. (jugar) ___jugemos___
5. (repetir) ___repitamos___
6. (tener) ___tenamos___

'lets

C. Marisa is suggesting that she and Josefina do the same things. Write the suggestion Marisa gives, using **nosotros** commands. Follow the model.

> Modelo   Josefina, no _____*miremos*_____ la tele hoy.

1. Josefina, ___*escuchar*___ la música clásica.

2. Josefina, _____ una explicación cuando tenemos un malentendido.

3. Josefina, _____ en el coro.

4. Josefina, _____ la tarea juntas.

- When you use a direct or indirect object pronoun with an affirmative **nosotros** command, attach it to the end of the verb.

  Resolvamos el problema. Resolvámoslo.

- With a negative **nosotros** command, place the object pronoun in front of the verb.

  No le digamos el secreto al chico chismoso.

D. Each time your parents make a suggestion, respond with an opposite suggestion. Replace the underlined word in each sentence with a direct object pronoun in your answer. Follow the model.

> Modelo   MAMÁ: Celebremos el cumpleaños de tu abuelita.
>
> TÚ: ___*No lo celebremos.*___

1. PAPÁ: Limpiemos el garaje.
   TÚ: *No lo limpiemos*

2. MAMÁ: Escuchemos música clásica.
   TÚ: *No lo escuchemos*

3. PAPÁ: Hagamos las paces.
   TÚ: *No los hagamos*

4. MAMÁ: Pidamos perdón.
   TÚ: *No lo pidamos*

- When the reflexive or reciprocal pronoun **nos** is used in an affirmative **nosotros** command, the final **-s** of the command is dropped before the pronoun. A written accent is added to maintain stress, usually on the third-to-last vowel.

  Contémonos los secretos.   *Divirtámonos.*

E. Complete each sentence using the **nosotros** command of the reflexive verb.

> Modelo   (**vestirse**) ___*Vistámonos*___.

1. (**cepillarse**) *cepillémonos* los dientes.

2. (**ponerse**) *ponamónos* los zapatos.

3. (**ducharse**) *duchémonos*.

4. (**lavarse**) *lavémos* las manos.

Pronombres posesivos (p. 190)

adj: describing word

pron.: replace nouns

eng: my, your, his, her, our, yalls, their

- Possessive pronouns help you avoid repetition in conversation by replacing nouns. They are usually preceded by a definite article, and must have the same gender and number as the nouns they replace.

Span: mi, tu, su, nuestro, vuestro, su

> **Mi mejor (amiga) es muy sincera. ¿Cómo es *la tuya?***
> *My best friend is very sincere. What is yours like?*

> **El (padre) de José es tan comprensivo como *el mío.***
> *José's father is as understanding as* mine.

Below are the possessive pronouns in Spanish.

eng: mines, yours, his, hers, ours, yalls, theirs

- **el mío / la mía / los míos / las mías:** *mine*
- **el tuyo / la tuya / los tuyos / las tuyas:** *yours*
- **el suyo / la suya / los suyos / las suyas:**
  his / hers / yours (sing. formal or plural) / theirs

span: mío, tuyo, suyo, nuestro, vuestro, suyo

- **el nuestro / la nuestra / los nuestros / las nuestras:** *ours*
- **el vuestro / la vuestra / los vuestros / las vuestras:** *yours (plural)*

A. Write the letter of the question that would most logically follow each statement below. The pronoun in the question should agree in gender and number with the underlined noun. The first one is done for you.

B 1.	<u>Mis padres</u> son muy serios.	A. ¿Y el suyo?
E 2.	<u>Mi mamá</u> es cariñosa.	B. ¿Y los tuyos?
D 3.	<u>Mis amigas</u> son deportistas.	C. ¿Y la suya?
A 4.	<u>Nuestro</u> hermano es chismoso.	D. ¿Y las tuyas?
F 5.	<u>Nuestras amigas</u> no nos hacen caso.	E. ¿Y la tuya?
C 6.	<u>Nuestra jefa</u> colabora con nosotros.	F. ¿Y las suyas?

- When the verb (ser) is used with a posse<u>ssive</u> pronoun, the definite article is commonly left out.

> *Esos textos son **nuestros.***   *Esa calculadora es **mía.***

B. Write the letter of the phrase that is the best completion for each statement. The first one is done for you.

B 1.	La corbata...	A. ...son suyos.
C 2.	El traje de baño...	B. ...es mía.
A 3.	Los anteojos...	C. ...es tuyo.
D 4.	Las joyas...	D. ...son nuestras.

C. The following pairs of statements are opposites. Complete the sentences with the correct form of the possessive pronoun **mío** or **tuyo**. Follow the models.

Modelos   Tu familia es unida. __La____ __mía__ es independiente.

Mi casa es pequeña. __La____ __tuya__ es grande.

1. Tus hermanas son divertidas. __las__ __mías__ son aburridas.

2. Mi computadora es vieja. __la__ __tuya__ es moderna.

3. Tus libros son grandes. __los__ __míos__ son pequeños.

4. Mis padres son atléticos. __los__ __tuyos__ son poco atléticos.

5. Mi perro es gordísimo. __el__ __tuyo__ es flaquito.

6. Tu carro es nuevo. __el__ __mío__ es viejo.

D. Create complete sentences by modifying the possessive pronoun, if necessary, to agree in gender and number with the noun it respresents. Follow the model.

Modelo   Los libros / de Cervantes / son / nuestro

Los libros de Cervantes son nuestros.

1. Las flores / bonitas / son / mío

_____

2. La culpa / es / tuyo

_____

3. Esas / pinturas / de Velázquez / son / suyo

_____

4. Los / zapatos / son / nuestro

_____

5. El perro / es / suyo

_____

6. La tarea / de / español / es / nuestro

_____

Puente a la cultura (pp. 192–193)

A. Scan the reading for names of people, and match each of the following artists with the type of art they made or make. (Hint: you will use one letter more than once!)

1. _____ Diego Rivera   **A.** la música

2. _____ Judith Francisca Baca   **B.** la pintura

3. _____ Augustín Lara   **C.** la literatura

4. _____ Gustavo Adolfo Bécquer

B. Look at the sentence starters below. Circle the best completion for each sentence based on each section of the reading. Use the reading subtitles to help you.

1. La pintura en murales ha sido otra forma de expresión artística...

   a. del amor.   **b.** de la madre.   **c.** de gente famosa.

2. La fuente de inspiración de la mayoría de sus [de Agustín Lara] canciones fue...

   a. el amor a la pintura.   **b.** el amor a México.   **c.** el amor a la mujer.

3. De todas las formas de expresar el amor en la literatura... la más apropiada es...

   a. la poesía.   **b.** el drama.   **c.** la naturaleza.

C. Look at the poem tled "*Amor eterno*" from your reading. Circle the words in the poem that have to do with nature.

> *Podrá nublarse el sol*
>
> *eternamente;*
>
> *Podrá secarse en un*
>
> *instante el mar;*
>
> *Podrá romperse el eje de la tierra*

Lectura (pp. 198–200)

A. You are about to read several poems about love and friendship. In the spaces provided, write three adjectives in Spanish that you associate with love and friendship. Think of ideals you might expect to see expressed in the poems. Use the models to get you started.

_____ *comprensivo* _____   _____ *íntima* _____   _____

_____   _____

B. Match each of the important vocabulary words with its synonym or definition. These words are from the two poems: *Poema No. 15,* on page 198, and *Homenaje a los padres chicanos* on page 199.

1. _____ callarse   **A.** tradición

2. _____ mariposa   **B.** lo que se oye cuando una persona habla

3. _____ voz   **C.** lo que tienes cuando crees en algo

4. _____ melancolía   **D.** no hablar

5. _____ sagrado   **E.** de muchísima importancia

6. _____ costumbre   **F.** respetar mucho y amar

7. _____ fe   **G.** un insecto bonito

8. _____ venerar   **H.** la tristeza fuerte

9. _____ chicano   **I.** mexicano americano

C. Circle the responses in parentheses that best complete the main ideas about the first two poems.

"Poema No. 15"

1. Al poeta le gusta que su novia (hable mucho / no hable mucho) porque (así él la aprecia más / ella no dice muchas cosas importantes).

"Homenaje a los padre chicanos"

2. El poeta quiere ilustrar que (es importante expresar el amor por los padres / los padres deben amar más a sus hijos) aunque en la cultura (gringa / chicana) no es tan común hacerlo.

D. Look at the following sets of key lines from each poem on page 200 and circle the phrase that best conveys the meaning of each quotation.

"Rimas"

1. *"Poesía ... eres tú."*

   a. La mujer escribe poesía como profesión.

   b. La mujer y la poesía son cosas bellas e imposibles de describir.

"El amor en preguntas"

2. *"¿Qué es necesario para ser amado,*
   para entender la vida y saber soñar?"

   a. Todos buscan el amor, pero a veces es difícil encontrarlo.

   b. El amor sólo existe en los sueños.

"Como tú"

3. *"Creo que el mundo es bello,*
   que la poesía es como el pan, de todos."

   a. La poesía es universal y crea conexiones entre las personas.

   b. Hay mucha hambre y pobreza en el mundo, y la poesía no ayuda con los problemas.

E. Roque Dalton named his poem "*Cómo tú*" because it is a comparison of himself with another person. Read the poem on page 200 and check off which of the following are comparisons Dalton actually uses in the poem.

_____ "amo el amor, la vida"

_____ "[amo] el paisaje celeste de los días de enero"

_____ "[amo] la poesía de ti"

_____ "creo que el mundo es bello"

_____ "[creo que] los suspiros son aire"

_____ "[creo que] la poesía es como el pan"

El participio presente (p. 209)

- The present participle is used to talk about actions that are in progress at the moment of speaking. To form the present participle of -**ar** verbs, add -**ando** to the stem. For -**er** and -**ir** verbs, add -**iendo** to the stem.

  cantar: cant**ando** insistir: insist**iendo** tener: ten**iendo**

- The present participle is frequently combined with the present tense of **estar** to talk about what someone *is doing*, or with the imperfect of **estar** to talk about what someone *was doing*.

  Estoy cort*ando* el césped.   *I am mowing the lawn.*

  Los niños estaban hac*iendo* sus quehaceres.   *The kids were doing their chores.*

A. Write the ending of the present participle for each of the following verbs to say what the following people are doing while you're at school. Follow the model.

Modelo (**sacar**) El fotógrafo está sac*ando* fotos.

1. (**trabajar**) El agente de viajes está trabaj_____ en su oficina.

2. (**beber**) El entrenador está beb_____ agua.

3. (**hacer**) El científico está hac_____ un experimento.

4. (**escribir**) El reportero está escrib_____ un artículo.

- Only -**ir** stem-changing verbs change in the present participle. In the present participle, the **e** changes to **i** and the **o** changes to **u**.

  serv**ir**: s*i*rviendo dorm**ir**: d*u*rmiendo despedir: desp*i*diendo

B. Write the present participles of the verbs in the chart below. The first row has been done for you. Remember that -**ar** and -**er** stem-changing verbs have <u>no stem changes</u> in the present participle.

-ar, -er	present participle	-ir	present participle
jugar	*jugando*	divertir	*divirtiendo*
sentar	1. _____	sentir	5. _____
contar	2. _____	morir	6. _____
volver	3. _____	preferir	7. _____
perder	4. _____	dormir	8. _____

C. Complete the sentences with the present progressive of the verb given (+ *present participle*) to say what the following people are doing. Follow the model.

> **Modelo** (decir) Yo ___estoy___ ___diciendo___ la verdad.

1. (**dormir**) Tú no _____ _____.

2. (**pedir**) Ellos no _____ _____ una pizza.

3. (**contar**) Nosotros _____ _____ chistes.

4. (**resolver**) Yo _____ _____ problemas de matemáticas.

- A spelling change occurs in the present participle of the verbs **ir, oír,** and verbs ending in **-aer, -eer,** and **-uir.** The ending becomes **-yendo.**

  creer: cre**yendo**   oír: o**yendo**   caer: ca**yendo**

  construir: constru**yendo**   ir: **yendo**

D. Complete the following sentences with the present progressive. Remember to use the verb **estar** along with the verb provided. Follow the model.

> **Modelo** Mis padres ___están___ ___trayendo___ (**traer**) el perro al veterinario.

1. El asistente _____ _____ (**oír**) las instrucciones del dentista.

2. La reportera dice que _____ _____ (**caer**) granizo y que _____ _____ (**destruir**) los coches de muchas personas.

3. Las vendedoras _____ _____ (**leer**) las etiquetas de la ropa.

4. Nadie _____ _____ (**creer**) lo que dice el atleta egoísta.

- In the progressive tenses, reflexive or object pronouns can be placed before the verb **estar,** or they can be attached to the end of the present participle. If they are attached to the present participle, a written accent is needed to maintain stress (usually over the third-to-last vowel).

  El bombero está ayudándome.   or   *El bombero **me** está ayudando.*

E. The sentences below each have a phrase using the present progressive tense and a pronoun. Each phrase is underlined. In the space provided, write the phrase in a different way, using what you learned about placement of pronouns. Follow the model.

> **Modelo** No puedo hablar porque <u>me estoy cepillando</u> los dientes. ___estoy cepillándome___

1. Mis abuelos <u>nos están felicitando</u> por la graduación. _____

2. A Juan no le gusta el postre, pero <u>está comiéndolo</u>. _____

3. Mi hermano está en el baño. <u>Está lavándose</u> las manos. _____

4. Mi profesora <u>me está dando</u> este libro para estudiar. _____

Dónde van los pronombres reflexivos y de complemento (p. 211)

- Deciding where to put object and reflexive pronouns can sometimes be confusing. Here is a summary of some of these rules.

- When a sentence contains two verbs in a row, as with a present participle or infinitive, the pronoun may be placed either in front of the first verb or be attached to the second verb. Note that the second example is negative.

  Nos vamos a duchar.   or   *Vamos a ducharnos.*

  *No **nos** vamos a duchar.*   or   *No vamos a ducharnos.*

- Adding a pronoun to the end of a present participle requires a written accent mark, while adding a pronoun to the end of an infinitive does not.

  Estoy pagándole.   *Voy a pagarle.*

A. Rewrite each phrase using the pronoun in parentheses in two different ways. In column A, place the pronouns before the first verb. In column B, attach them to the second verb. Remember, if you add a pronoun to the end of a present participle, you need to include an accent mark. Follow the model.

	A	B
Modelo van a regalar (me)	*me van a regalar*	*van a regalarme*
1. vamos a dar (le)	_____	_____
2. debo encontrar (lo)	_____	_____
3. estamos registrando (nos)	_____	_____
4. van a dormir (se)	_____	_____

- When you give an affirmative command, you must attach any pronouns to the end of the verb and add an accent mark if the verb has two or more syllables.

  Permítelo.   *Ganémoslas.*

  In negative commands, place the pronoun between **no** and the verb. No written accent mark is needed.

  *No **lo** hagan.*   *No **te** laves el pelo ahora.*

B. Combine the following affirmative commands and pronouns. Remember to write an accent mark on the stressed syllable. Follow the model.

Modelo   lava + te = _____ *lávate* _____

1. ponga + se = _____   4. ayuden + me = _____

2. vean + los = _____   5. consigamos + la = _____

3. despierten + se = _____

C. For each question, write an answer using one of the affirmative **tú** commands with the correct direct object pronoun (**lo, la, los, las**). Use the word bank to help you choose the correct forms. Add accents as needed. Follow the model.

| haz | pide | ~~cocina~~ | enciende | trae | pon |

Modelo ¿Cocino el pavo? Sí, _____*cocínalo*_____.

1. ¿Enciendo las velas? Sí, _____.

2. ¿Pido unas flores? Sí, _____.

3. ¿Hago el menú? Sí, _____.

4. ¿Pongo la mesa? Sí, _____.

5. ¿Traigo una botella de vino? Sí, _____.

D. Write the negative command that corresponds to each affirmative command below. Follow the model.

Modelo Córtense las uñas. No __*se*__ __*corten*__ el pelo.

1. Vístanse con la ropa suya. No _____ _____ con la ropa de sus amigos.

2. Pónganse las chaquetas. No _____ _____ las joyas.

3. Báñense por la tarde. No _____ _____ por la mañana.

4. Levántense a las ocho. No _____ _____ tarde.

5. Cepíllense los dientes. No _____ _____ los dedos.

Capítulo 5

Write the Spanish vocabulary word below each picture. If there is a word or phrase, copy it in the space provided. Be sure to include the article for each noun.

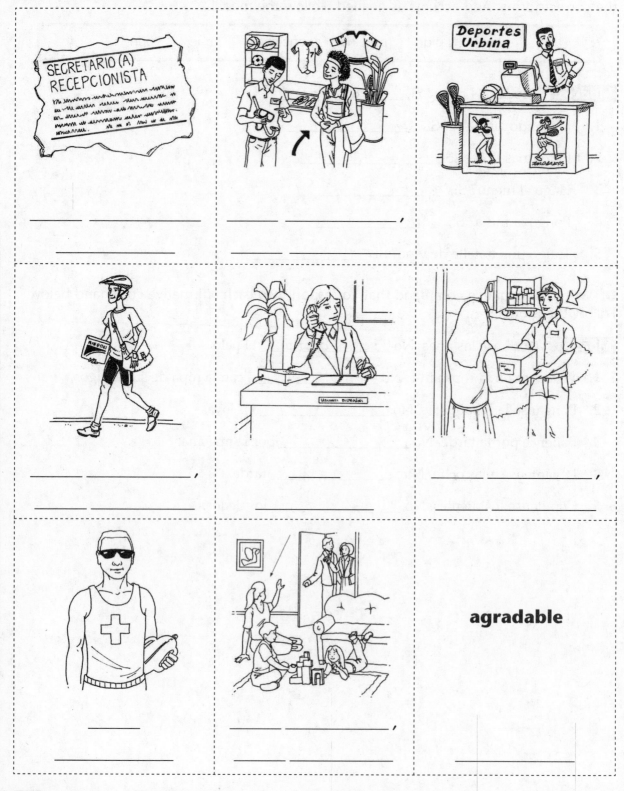

SECRETARIO (A) RECEPCIONISTA

Deportes Urbina

agradable

Copy the word or phrase in the space provided. Be sure to include the article for each noun.

atender	**a tiempo completo**	**a tiempo parcial**
_____	____ _____ _____	____ _____ _____
beneficiar	**los beneficios**	**la compañía**
_____	_____ _____	_____ _____
la computación	**el consejero, la consejera**	**los conocimientos**
_____ , _____	____ _____ , ____ _____	_____ _____

Copy the word or phrase in the space provided. Be sure to include the article for each noun.

cumplir con

_____

_____

dedicado, dedicada

_____,

_____

el dueño, la dueña

_____ _____,

_____

encargarse (de)

_____

la entrevista

_____

_____

la fecha de nacimiento

_____ _____

_____

_____

flexible

_____

la habilidad

_____

_____

el puesto

_____

_____

Copy the word or phrase in the space provided. Be sure to include the article for each noun.

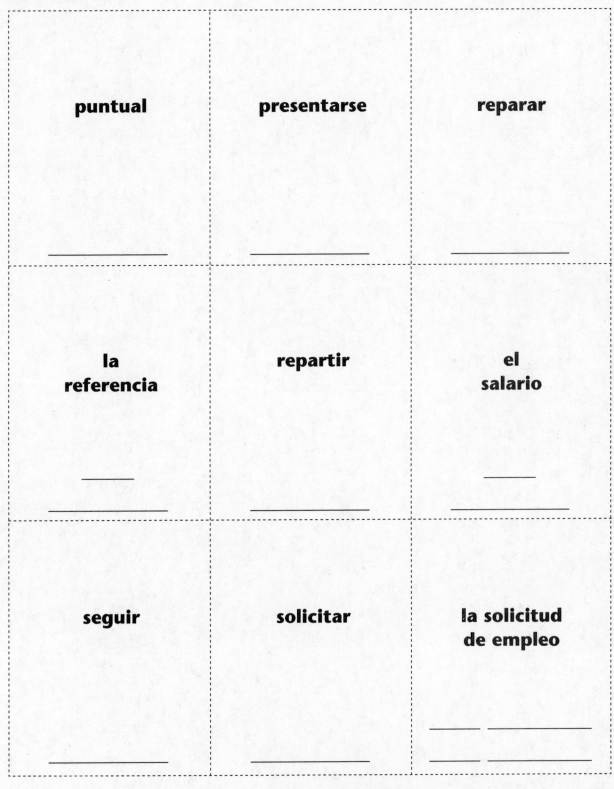

puntual

_____

presentarse

_____

reparar

_____

la referencia

_____

repartir

_____

el salario

_____

seguir

_____

solicitar

_____

la solicitud de empleo

_____

These blank cards can be used to write and practice other Spanish vocabulary for the chapter.

Capítulo 5

Tear out this page. Write the English words on the lines. Fold the paper along the dotted line to see the correct answers so you can check your work.

a tiempo completo _____

a tiempo parcial _____

agradable _____

el anuncio clasificado _____

atender _____

los beneficios _____

el cliente, la clienta _____

la compañía _____

el consejero,
la consejera _____

los conocimientos _____

cumplir con _____

dedicado, dedicada _____

el dueño, la dueña _____

encargarse (de) _____

la entrevista _____

la fecha de nacimiento _____

el/la gerente _____

la habilidad _____

Fold In

Tear out this page. Write the Spanish words on the lines. Fold the paper along the dotted line to see the correct answers so you can check your work.

full time _____

part time _____

pleasant _____

classified ad _____

to help, assist _____

benefits _____

client _____

firm/company _____

counselor _____

_____

knowledge _____

to carry out, to perform _____

dedicated _____

owner _____

to be in charge (of) _____

interview _____

date of birth _____

manager _____

skill _____

Fold In ←

Tear out this page. Write the English words on the lines. Fold the paper along the dotted line to see the correct answers so you can check your work.

el mensajero,
la mensajera   _____

el niñero, la niñera   _____

presentarse   _____

repartir   _____

el puesto   _____

puntual   _____

el/la recepcionista   _____

reparar   _____

el repartidor,
la repartidora   _____

el requisito   _____

la responsabilidad   _____

el salario   _____

el/la salvavida   _____

seguir (+ *gerund*)   _____

soler (*o→ue*)   _____

la solicitud de empleo   _____

solicitar   _____

Fold In

Tear out this page. Write the Spanish words on the lines. Fold the paper along the dotted line to see the correct answers so you can check your work.

messenger _____

_____

babysitter _____

to apply for a job _____

to deliver _____

position _____

punctual _____

receptionist _____

to repair _____

delivery person _____

_____

requirement _____

responsibility _____

salary _____

lifeguard _____

to keep on (doing) _____

to usually do something _____

job application _____

to request _____

Fold In ←

El presente perfecto (p. 222)

- In Spanish, the *present perfect* tense is used to talk about what someone *has done* in the past without necessarily telling the time when they did it.

  Yo *he trabajado en* una tienda de bicicletas.   *I have worked at a bicycle store.*

- The present perfect is formed by using the present tense forms of the irregular verb **haber** plus the *past participle* of another verb. Remember that the past participle is formed by adding **-ado** to the stem of an **-ar** verb or **-ido** to the stem of an **-er** or **-ir** verb. Below is the verb **cantar** conjugated in the present perfect.

cantar	
he cantado	**hemos** cantado
has cantado	**habéis** cantado
ha cantado	**han** cantado

- Notice that each conjugation has two parts, and that the second part (in this case, **cantado**) is the <u>same</u> in all forms.

- Remember that direct and indirect object pronouns, reflexive pronouns, and negative words are placed before the first part of the conjugation.

  ***Me* he encargado del trabajo.**   or   ***No se* ha afeitado todavía.**

A. Complete the sentences with the correct form of the verb **haber**. The first one has been done for you.

1. Yo ____*he*____ comido.

2. Ellas _____ trabajado.

3. Nosotros _____ permitido.

4. José _____ aprendido.

5. Tú te _____ dormido.

6. Yo me _____ lavado.

7. María no se _____ presentado.

8. Nosotros no lo _____ repartido.

B. Complete each sentence with the correct present perfect form of the verb. Follow the model. Note that the past participle always ends in **-o**.

Modelo   Margarita Arroyo ___*ha*___ ___*repartido*___ pizzas. (**repartir**)

1. El Sr. Flores _____ _____ a los niños de sus vecinos. (**cuidar**)

2. Las empleadas _____ _____ experiencia con la computación. (**tener**)

3. Marisol y yo _____ _____ muchas clases de arte. (**tomar**)

4. ¿Uds. _____ _____ un trabajo? (**solicitar**)

5. Yo _____ _____ computadoras. (**reparar**)

6. Y tú, ¿_____ _____ con tu trabajo? (**cumplir**)

El presente perfecto (*continued*)

- Verbs that end in **-aer**, **-eer**, and **-eír**, as well as the verb **oír**, have a written accent mark on the *i* in the past participle.

  leer: leído   oir: oído

  sonreír: sonreído   caer: caído

  Verbs that end in **-uir** do <u>not</u> get a written accent mark in the past participle.

C. Complete the following sentences with the present perfect of the verb. **¡Cuidado!** Remember that verbs that end in **-uir**, do not require an accent mark. Follow the model.

Modelo (Yo) ___*he*___ _____*leído*_____ los anuncios clasificados. (**leer**)

1. Tú _____ _____ que esta compañía es buena. (**oír**)

2. Mateo Ortega se _____ _____ de su bicicleta. (**caer**)

3. La jefa _____ _____ dos cartas de recomendación. (**incluir**)

4. Los hermanos García _____ _____ una casa. (**construir**)

- Remember that several Spanish verbs have irregular past participles.

  decir: **dicho**   hacer: **hecho**

  poner: **puesto**   ver: **visto**

  escribir: **escrito**   morir: **muerto**

  abrir: **abierto**   ser: **sido**

  resolver: **resuelto**   romper: **roto**

  volver: **vuelto**

D. Tell what the following job candidates have done by writing the irregular present perfect of the verb given. Follow the model.

Modelo (**escribir**) Verónica Sánchez _____*ha*_____ _____*escrito*_____ una descripción de todos sus trabajos.

1. Héctor Pérez y Miguel Díaz _____ _____ que son muy puntuales. (**decir**)

2. Juanita Sánchez y Lidia Rivera _____ _____ mucha información en sus solicitudes de empleo. (**poner**)

3. Raúl Ramírez y yo _____ _____ un vaso en la oficina. (**romper**)

4. Marcos Ortiz _____ _____ su carta de recomendación. (**abrir**)

5. Ud. _____ _____ un problema importante con su horario. (**resolver**)

El pluscuamperfecto (p. 225)

- In Spanish, the *pluperfect* tense is used to tell about an action in the past that happened *before* another action in the past. It can generally be translated with the words "had done" in English.

  Cuando los empleados llegaron a la oficina, su jefe ya *había empezado* a trabajar.
  When the employees arrived at the office, their boss had already started to work.

- You form the pluperfect tense by combining the imperfect forms of the verb **haber** with the past participle of another verb. Here are the pluperfect forms of the verb **repartir**:

  había repartido   **habíamos** repartido
  habías repartido   **habíais** repartido
  había repartido   **habían** repartido

A. What had everyone done prior to their job interviews? Complete the sentences with the correct imperfect form of the verb **haber**. Follow the model.

Modelo   El gerente _____*había*_____ leído las solicitudes de empleo.

1. El dueño _____ hecho una lista de requisitos.

2. Las recepcionistas _____ copiado las solicitudes de empleo.

3. Elena y yo _____ traído una lista de referencias.

4. (Yo) _____ practicado unas preguntas con mi mamá.

5. Y tú, ¿te _____ preparado antes de la entrevista?

B. Why was Mr. Gutiérrez so nervous before beginning his first day at his new job? Complete each sentence with the correct regular past participles. Follow the model.

Modelo   Había _____*mentido*_____ en su solicitud de empleo. (**mentir**)

1. No había _____ a los otros empleados. (**conocer**)

2. No había _____ si había una cafetería en el edificio. (**preguntar**)

3. Había _____ la dirección incorrecta en su solicitud. (**dar**)

4. No había _____ mucho. (**dormir**)

5. Había _____ sus cartas de recomendación. (**olvidar**)

C. Complete each sentence with the pluperfect tense of the verb in parentheses to tell what people had done before their first day of work. Follow the model.

¡Cuidado! Some past participles require an accent mark and some have completely irregular forms.

Modelo (**escribir**) Carlos ___*había*___ ___*escrito*___ en una tarjeta todo lo que quería recordar.

1. (**oír**) Nosotros _____ _____ muchos comentarios positivos sobre la compañía.

2. (**poner**) Yo _____ _____ unos bolígrafos y un calendario en mi mochila.

3. (**leer**) Todos los nuevos empleados _____ _____ el manual de trabajo.

4. (**decir**) La jefa de la compañía _____ _____ "Bienvenidos a nuestra oficina."

5. (**sonreír**) Tú _____ _____ durante la entrevista.

D. Based on the pictures, tell what each person had done before leaving for work. You can use the verbs in the word bank to help you describe the actions.

¡Cuidado! Reflexive pronouns, object pronouns, and negative words go in front of the conjugated form of **haber** in the pluperfect.

levantarse	~~secarse~~	lavarse	afeitarse	cepillarse	ponerse

Modelo Marta __*se*__ __*había*__ __*secado*__ el pelo.

1. Los gemelos _____ _____ _____ los dientes.

2. Luis _____ _____ _____ temprano.

3. Yo _____ _____ _____ la camisa.

4. Tú _____ _____ _____ .

5. Nosotros _____ _____ _____ las manos.

160 *Guided Practice Activities* — *5-4*

Write the Spanish vocabulary word below each picture. If there is a word or phrase, copy it in the space provided. Be sure to include the article for each noun.

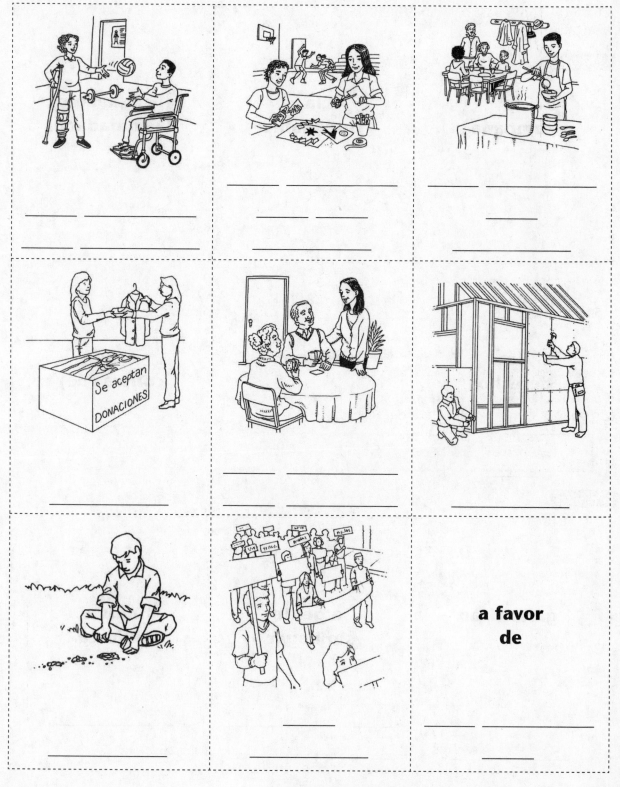

a favor
de

Nombre _____   Hora _____

Capítulo 5   Fecha _____   **Vocabulary Flash Cards, Sheet 7**

Copy the word or phrase in the space provided. Be sure to include the article for each noun.

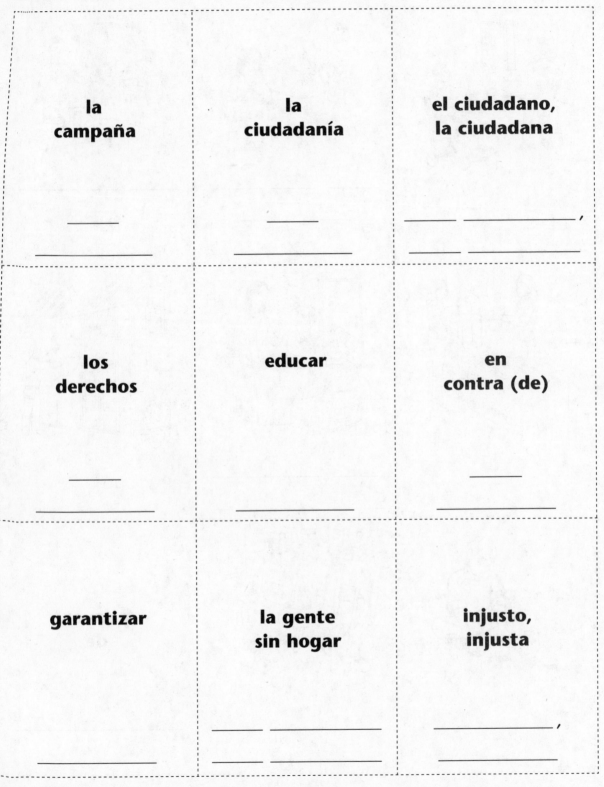

la campaña	la ciudadanía	el ciudadano, la ciudadana
los derechos	educar	en contra (de)
garantizar	la gente sin hogar	injusto, injusta

Copy the word or phrase in the space provided. Be sure to include the article for each noun.

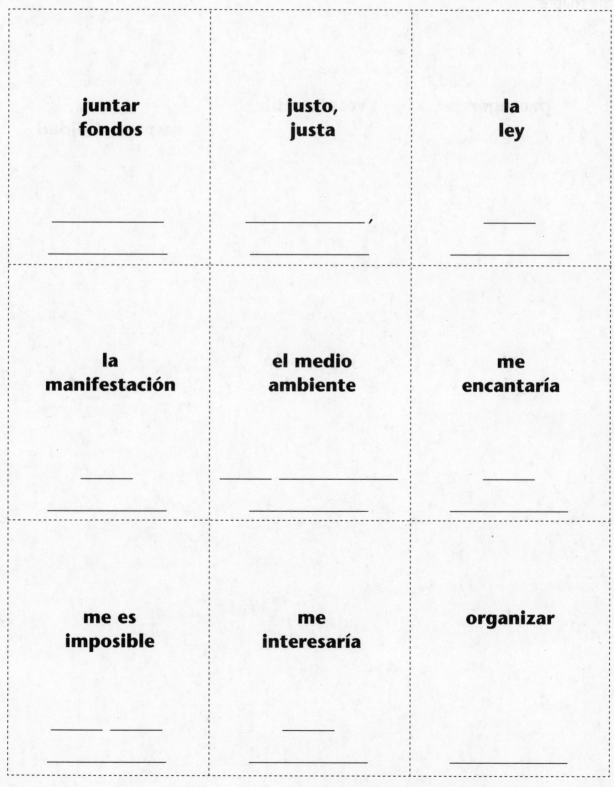

juntar fondos

_____
_____

justo, justa

_____,
_____

la ley

_____
_____

la manifestación

_____
_____

el medio ambiente

_____
_____

me encantaría

_____
_____

me es imposible

_____
_____

me interesaría

_____
_____

organizar

_____
_____

Copy the word or phrase in the space provided. Be sure to include the article for each noun. The blank cards can be used to write and practice other Spanish vocabulary for the chapter.

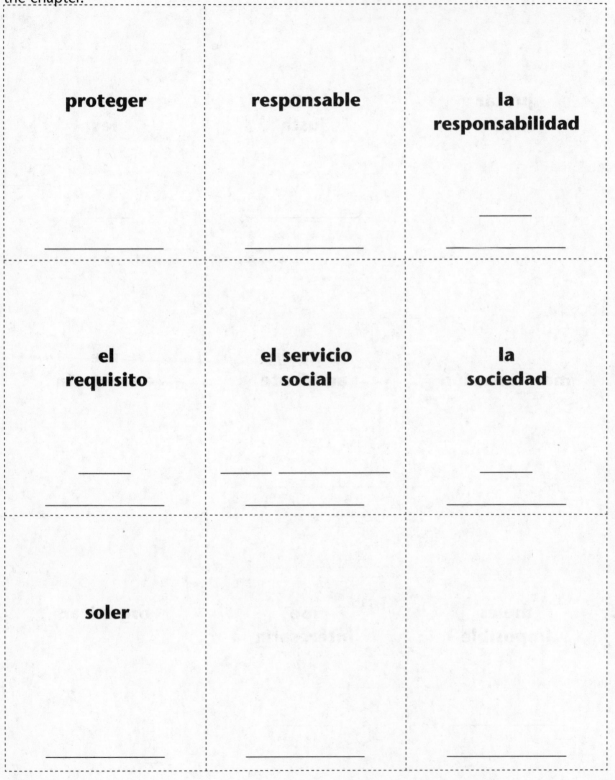

proteger	responsable	la responsabilidad
el requisito	el servicio social	la sociedad
soler		

Tear out this page. Write the English words on the lines. Fold the paper along the dotted line to see the correct answers so you can check your work.

a favor de _____

la campaña _____

el centro de la
comunidad _____

el centro de
rehabilitación _____

el centro recreativo _____

la ciudadanía _____

el ciudadano,
la ciudadana _____

el comedor de
beneficencia _____

construir (*i*➔*y*) _____

los derechos _____

donar _____

educar _____

en contra (de) _____

garantizar _____

la gente sin hogar _____

Fold In ←

Tear out this page. Write the Spanish words on the lines. Fold the paper along the dotted line to see the correct answers so you can check your work.

in favor of _____

campaign _____

community center _____
_____

rehabilitation center _____
_____

recreation center _____

citizenship _____

citizen _____
_____

soup kitchen _____
_____

to build _____

rights _____

to donate _____

to educate _____

against _____

to guarantee _____

homeless people _____

Fold In

Tear out this page. Write the English words on the lines. Fold the paper along the dotted line to see the correct answers so you can check your work.

el hogar de ancianos _____

injusto, injusta _____

juntar fondos _____

justo, justa _____

la ley _____

la manifestación _____

la marcha _____

el medio ambiente _____

me es imposible _____

me encantaría _____

me interesaría _____

organizar _____

proteger _____

sembrar (*e*➔*ie*) _____

el servicio social _____

la sociedad _____

Fold In

Tear out this page. Write the Spanish words on the lines. Fold the paper along the dotted line to see the correct answers so you can check your work.

home for the elderly   _____

unfair   _____

to fundraise   _____

fair   _____

law   _____

demonstration   _____

march   _____

environment   _____

It is impossible for me...   _____

I would love to...   _____

I would be interested...   _____

to organize   _____

to protect   _____

to plant   _____

social service   _____

society   _____

Fold In

El presente perfecto del subjuntivo (p. 235)

- The present perfect subjunctive is used to talk about actions or situations that may have occurred before the action of the main verb. The present perfect subjunctive often follows expressions of emotion like those you used for the present subjunctive. To review present subjunctive with emotions, see pages 168–170 of your textbook.

    Es bueno que tú *hayas ayudado* **en el comedor de beneficencia.**

    It is good that you have helped out at the soup kitchen.

- You form the present perfect subjunctive by combining the present subjunctive of the verb **haber** with the past participle of another verb. The verb **educar** has been conjugated as an example below.

haya educado	**hayamos** educado
hayas educado	**hayáis** educado
haya educado	**hayan** educado

A. Read each sentence and underline the expression of emotion that indicates the subjunctive should be used. Then, circle the correct form of **haber** that is used in the present perfect subjunctive. Follow the model.

Modelo   <u>Me alegro</u> de que muchos (**han** / (**hayan**)) participado en la manifestación.

1. Es bueno que estos programas (**han** / **hayan**) ayudado a tantas personas.

2. Me sorprende que los estudiantes (**hayas** / **hayan**) trabajado en el hogar de ancianos.

3. Siento que tú no (**haya** / **hayas**) recibido ayuda.

4. Es interesante que el presidente (**hayan** / **haya**) protegido los derechos de los niños.

5. A mí me gusta que nosotros (**hayamos** / **hayan**) sembrado árboles hoy.

B. Complete each sentence about what volunteers have done, using the present perfect of the subjunctive of the verb. Follow the model.

Modelo   Es maravilloso que muchos ____*hayan*____ ____*trabajado*____ en el comedor de beneficencia. (**trabajar**)

1. Estamos orgullosos de que los jóvenes _____ _____ en la marcha. (**participar**)

2. Es una lástima que ese político no _____ _____ el movimiento por los derechos de los ancianos. (**apoyar**)

3. Ojalá que nosotros _____ _____ con nuestras responsabilidades. (**cumplir**)

4. Estamos contentos de que esta organización _____ _____ construir un centro recreativo nuevo. (**decidir**)

- **¡Recuerda!** Some past participles require an accent mark and some have completely irregular forms. Look back at page 61 of your workbook for a reminder of these verbs.

C. Complete each sentence with the present perfect subjunctive. Follow the model. **¡Cuidado!** The past participles used are irregular.

Modelo   (**abrir**) Me alegro de que Uds. les ___*hayan*___ ___*abierto*___ las puertas a esas personas.

1. (**escribir**) Es excelente que tú _____ _____ una composición sobre los derechos humanos.

2. (**hacer**)   Nos gusta que los enemigos _____ _____ las paces.

3. (**ver**)   Espero que José _____ _____ el nuevo centro de la comunidad.

4. (**resolver**) Me preocupa que el gobierno no _____ _____ los problemas de la contaminación del medio ambiente.

5. (**decir**)   Es triste que el presidente _____ _____ que hay tanta gente sin hogar en nuestro país.

D. Create complete sentences by conjugating the verbs in the present perfect subjunctive. Follow the model.

Modelo   Es una lástima / que / los estudiantes / no (**donar**) / mucha comida / a la gente pobre

*Es una lástima que los estudiantes no hayan donado mucha comida*
*a la gente pobre.*

1. Es mejor / que / mi amigo / (**aprender**) / más / sobre la campaña

_____

2. Es terrible / que / la comunidad / (**eliminar**) / los servicios sociales

_____

3. Nos sorprende / que / nadie / (**escribir**) / cartas / para apoyar / a los inmigrantes

_____

4. Esperamos / que / los estudiantes / (**hacer**) / proyectos / para beneficiar / a la comunidad

_____

5. El director de escuela / se alegra de / que / nosotros / (**ir**) / al centro recreativo

_____

Capítulo 5

Los adjetivos y los pronombres posesivos (p. 237)

- In Spanish, demonstrative adjectives are used to indicate things that are near or far from the speaker. Demonstrative adjectives are placed in front of a noun and agree with the noun in gender and number.

  Este **árbol es muy alto.**   *This tree is very tall.*

  Below is a list of the forms of demonstrative adjectives used to say *this/these (near you)*, *that/those (near the person you're speaking with)*, and *that/those (far away)*.

this: **este, esta**	these: **estos, estas**
that (near): **ese, esa**	those (near): **esos, esas**
that (far): **aquel, aquella**	those (far): **aquellos, aquellas**

A. Your friend is telling you about several of the students below and their accomplishments. Decide which pair of students she is talking about.

1. __*A*__ Estos estudiantes han construido un centro de donaciones en su escuela.

2. _____ Aquellos jóvenes han hecho mucho trabajo para el centro recreativo.

3. _____ Sé que esos muchachos juntan fondos para el medio ambiente todos los años.

4. _____ Aquellos chicos suelen participar en muchas marchas.

5. _____ ¿Han cumplido estos jóvenes con sus responsabilidades como voluntarios?

B. Circle the demonstrative adjective needed to complete each sentence.

Modelo (**Esos** / (**Esas**)) donaciones son para el centro de la comunidad.

1. ¿Adónde vas con (**estos / estas**) cajas de ropa?

2. (**Aquellas / Aquellos**) chicas tienen que solicitar más donaciones.

3. Queremos felicitar a (**ese / esos**) voluntarios.

4. Necesitan proteger (**esta / estas**) leyes.

Capítulo 5

- Demonstrative <u>pronouns</u> take the place of nouns. The pronouns must agree in gender and number with the nouns they replace.

  No quiero este documento. Quiero **ése.**

- Demonstrative pronouns all have written accent marks. Look at the list below:

  this; these: **éste, ésta; éstos, éstas**

  that; those (near the person you're speaking with): **ése, ésa; ésos, ésas**

  that; those (far away): **aquél, aquélla; aquéllos, aquéllas**

C. Underline the correct demonstrative pronoun based on the questions asked. Follow the model.

| Modelo | A: ¿Qué libro prefieres? | B: Prefiero (<u>ése</u> / **ésos**) porque es para niños. |

1. A: ¿Quieres una de las camisas?   B: Sí, quiero (**éste** / **ésta**).

2. A: ¿Con qué grupo voy a trabajar?   B: Vas a trabajar con (**aquél** / **aquella**).

3. A: ¿Qué casas vamos a reparar?   B: Vamos a reparar (**aquéllas** / **aquél**).

4. A: ¿Cuál es el documento que vamos a entregar?   B: Es (**ése** / **ésa**).

D. Identify the noun in the first part of the sentence that is being omitted in the second part. Circle the noun. Then, write the correct form of the demonstrative pronoun.

| Modelo | Me gusta esta (camisa) pero no me gusta _____*ésa*_____ (*that one*). |

1. No voy a comer esas fresas pero sí voy a comer _____ (*these*).

2. No pensamos comprar estos libros pero nos interesan mucho _____ (*those over there*).

3. Ellas no quieren marchar por estas calles sino por _____ (*those*).

4. Mis amigos van a llenar esos documentos y yo voy a llenar _____ (*this one*).

- There are also three "neutral" demonstrative pronouns that do not have a gender or number. They refer to an idea or to something that has not yet been mentioned.

  ¿Qué es **eso?**   *What is **that?***

  Esto es un desastre.   ***This** is a disaster.*

  ¿Aquello es un centro recreativo?   *Is **that (thing over there)** a rec center?*

  These do not have accent marks and <u>never</u> appear immediately before a noun.

E. Choose whether the demonstrative adjective or the demonstrative pronoun would be used in each of the following situations. Circle your choice.

1. ¿Qué es (**este** / **esto**)?

3. Traigamos (**aquel** / **aquello**) libro al centro recreativo.

2. Discutamos (**ese** / **eso**) más.

4. ¿Quién ha donado (**esa** / **eso**) computadora?

Puente a la cultura (pp. 240–241)

A. There are photos of various people mentioned in the reading in your textbook. Match the names of the people with the area of society with which they are paired.

1. _____ Julián Castro   **A.** los negocios

2. _____ Sonia Sotomayor   **B.** la política

3. _____ Linda Alvarado   **C.** las ciencias

4. _____ Mario Molina

5. _____ Hilda Solís

B. Read the section titled **La población** on page 240 of your textbook. Say whether the following statements are true (**cierto**) or false (**falso**).

1. Más de 50 por ciento de la población de los Estados Unidos
   es hispano.   cierto   falso

2. Hay más de 50 millones de hispanohablantes en los
   Estados Unidos.   cierto   falso

3. Un diez por ciento de los ciudadanos de los Estados Unidos
   habla español.   cierto   falso

4. Hay más hispanohablantes en los Estados Unidos que
   personas que hablan inglés.   cierto   falso

5. El español influye en muchos campos de los Estados Unidos.   cierto   falso

C. Match the three Hispanic women discussed in the sections titled **La política, Los negocios,** and **Las ciencias** with the reason for which they are considered successful.

_____ Sonia Sotomayor   **A.** primera mujer hispana que trabajó
                                 para el Senado de California y para
                                 el gobierno de Obama

_____ Hilda Solís   **B.** presidenta de su propia compañía y
                                 cinco compañías más

_____ Linda G. Alvarado   **C.** primera jueza hispana de la Corte
                                 Suprema

Lectura (pp. 246–248)

A. Look at the title of the reading and the drawings on pages 246–248 in order to make predictions about what you will read. Then, place a checkmark next to the type of reading you think this will be.

_____ una biografía realista

_____ una leyenda imaginativa

B. Several key words to understanding the relationships between the characters appear on the first page. Choose the right meaning for each underlined phrase.

> *Manuela [...] fue a decir adiós a su madre. El encuentro fue muy <u>doloroso</u>, pues no sabían si <u>volverían a verse</u> en vida.*

1. doloroso   **a.** glorioso   **b.** difícil

2. volverían a verse   **a.** se verían otra vez   **b.** se encontraron una vez

> *Pronto <u>nació</u> entre ambas mujeres una amistad sincera y un <u>cariño profundo</u>.*

3. nació   **a.** empezó   **b.** terminó

4. un cariño profundo   **a.** un amor especial   **b.** una fuerte desconfianza

C. In this chapter, you learned about the present and past perfect tenses. For each sentence circle the correct form of *haber*.

1. *Nada de lo que hacía era como lo que ha / había soñado.*

2. *—¡Ibotí! ¿Qué es esto? [...] ¿De dónde ha / había salido esta mantilla?*

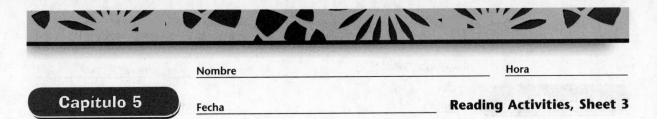

D. Imagine that the legend "Ñandutí" is a four-act play. Complete the description of each act using words from the legend.

araña	baúles	mantilla	deshilachada	casona	expedición

Primer acto *La despedida* Manuela le dice adiós a su madre, y su madre le regala una _____.

Segundo acto *Nace una amistad* Manuela y su marido llegan a Itaguá. Ibotí llega a vivir a la _____ para ayudar con las tareas de la casa. Ibotí y Manuela se hacen amigas.

Tercer acto *La vieja mantilla* El marido se va a una _____ militar y Manuela se queda triste. Manuela comienza a sacar cosas de sus _____ que le traen recuerdos del pasado. Encuentra la vieja mantilla que le dio su madre. Ibotí lava la mantilla, pero esta termina completamente _____. Ibotí trata de hacer una mantilla nueva, pero no puede.

Cuarto acto *Una nueva mantilla* Ibotí aprende a hacer la mantilla al observar cómo teje su tela una _____.

E. Read the legend again. Find the place where each of the four acts from activity D begins and write the first line of each act.

Acto 1: _____

Acto 2: _____

Acto 3: _____

Acto 4: _____

Saber vs. conocer (p. 257)

- The verbs **saber** and **conocer** both mean "to know," but they are used in different contexts.

  Saber is used to talk about knowing a fact or a piece of information, or knowing how to do something.

    *Yo **sé** que Madrid es la capital de España.*

    *Los bomberos **saben** apagar un incendio.*

  Conocer is used to talk about being acquainted or familiar with a person, place, or thing.

    *Yo **conozco** a un policía.*

    *Nosotros **conocemos** la ciudad de Buenos Aires.*

A. Read each of the following pieces of information. Decide if "knowing" each one would use the verb **saber** or the verb **conocer** and mark your answer. Follow the model.

Modelo	una actriz famosa	_____ saber	✓ conocer

1. reparar coches   _____ saber   _____ conocer

2. la música latina   _____ saber   _____ conocer

3. dónde está San Antonio   _____ saber   _____ conocer

4. la ciudad de Nueva York   _____ saber   _____ conocer

5. el dentista de tu comunidad   _____ saber   _____ conocer

6. cuándo es el examen final   _____ saber   _____ conocer

B. Your school recently hired a new principal. Circle the verb that best completes each statement or question about his qualifications.

Modelo ¿(Sabes /(Conoces)) la Universidad de Puerto Rico?

1. Él (**sabe** / **conoce**) mucho del mundo de negocios.

2. También (**sabe** / **conoce**) a muchos miembros de nuestra comunidad.

3. Mis padres lo (**saben** / **conocen**).

4. Él (**conoce** / **sabe**) bien nuestra ciudad.

5. Él (**conoce** / **sabe**) trabajar con los estudiantes y los maestros.

C. Complete each sentence with **conozco** or **sé**. Your sentences can be affirmative or negative, based on your own experiences. Follow the model.

Modelo _Conozco (No conozco)_ bien a Jennifer López.

1. _____ cuándo van a encontrar una cura contra el cáncer.

2. _____ a una mujer de negocios muy inteligente.

3. _____ usar muchos programas en la computadora.

4. _____ Puerto Rico.

D. Complete the sentences below with the correct form of **saber** or **conocer** to discuss jobs and professionals in the community. Follow the model.

Modelo Patricia, tú _____conoces_____ al veterinario, el Sr. Hernández, ¿no?

1. Sí, nosotros lo _____ (a él) muy bien.

2. Nosotros no _____ cuál es el nombre del gerente de esa compañía.

3. ¿_____ (tú) contar dinero tan rápidamente como ese cajero?

4. ¿_____ (Uds.) un buen sitio Web para encontrar trabajos?

5. Yo _____ al secretario de ese grupo político.

6. Esos mecánicos no _____ reparar los motores de los coches.

• In the preterite, **conocer** means "to meet someone for the first time."

   *Mis padres **conocieron** al veterinario la semana pasada cuando mi gato se enfermó.*

E. Create sentences with the preterite form of **conocer** about when various people met. Follow the model.

Modelo Mi tío / conocer / al presidente / el año pasado.

   Mi tío conoció al presidente el año pasado.

1. El dependiente / conocer / al dueño / hace dos años

_____

2. Yo / conocer / a mi profesora de español / en septiembre

_____

3. Nosotros / conocer / a una actriz famosa / el verano pasado

_____

4. Mis amigos / conocer / al médico / el miércoles pasado

_____

El *se* impersonal (p. 259)

- When speaking in English, we often say "they do (something)," "you do (something)," "one does (something)," or "people do (something)" to talk about people in general. In Spanish, you can also talk about people in an impersonal or indefinite sense. To do so, you use *se* + the **Ud./él/ella** or the **Uds./ellos/ellas** form of the verb.

    Se venden videos aquí.   *They sell videos here.*

    Se pone el aceite en la sartén.   *You put (One puts) oil in the frying pan.*

  In the sentences above, note that you don't know who performs the action. The word or words that come *after* the verb determine whether the verb is singular or plural.

A. First, underline the *impersonal se* expression in each sentence. Then, write the letter of the English translation that might be used for it from the list below. Follow the model.

A. They dance	~~**C.** They eat~~	**E.** They sell
B. One finds / You find	**D.** One talks / They talk	**F.** They celebrate

Modelo   En España <u>se cena</u> muy tarde.   *C*

1. En México se celebran muchos días festivos.   _____

2. Se encuentran muchos animales en Costa Rica.   _____

3. En Colombia se habla mucho de los problemas políticos. _____

4. Se baila el tango en Argentina.   _____

5. En Perú se venden muchas artesanías indígenas.   _____

B. Choose the correct verb to complete each description of services offered at the local community center. Follow the model.

Modelo   Se ((habla)/ hablan) español.

1. Se (**vende / venden**) refrescos.

2. Se (**ofrece / ofrecen**) información.

3. Se (**mejora / mejoran**) las vidas.

4. Se (**sirve / sirven**) café.

5. Se (**toma / toman**) clases de arte.

6. Se (**construye / construyen**) casas para la gente sin hogar.

C. Combine the verbs and objects given to create sentences using **se**. Follow the model.

| Modelo | reparar / televisores 3D | *Se reparan televisores 3D.* |

1. beber / agua _____

2. eliminar / contaminantes _____

3. vender / ropa _____

4. servir / comida _____

5. sembrar / plantas _____

6. leer / poemas _____

- When the word following the conjugated verb in an *impersonal se* expression is an infinitive, the verb form is singular.

  Se necesita **encontrar un apartamento.**   *One needs to find an apartment.*

D. Use the *impersonal se* with the two verbs given to create sentences. Use the singular form of the first verb and the infinitive of the second verb. Follow the model.

| Modelo | (**necesitar / proteger**) la naturaleza |

  Se necesita proteger la naturaleza. _____

1. (**poder / beneficiar**) del aire fresco

   _____

2. (**deber / eliminar**) el estrés

   _____

3. (**acabar de / terminar**) la página web

   _____

4. (**no necesitar / construir**) la casa

   _____

5. (**poder / cambiar**) la vida

   _____

Write the Spanish vocabulary word below each picture. Be sure to include the article for each noun.

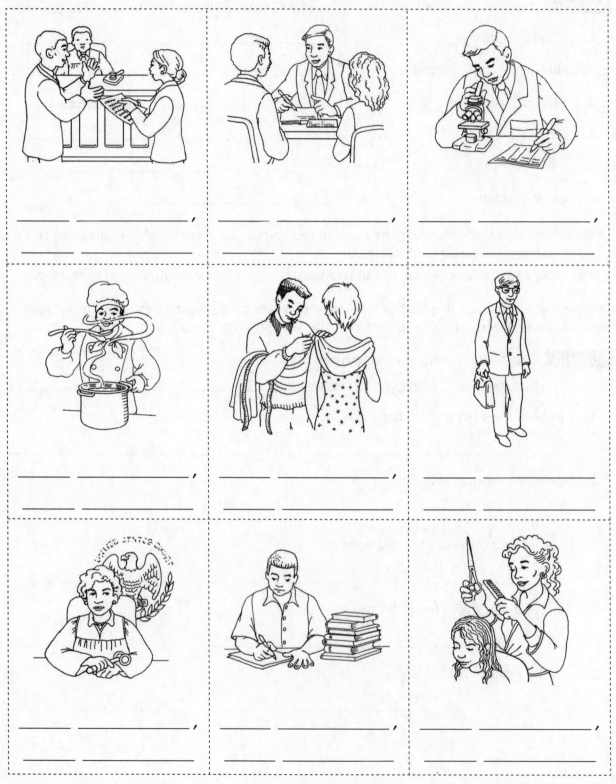

_____ ,
_____

_____ ,
_____

_____ ,
_____

_____ ,
_____

_____ ,
_____

_____ ,
_____

_____ ,
_____

_____ ,
_____

_____ ,
_____

Write the Spanish vocabulary word below each picture. If there is a word or phrase, copy it in the space provided. Be sure to include the article for each noun.

_____ _____	_____ _____ ,	**además de** _____
_____	_____ _____	
ahorrar _____	**ambicioso, ambiciosa** _____ ,	**así que** _____
averiguar _____	**capaz** _____	**casado, casada** _____ ,

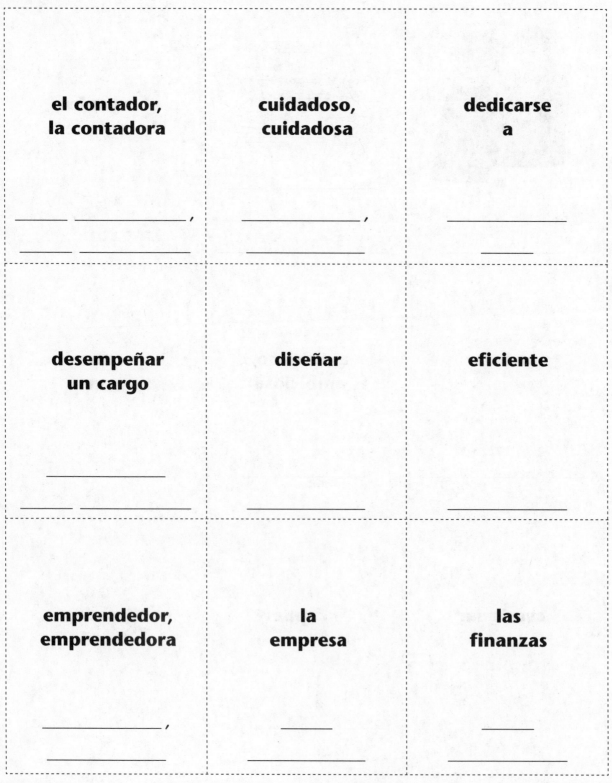

Copy the word or phrase in the space provided. Be sure to include the article for each noun.

el contador, la contadora	cuidadoso, cuidadosa	dedicarse a
_____ _____, _____	_____,	_____
_____ _____		_____

desempeñar un cargo	diseñar	eficiente
_____	_____	_____
_____ _____		

emprendedor, emprendedora	la empresa	las finanzas
_____,	_____	_____
_____		

Copy the word or phrase in the space provided. Be sure to include the article for each noun.

hacerse	haré lo que me dé la gana	el ingeniero, la ingeniera
el jefe, la jefa	lograr	maduro, madura
mudarse	la mujer de negocios	por lo tanto

Copy the word or phrase in the space provided. Be sure to include the article for each noun. The blank cards can be used to write and practice other Spanish vocabulary for the chapter.

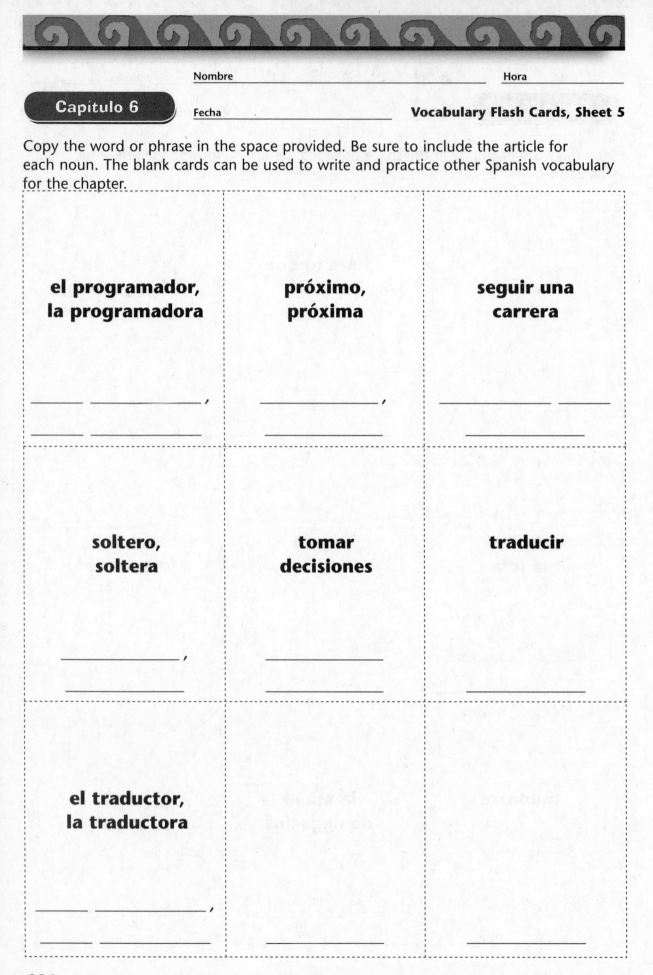

el programador, la programadora

_____ _____,

_____ _____

próximo, próxima

_____,

_____

seguir una carrera

_____ _____

_____

soltero, soltera

_____,

_____

tomar decisiones

_____

_____

traducir

_____

el traductor, la traductora

_____ _____,

_____ _____

Tear out this page. Write the English words on the lines. Fold the paper along the dotted line to see the correct answers so you can check your work.

ahorrar _____

el banquero,
la banquera _____

capaz _____

casado, casada _____

el científico,
la científica _____

el cocinero,
la cocinera _____

el contador,
la contadora _____

cuidadoso,
cuidadosa _____

dedicarse a _____

desempeñar un cargo _____

el diseñador,
la diseñadora _____

diseñar _____

emprendedor,
emprendedora _____

la empresa _____

las finanzas _____

Fold In

Tear out this page. Write the Spanish words on the lines. Fold the paper along the dotted line to see the correct answers so you can check your work.

to save _____

banker _____
_____

able _____

married _____

scientist _____
_____

cook _____
_____

accountant _____
_____

careful _____
_____

to dedicate oneself to _____

to hold a position _____

designer _____
_____

to design _____

enterprising _____
_____

business _____

finance _____

Fold In

Tear out this page. Write the English words on the lines. Fold the paper along the dotted line to see the correct answers so you can check your work.

graduarse (u➔ú) _____

hacerse _____

el hombre de negocios, _____
la mujer de negocios

el ingeniero, _____
la ingeniera

el jefe, la jefa _____

el juez, la jueza _____

lograr _____

maduro, madura _____

mudarse _____

el peluquero, _____
la peluquera

el programador, _____
la programadora

el redactor, la redactora _____

seguir una carrera _____

soltero, soltera _____

el traductor, _____
la traductora

traducir (zc) _____

Fold In

Tear out this page. Write the Spanish words on the lines. Fold the paper along the dotted line to see the correct answers so you can check your work.

to graduate _____

to become _____

businessman, businesswoman _____ _____

engineer _____ _____

boss _____

judge _____

to achieve, to manage to _____

mature _____

to move to _____

hairstylist _____ _____

programmer _____ _____

editor _____

to pursue a career _____

single _____

translator _____ _____

to translate _____

Fold In

El futuro (p. 270)

- You already know at least two ways to express the future in Spanish: by using the present tense or by using **ir** + **a** + *infinitive*:

  Mañana *tengo* **una entrevista.**   *I have an interview tomorrow.*

  ***Vamos a* traducir el documento.**   *We are going to translate the document.*

- The future can also be expressed in Spanish by using the *future tense*. The endings for the future tense are the same for regular -**ar**, -**er**, and -**ir** verbs. For regular verbs, the endings are attached to the infinitive. See two examples below:

estudiar		repetir	
estudiar**é**	estudiar**emos**	repetir**é**	repetir**emos**
estudiar**ás**	estudiar**éis**	repetir**ás**	repetir**éis**
estudiar**á**	estudiar**án**	repetir**á**	repetir**án**

A. Read each of the following statements and decide if it describes something that took place in the past, or something that will take place in the future. Mark your answer. Follow the model.

Modelo   Montaba en triciclo.   ✓ en el pasado   _____ en el futuro

1. Manejaremos coches eléctricos.   _____ en el pasado   ✓ en el futuro

2. Nadábamos en la piscina.   ✓ en el pasado   _____ en el futuro

3. Todos viajarán a otros planetas.   _____ en el pasado   ✓ en el futuro

4. Los teléfonos no existían.   ✓ en el pasado   ✓ en el futuro

5. Las enfermedades serán eliminadas.   _____ en el pasado   ✓ en el futuro

B. Choose the correct verb form to complete each prediction about what will happen in the year 2025. Follow the model.

Modelo   Los estudiantes ((usarán) / usará) computadoras todos los días.

1. Yo (será / (seré)) banquero.

2. Mi mejor amigo y yo (vivirá / (viviremos)) en la Luna.

3. Mi profesor/a de español ((conseguirá) / conseguirás) un puesto como director/a.

4. Mis padres (estarás / (estarán)) jubilados.

5. Tú ((hablarás) / hablarán) con los extraterrestres.

6. Nosotros ((disfrutaremos) / disfrutarán) mucho.

C. Complete each sentence with the correct form of the future tense of the verb given. Follow the model. **¡Recuerda!** All forms except **nosotros** have an accent mark.

| Modelo | Nosotros ___trabajaremos___ en una oficina. (**trabajar**) |

1. Lidia __será__ una madre estupenda. (**ser**)

2. Mi familia __se mudará__ a una ciudad más grande. (**mudarse**)

3. Yo __desempeñaré__ un cargo de contadora. (**desempeñar**)

4. Nosotros __ahorraremos__ mucho dinero en el banco. (**ahorrar**)

5. Tú __seguirás__ una carrera muy interesante. (**seguir**)

- Some verbs have irregular stems in the future tense. You will use these stems instead of the full infinitive. Note that the irregular verbs have the same future endings as regular verbs. Look at the list of irregular stems below.

tener: **tendr-**	decir: **dir-**	
salir: **saldr-**	poder: **podr-**	
venir: **vendr-**	haber: **habr-**	-é, -ás, -á, -emos, -éis, -án
poner: **pondr-**	hacer: **har-**	• no accent mark on "emos"
saber: **sabr-**	querer: **querr-**	

D. Write the irregular future tense verbs for each subject and infinitive.

| Modelo | nosotros (**salir**) ___saldremos___ |

1. yo (**poder**) __podré__

2. ellas (**querer**) __querrán__

3. él (**hacer**) __hará__

4. tú (**tener**) __tendrás__

5. Uds. (**decir**) __dirán__

6. yo (**saber**) __sabré__

7. nosotras (**poner**) __pondremos__

8. ella (**venir**) __vendrá__

E. Complete each sentence about your hopes for the future using the future tense of the irregular verbs in parentheses.

| Modelo | Mis padres ___podrán___ mandarme a una universidad famosa. (**poder**) |

1. Mis amigos __sabrán__ mucho sobre tecnología. (**saber**)

2. Mi esposo y yo __tendremos__ una casa grande. (**tener**)

3. __habrá__ un robot que limpie toda la casa. (**haber**)

4. Mis colegas y yo __saldremos__ de la oficina temprano los viernes. (**salir**)

5. Mi jefa __dirá__ que yo soy más capaz que los otros. (**decir**)

El futuro (*continued*)

F. Write sentences based upon the pictures. Use the information in parentheses in your sentences, including the future tense of the infinitives.

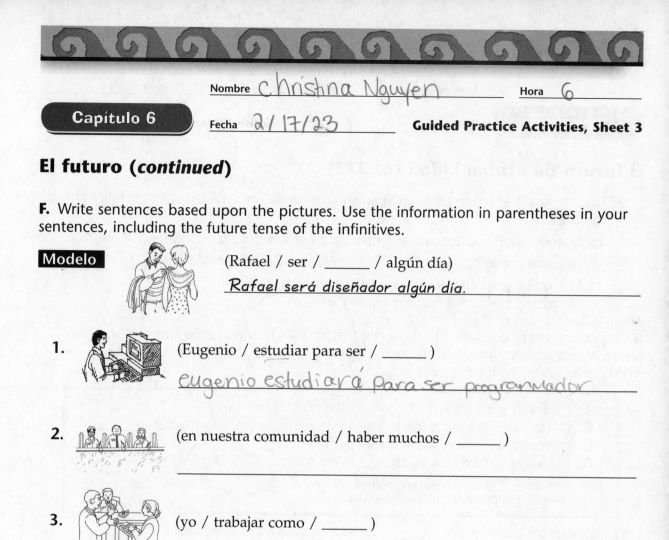

Modelo   (Rafael / ser / _____ / algún día)

Rafael será diseñador algún día.

1.   (Eugenio / estudiar para ser / _____)

Eugenio estudiará para ser programador

2.   (en nuestra comunidad / haber muchos / _____)

_____

3.   (yo / trabajar como / _____)

_____

4.   (nosotros / conocer a / _____ / muy capaz)

_____

5.   (el autor / querer trabajar con / _____ / bueno)

_____

6.   (tú / hacerse / _____)

_____

El futuro de probabilidad (p. 273)

- You can use the future tense in Spanish to express uncertainty or probability about the present.

  Some equivalent expressions in English are *I wonder, it's probably,* and *it must be.*

  ¿Hará frío hoy?   *I wonder if it's cold today.*

  Mis guantes y mi chaqueta *estarán* en el armario.
  My gloves and jacket must be in the closet.

A. A person is very disoriented. Underline the phrases in their sentences that use the future of probability. Then find the best way of expressing this phrase in English in the word bank. Write the letter of the English phrase.

> **A.** I wonder what time it is. / What time must it be?
> **B.** I wonder where my parents are. / Where might my parents be?
> **C.** I wonder why there are so many people here.
> **D.** I wonder what today's date is. / What must today's date be?
> **E.** I wonder who he is. / Who could he be?
> **F.** I wonder what my brothers are doing.

1. ¿Qué harán mis hermanos? _____   4. ¿Cuál será la fecha de hoy? _____

2. ¿Qué hora será? _____   5. ¿Por qué habrá tantas personas aquí? _____

3. ¿Dónde estarán mis padres? _____   6. ¿Quién será él? _____

B. You are daydreaming during your Spanish class. Use the elements given and the future of probability to tell what you imagine your friends and family must be doing. Follow the model.

Modelo   Mi madre / estar / en su oficina   *Mi madre estará en su oficina.*

1. Mis amigos / jugar fútbol / en la clase de educación física

   _____

2. Mi perro / dormir / en el sofá _____

3. Mis abuelos / dar una caminata / por el parque

   _____

4. ¿Qué / hacer / mi padre? _____

5. Mi mejor amiga / dar / un examen difícil / en la clase de matemáticas

   _____

Write the Spanish vocabulary word below each picture. If there is a word or phrase, copy it in the space provided. Be sure to include the article for each noun.

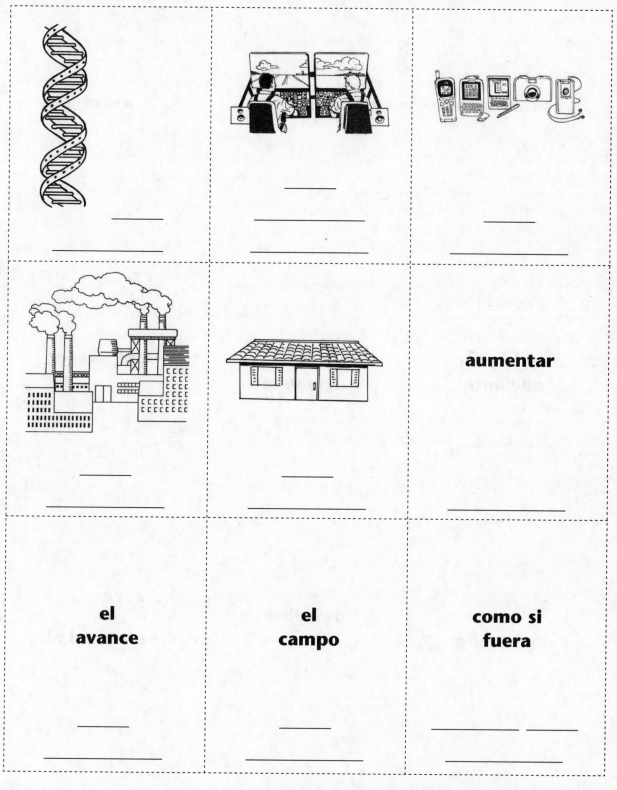

aumentar

_____

el
avance

_____

el
campo

_____

como si
fuera

_____

Copy the word or phrase in the space provided. Be sure to include the article for each noun.

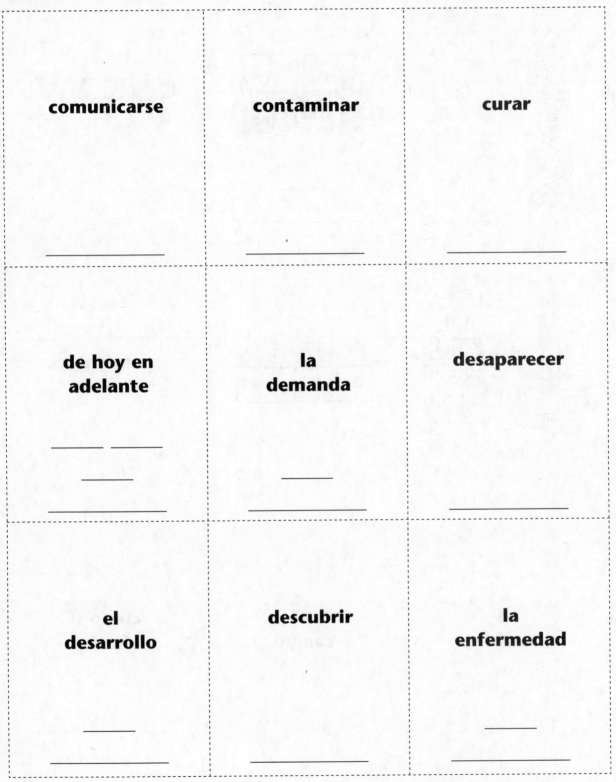

comunicarse	contaminar	curar
de hoy en adelante	la demanda	desaparecer
el desarrollo	descubrir	la enfermedad

Copy the word or phrase in the space provided. Be sure to include the article for each noun.

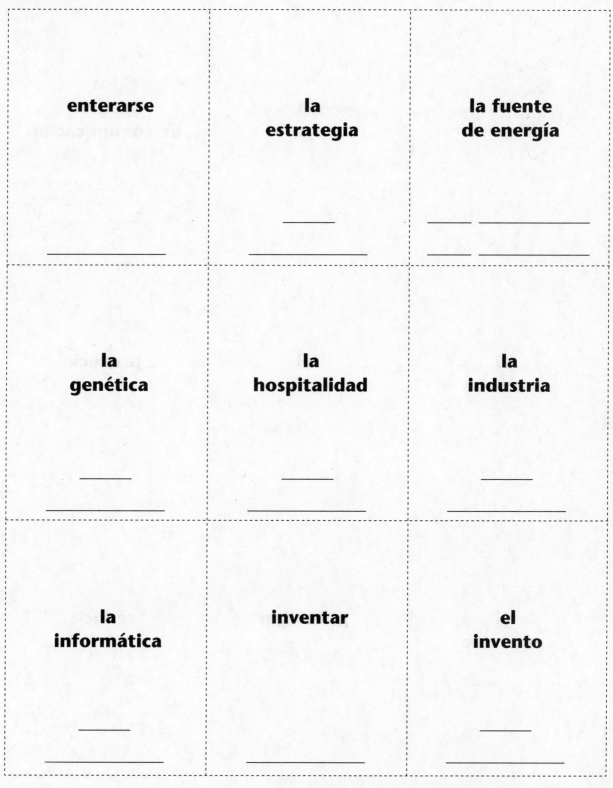

enterarse	la estrategia	la fuente de energía
_____	_____	_____ _____
la genética	la hospitalidad	la industria
_____	_____	_____
la informática	inventar	el invento
_____	_____	_____

Copy the word or phrase in the space provided. Be sure to include the article for each noun.

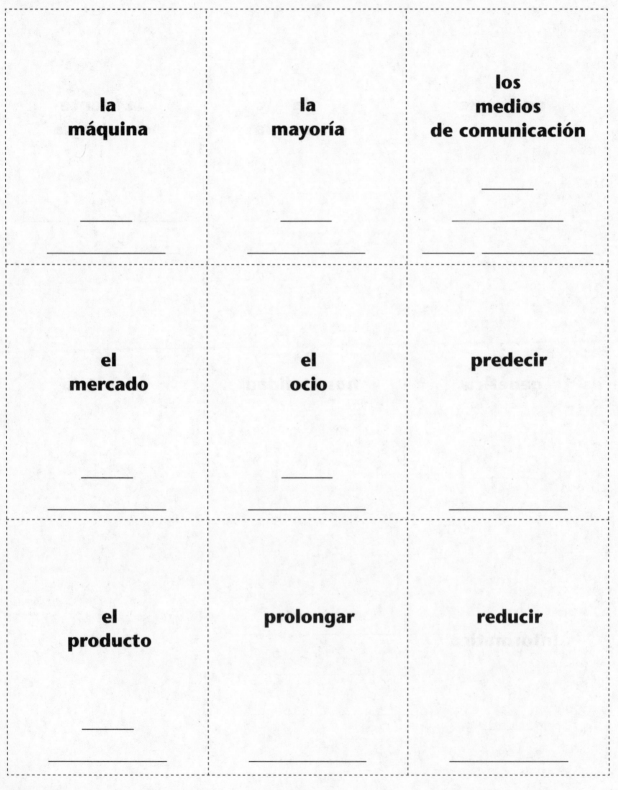

la
máquina

_____

_____

la
mayoría

_____

_____

los
medios
de comunicación

_____

_____   _____

el
mercado

_____

_____

el
ocio

_____

_____

predecir

_____

el
producto

_____

_____

prolongar

_____

reducir

_____

Tear out this page. Write the English words on the lines. Fold the paper along the dotted line to see the correct answers so you can check your work.

el aparato _____

aumentar _____

el avance _____

averiguar _____

el campo _____

comunicarse _____

curar _____

desaparecer _____

el desarrollo _____

descubrir _____

enterarse _____

la estrategia _____

la fábrica _____

la fuente de energía _____

el gen (*pl.* los genes) _____

la genética _____

la hospitalidad _____

la industria _____

Fold In →

Tear out this page. Write the Spanish words on the lines. Fold the paper along the dotted line to see the correct answers so you can check your work.

gadget _____

to increase _____

advance _____

to find out (inquire) _____

field _____

to communicate _____

to cure _____

to disappear _____

development _____

to discover _____

to find out _____

strategy _____

factory _____

energy source _____

gene (genes) _____

genetics _____

hospitality _____

industry _____

Fold In ←

Tear out this page. Write the English words on the lines. Fold the paper along the dotted line to see the correct answers so you can check your work.

la informática _____
_____

el invento _____

la máquina _____

la mayoría _____

los medios de comunicación _____

el mercadeo _____

el ocio _____

predecir _____

prolongar _____

la realidad virtual _____

reducir (zc) _____

reemplazar _____

el servicio _____

tener en cuenta _____

vía satélite _____

la vivienda _____

Fold In →

Nombre ______________________ Hora ______

Capítulo 6

Fecha ______________________

Vocabulary Check, Sheet 8

Tear out this page. Write the Spanish words on the lines. Fold the paper along the dotted line to see the correct answers so you can check your work.

information technology ______________

invention ______________

machine ______________

the majority ______________

media ______________
____

marketing ______________

free time ______________

to predict ______________

to prolong, to extend ______________

virtual reality ______________

to reduce ______________

to replace ______________

service ______________

to take into account ______________

via satellite ______________

housing ______________

Fold In ←

El futuro perfecto (p. 283)

- The future perfect tense is used to talk about what *will have happened* by a certain time. You form the future perfect by using the future of the verb **haber** with the past participle of another verb. Below is the future perfect of the verb **ayudar**.

ayudar	
habré ayudado	habremos ayudado
habrás ayudado	habréis ayudado
habrá ayudado	habrán ayudado

- The future perfect is often used with the word **para** to say "by (a certain time)" and with the expression **dentro de** to say "within (a certain time)".

  Para el año 2050 *habremos reducido* la contaminación del aire.
  By the year 2050, we will have reduced air pollution.

  Los médicos *habrán eliminado* muchas enfermedades *dentro de* 20 años.
  Doctors will have eliminated many illnesses within 20 years.

A. Read each statement and decide if it will happen in the future (future tense), or if it will have happened by a certain point of time in the future (future perfect). Check the appropriate column.

Modelo   Cada estudiante habrá comprado
un teléfono celular para el año 2016.   ____ futuro   ✓ futuro perfecto

1. Los estadounidenses trabajarán menos horas.   ____ futuro   ____ futuro perfecto

2. Todas las escuelas habrán comprado una
computadora para cada estudiante.   ____ futuro   ____ futuro perfecto

3. Los coches volarán.   ____ futuro   ____ futuro perfecto

4. Alguien habrá inventado un robot que
maneje el carro.   ____ futuro   ____ futuro perfecto

B. Circle the correct form of the verb **haber** to complete each sentence.

Modelo   Los médicos (**habrá** / **habrán**) descubierto muchas medicinas nuevas antes del
fin del siglo.

1. Nosotros (**habrán** / **habremos**) conseguido un trabajo fantástico dentro de diez años.

2. Los científicos (**habrás** / **habrán**) inventado muchas máquinas nuevas dentro de
cinco años.

3. Tú (**habrá** / **habrás**) aprendido a usar la energía solar antes del fin del siglo.

4. Yo (**habré** / **habrá**) traducido unos documentos antes de graduarme.

C. Complete each sentence with the future perfect of the verb in parentheses.
¡Cuidado! Some verbs have irregular past participles. Refer to page 81 in your textbook for the list of irregular forms.

Modelo   (**decir**) La presidente ___*habrá*___ ___*dicho*___ que es necesario usar otras fuentes de energía.

1. (**poner**)   Yo _____ _____ agua en mi coche en vez de gasolina.

2. (**reemplazar**) Los robots _____ _____ a muchos trabajadores humanos dentro de 100 años.

3. (**empezar**)   Nosotros _____ _____ a usar muchas fuentes de energía dentro de poco tiempo.

4. (**curar**)   Los médicos _____ _____ muchas enfermedades graves para el año 2025.

5. (**volver**)   Tú _____ _____ de un viaje a Marte con una novia extraterrestre.

6. (**descubrir**)   Alguien _____ _____ una cura para el resfriado.

• The future perfect tense is also used to speculate about something that may have happened in the past.

> **Mis amigos no están aquí. ¿Adónde habrán ido?**
> *My friends are not here. I wonder where they might have gone.*

D. Your Spanish teacher is not at school today. You and other students are discussing what may have happened to her. Write complete sentences below with the future perfect tense. Follow the model.

Modelo   ir a una conferencia ___*Habrá ido a una conferencia.*___

1. visitar a un amigo en otra ciudad _____

2. enfermarse _____

3. salir para una reunión importante _____

4. hacer un viaje a España _____

Uso de los complementos directos e indirectos (p. 285)

- Review the list of direct and indirect object pronouns. You may remember them from Chapter 3 in your textbook.

Direct Object Pronouns	
me	nos
te	os
lo / la	los / las

Indirect Object Pronouns	
me	nos
te	os
le	les

- You can use a direct and an indirect object pronoun together in the same sentence. When you do so, place the indirect object pronoun before the direct object pronoun.

   La profesora me dio un examen. *Me lo* dio el martes pasado.
   The teacher gave me an exam. She gave <u>it to me</u> last Tuesday.

A. Marcos was very busy yesterday. Complete each sentence with the correct direct object pronoun: **lo, la, los, las.** Follow the model.

Modelo   Marcos compró un libro de cocina española ayer. __*Lo*__ compró en la Librería Central.

1. Preparó una paella deliciosa. _____ preparó en la cocina de su abuela.

2. Encontró unas flores en el jardín y _____ trajo para poner en el centro de la mesa.

3. Decidió comprar unos tomates. _____ compró para preparar una ensalada.

4. Encontró una botella de vino y _____ abrió.

5. Marcos terminó de cocinar el pan y _____ sirvió.

B. Read the sentences again in exercise A and look at the direct object pronouns you wrote. Then, based on the cue in parentheses, add the indirect object pronoun **me, te,** or **nos** to create new sentences telling whom Marcos did these things for. Write both pronouns in the sentence. Follow the model.

Modelo   (para ti)   __*Te*__ __*lo*__ compró en la Librería Central.

1. (para nosotros) _____ _____ preparó en la cocina de su abuela.

2. (para mí) _____ _____ trajo para poner en el centro de la mesa.

3. (para ti) _____ _____ compró para preparar una ensalada.

4. (para mí) _____ _____ abrió.

5. (para nosotros) _____ _____ sirvió.

- In sentences with two object pronouns, sometimes the pronouns **le** and **les** have to be changed. If the **le** or **les** comes before the direct object pronoun **lo, la, los,** or **las,** the **le** or **les** must change to **se.**

  Le compré unas flores a mi madre. Se las di esta mañana.
  I bought flowers for my mother. I gave <u>them to her</u> *this morning.*

- You often add the personal **a** + a pronoun, noun, or person's name to make it more clear who the **se** refers to.

  Mi tía Gloria le trajo regalos a Lupita. Se los dio *a ella* después de la fiesta.
  My aunt Gloria brought gifts for Lupita. She gave them <u>to her</u> *after the party.*

C. Read the first sentence in each pair and underline the ⟨direct object.⟩ Then, circle the correct combination of indirect and direct object pronouns to complete the second sentence. Follow the model.

> **Modelo**   Patricia le comprará <u>un anillo</u> a su hermana. ((**Se lo**)/ **Se la**) comprará en Madrid.

1. El Sr. Gómez les escribirá unas <u>cartas de recomendación</u> a sus estudiantes. (**Se lo** / (**Se las**)) escribirá el próximo fin de semana.

2. Nosotros le enviaremos <u>regalos</u> a nuestra prima. ((**Se los** / **Se las**) enviaremos muy pronto.

3. Yo les daré unas <u>tareas</u> a mis maestros. (**Se la** / (**Se las**)) daré en la próxima clase.

4. ¿Tú le prepararás <u>un pastel</u> a tu papá? ¿(**Se la** / (**Se lo**)) prepararás para su cumpleaños?

5. Le pagaremos <u>dinero</u> a la contadora. (**Se la** / (**Se lo**)) pagaremos por su dedicación en el trabajo.

D. Complete each rewritten sentence using both indirect and direct object pronouns. Follow the model.

> **Modelo**   La profesora les leyó un cuento muy cómico a los estudiantes. La profesora _se_ _lo_ leyó.

1. Mis padres le dieron unos regalos a mi profesora. Mis padres _se_ _los_ dieron.

2. Yo te compré unas camisetas nuevas. Yo _te_ _las_ compré.

3. Nuestra directora nos explicó las reglas de la escuela. _nos_ _las_ explicó.

4. El científico les enseño una técnica a sus asistentes. Él _se_ _la_ enseñó.

5. Mi profesora me escribió unos comentarios. Ella _me_ _los_ escribió.

Puente a la cultura (pp. 288–289)

A. This reading is about the buildings of the future. Write three characteristics that you would expect the buildings of the future to have. Look at the photos in the reading to help you think of ideas. One example has been done for you.

buildings will use more technology _____

_____   _____

B. Look at the excerpt from the reading in your textbook. Try to figure out what the highlighted phrase means by using the context of the reading. Answer the questions below.

> «*Cada vez habrá más edificios "inteligentes", en otras palabras, edificios en los que una computadora central controla todos los aparatos y servicios para aprovechar (utilize) mejor la energía eléctrica...*»

1. What does the phrase **edificios "inteligentes"** mean in English?

_____   _____

2. What does this phrase mean in the context of this reading?

a. usarán más ladrillo   **b.** serán más altos   **c.** usarán mejor tecnología

C. Use the following table to help you keep track of the architects and one important characteristic of each of the buildings mentioned in the reading. The first one has been done for you.

Edificio	Arquitecto	Característica importante
1. las Torres Petronas	*César Pelli*	*los edificios más altos del mundo*
2. el Faro de Comercio		
3. el Hotel Camino Real		
4. el World Trade Center		

Lectura (pp. 294–296)

A. You will encounter many words in this reading that you do not know. Sometimes these words are cognates, which you can get after reading them alone. Look at the following cognates from the reading and write the corresponding English word.

1. superiores _____
2. la indignación _____
3. contemplado _____

4. ambiciones _____
5. una trayectoria _____
6. entusiasmo _____

B. This story contains a great deal of dialogue, but quotation marks are not used. Instead, Spanish uses another type of mark, **la raya** (—), to indicate direct dialogue. In the following paragraph, underline the section of text that is dialogue. Look for verbs such as **dijo** and **expresó** to help you determine where dialogue appears.

1. —¡Hoy es el día! —el tono de Rosa expresó cierta zozobra, la sensación de una derrota ineludible.

   —¿Por qué habrán decidido eso?

2. —A cualquiera le gustaría estar allí —dijo Rosa sin énfasis—. Pero creo que ya soy demasiado vieja.

C. Look at the following excerpts from page 295 of your reading. Circle the best translation for each by deciding whether it expresses a definite future action or a probability. Also use context clues to help you with meaning.

1. ‖ —Por eso **querrán** trasladarte. **Necesitarán** tus servicios en otra parte. Quizá te lleven al Centro Nacional de Comunicaciones. ‖

   a. That is why they will want to move you. They will need your services somewhere else. Perhaps they will bring you to the National Center for Communications.

   b. That must be why they want to move you. They probably need your services somewhere else. They might bring you to the National Center for Communications.

2. ‖ —Siempre serás un ejemplo para nosotras, Rosa.
   —Nadie será capaz de reemplazarte. Estamos seguras. ‖

   a. You will always be an example for us, Rosa. No one will be able to replace you. We are sure.

   b. You most likely will always be an example for us, Rosa. No one may be able to replace you. We are sure.

D. Decide whether the following statements are true or false about what happens in the story. Write **C** for **cierto** or **F** for **falso**. Then, correct the false statements to make them true.

1. _____ Rosa está nerviosa porque tiene que ir a un lugar desconocido.

   _____

2. _____ Las amigas de Rosa se llaman Marta y Pancha.

   _____

3. _____ Rosa ha trabajado en su compañía por treinta años.

   _____

4. _____ Rosa ha sido una buena trabajadora.

   _____

5. _____ Las amigas piensan que Rosa recibirá un mejor trabajo.

   _____

6. _____ Cinco robots vienen a sacar a Rosa de su trabajo.

   _____

7. _____ Rosa recibe un buen trabajo nuevo al final del cuento.

   _____

E. This story has a surprise ending. Finish the following sentence by circling the correct answers to explain what the "twist" ending reveals.

*Rosa no es un ser humano. Ella es (**una computadora / un animal**) y los hombres del cuento van a (**darle un premio / destruirla**) porque en el futuro (**los seres humanos / las máquinas**) controlarán el mundo.*

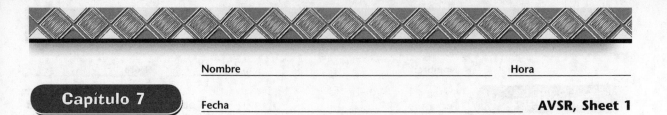

Las construcciones negativas (p. 305)

- Look at the following lists of affirmative and negative words.

Affirmative		Negative	
algo	*something*	nada	*nothing*
alguien	*someone*	nadie	*no one*
alguno/a (*pron.*)	*some*	ninguno/a	*none, not any*
algún/alguna (*adj.*)	*some*	ningún/ninguna	*none, not any*
algunos/as (*pron/adj*)	*some*	ningunos/as (*pron/adj*)	*none, not any*
siempre	*always*	nunca	*never*
también	*also*	tampoco	*either, neither*

A. Learning words as opposites is a good strategy. Match each of the following affirmative words with the negative word that means the opposite.

____ **1.** alguien

____ **2.** algo

____ **3.** algunos

____ **4.** siempre

____ **5.** también

A. nada

B. tampoco

C. nadie

D. ningunos

E. nunca

B. Circle the correct affirmative or negative word to complete each sentence. Follow the model.

Modelo No hay (**algo** /(nada)) interesante en esa plaza. Salgamos ahora.

1. (**Siempre / Nunca**) voy al desierto porque no me gusta el calor.

2. El Sr. Toledo encontró (**algún / ningún**) artefacto de oro por estas partes.

3. —Me encanta acampar en las montañas.

—A mí (**también / tampoco**).

4. Mis vecinos se mudaron y ahora no vive (**nadie / alguien**) en esa casa.

5. (**Ningún / Algún**) día voy a ser un cantante famoso porque practico todos los días.

- It is important to remember that the adjectives **algún, alguna, algunos, algunas** and **ningún, ninguna, ningunos, ningunas** agree in number and gender with the noun they modify.

  *Hay **algunas** esculturas en el templo.*

  *No hay **ningún** bosque en esa parte del país.*

C. Complete the sentences with the correct affirmative word (**algún, alguna, algunos, algunas**) or negative word (**ningún, ninguna, ningunos, ningunas**). Follow the model.

Modelo   Vimos _____*algunos*_____ ríos muy impresionantes.

1. No había _____ palacio antiguo en la ciudad.

2. Visitamos _____ montañas muy altas y bonitas.

3. ¿Hay _____ edificio de piedra por aquí?

4. No conocíamos a _____ persona en el pueblito.

5. Los arquitectos no han encontrado _____ objeto interesante en ese sitio.

6. Descubrimos _____ monumentos hermosos en el centro.

- Remember that to make a sentence negative in Spanish, you must put **no** in front of the conjugated verb.

  ***No** olvidé nada para mi viaje.*

- However, if a sentence starts with a negative word, like **nunca** or **nadie**, do not use the word **no** in front of the verb.

  ***Nadie** puede explicar ese fenómeno increíble.*

D. Change each of the following statements so they mean exactly the opposite.

Modelo   Conocimos a alguien interesante en la plaza.

   No conocimos a nadie interesante en la plaza.

1. Siempre llevo aretes de plata. _____

2. Hay algún río por aquí. _____

3. Nadie sube la escalera. _____

4. No hay nada en ese castillo. _____

5. Quiero hacer algo. _____

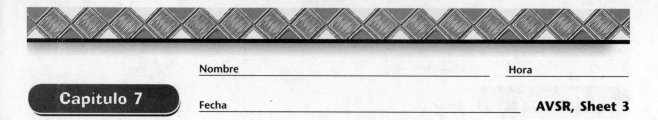
Los adjetivos usados como sustantivos (p. 307)

- When speaking about two similar things in Spanish you can avoid repetition by using the adjective as a noun. Look at the examples below.

    ¿Te gustan más los perros grandes o _los pequeños?_
    Do you like big dogs more or little ones?

    Tengo un pájaro blanco y _uno rojo._
    I have a white bird and a red one.

- Note that you use the definite article (**el, la, los, las**) or indefinite article (**un, una, unos, unas**) and an adjective that agrees in gender and number with the noun it replaces.

- Note also that **un** becomes **uno** when it is not followed by a noun.

A. Read each sentence. The underlined adjective is being used as a noun to avoid repeating the original noun in the sentence. Circle the original noun. Follow the model.

Modelo   Me gustan (las camisas) azules pero no me gustan nada <u>las amarillas</u>.

1. Tengo miedo de los animales grandes pero no me molestan <u>los pequeños</u>.

2. Anoche hubo una tormenta fuerte y esta noche va a haber <u>una pequeña</u>.

3. En el parque zoológico hay un elefante viejo y <u>uno joven</u>.

4. Las hormigas negras no pican pero <u>las rojas</u> sí.

5. La cebra flaca no come mucho porque <u>la gorda</u> se come toda la comida.

6. En ese acuario hay unos peces anaranjados y <u>unos azules</u>.

B. Choose the correct form of each adjective being used as a noun. Follow the model.

Modelo   Los osos de color café son más grandes que ((**los blancos**) / **las blancas**).

1. No quiero un cuaderno rojo. Quiero (**uno gris / una gris**).

2. Las moscas grandes me molestan más que (**los pequeños / las pequeñas**).

3. El mono gris es más agresivo que (**la negra / el negro**).

4. Hubo un incendio pequeño en la ciudad y (**una grande / uno grande**) en el campo.

5. Va a haber muchas flores de color rosa y (**unas amarillas / unos amarillos**) en mi jardín esta primavera.

- You can also use the definite or indefinite article with a prepositional phrase beginning with **a, de,** or **para** to avoid repetition.

  *¿Son más grandes los pájaros de Guatemala o **los de Costa Rica?***

  *Esta comida es para un perro joven, no **para uno viejo.***

C. Cross out the noun that is repeated in each sentence. Then, write the remaining phrase including **a, de,** or **para** that replaces the repeated noun. Follow the model.

Modelo   La entrenadora de fútbol y la ~~entrenadora~~ de béisbol son buenas amigas.
   la de béisbol

1. Las entradas del cine cuestan menos que las entradas de la obra de teatro.

   _____

2. Unos estudiantes de primer año y unos estudiantes de tercer año están de excursión hoy.

   _____

3. La clase de literatura y la clase de ciencias sociales tienen lugar en el teatro de la escuela.

   _____

4. El profesor de inglés es más exigente que el profesor de anatomía.

   _____

5. Nos quedamos para este mes y no para el mes que viene.

   _____

- You can also place **lo** in front of a masculine singular adjective to make it into a noun. This creates the equivalent of "the (adjective) thing . . ." in English.

  Lo bueno del verano es que no hay clases.
  The good thing about summer is that there are no classes.

D. Use the adjectives in parentheses as nouns at the beginning of each of the following sentences. Follow the model.

Modelo   __Lo__ __cómico__ de la situación es que Lidia no es profesora. (**cómico**)

1. _____ _____ de la clase es que hay mucha tarea. (**malo**)
2. _____ _____ del libro es que no tiene narrador. (**interesante**)
3. _____ _____ del invierno es que podemos esquiar. (**divertido**)
4. _____ _____ de esta tarea es que no comprendo el vocabulario. (**difícil**)
5. _____ _____ de esos pájaros es que pueden volar por varias millas sin descansar. (**impresionante**)

Write the Spanish vocabulary word or phrase below each picture. Be sure to include the article for each noun.

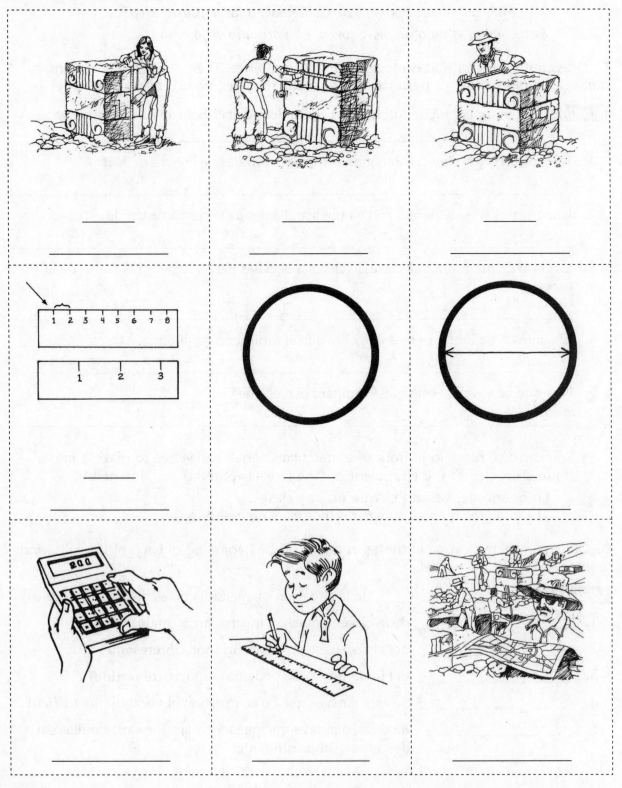

_____   _____   _____

_____   _____   _____

_____   _____   _____

_____   _____   _____

Write the Spanish vocabulary word or phrase below each picture. Be sure to include the article for each noun.

Write the Spanish vocabulary word below each picture. If there is a word or phrase, copy it in the space provided. Be sure to include the article for each noun.

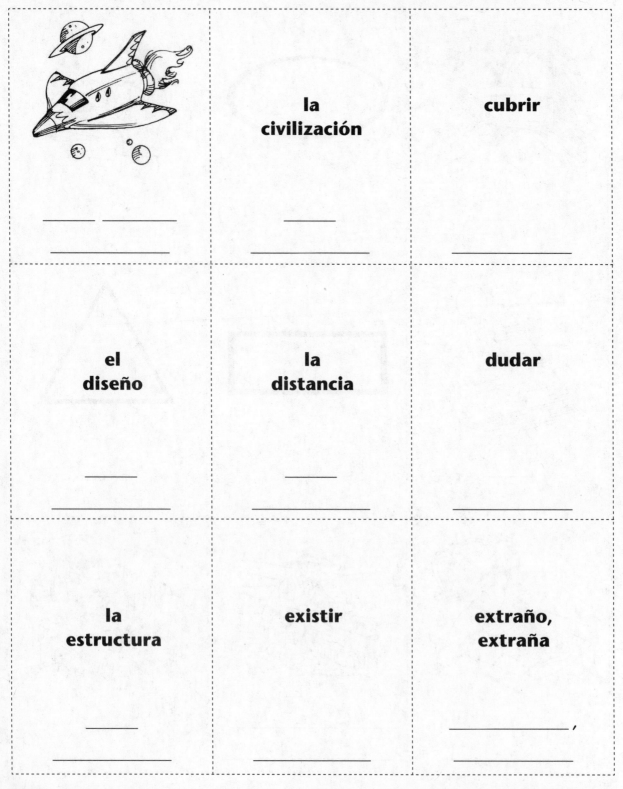

la
civilización

cubrir

el
diseño

la
distancia

dudar

la
estructura

existir

extraño,
extraña

Copy the word or phrase in the space provided. Be sure to include the article for each noun.

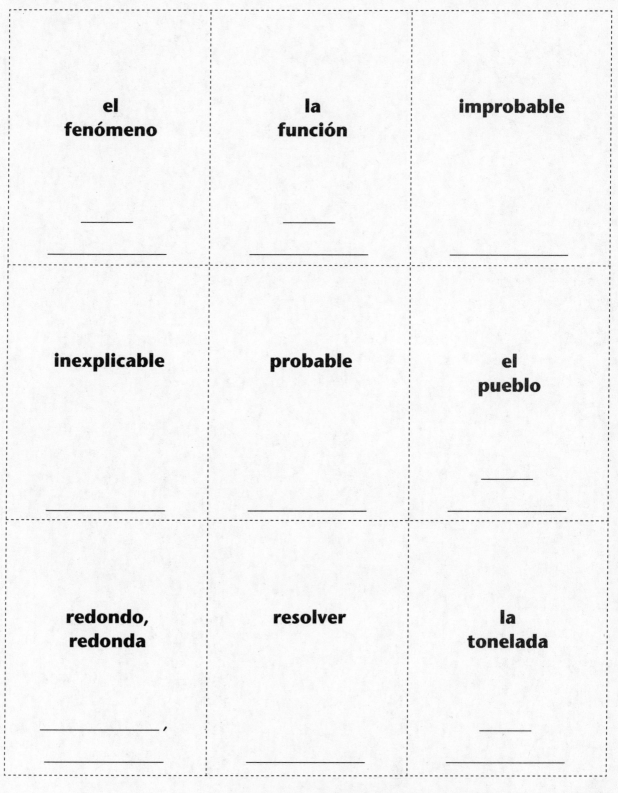

el fenómeno	la función	improbable
____ _____	____ _____	_____
inexplicable	probable	el pueblo
_____	_____	____ _____
redondo, redonda	resolver	la tonelada
_____, _____	_____	____ _____

These blank cards can be used to write and practice other Spanish vocabulary for the chapter.

Capítulo 7

Tear out this page. Write the English words on the lines. Fold the paper along the dotted line to see the correct answers so you can check your work.

el alto _____

el ancho _____

el arqueólogo,
la arqueóloga _____

calcular _____

_____

el círculo _____

la civilización _____

cubrir _____

el diámetro _____

el diseño _____

la distancia _____

excavar _____

dudar _____

extraño, extraña _____

el fenómeno _____

la función _____

geométrico,
geométrica _____

improbable _____

Fold In

Nombre Hora

Capítulo 7

Fecha

Vocabulary Check, Sheet 2

Tear out this page. Write the Spanish words on the lines. Fold the paper along the dotted line to see the correct answers so you can check your work.

height ____________________

width ____________________

archaeologist ____________________
____

to calculate, to compute ____________________

circle ____________________

civilization ____________________

to cover ____________________

diameter ____________________

design ____________________

distance ____________________

to dig ____________________

to doubt ____________________

strange ____________________

phenomenon ____________________

function ____________________

geometric(al) ____________________
____

unlikely ____________________

Fold In ←

Tear out this page. Write the English words on the lines. Fold the paper along the dotted line to see the correct answers so you can check your work.

inexplicable _____

el largo _____

medir (e➜i) _____

la nave espacial _____

el observatorio _____

el óvalo _____

pesar _____

la pirámide _____

probable _____

el pueblo _____

el rectángulo _____

redondo, redonda _____

resolver (o➜ue) _____

las ruinas _____

la tonelada _____

el triángulo _____

trazar _____

Fold In ←

Nombre ______________________ Hora ______________

Capítulo 7

Fecha ______________________

Vocabulary Check, Sheet 4

Tear out this page. Write the Spanish words on the lines. Fold the paper along the dotted line to see the correct answers so you can check your work.

inexplicable ______________

length ______________

to measure ______________

spaceship ______________

observatory ______________

oval ______________

to weigh ______________

pyramid ______________

likely ______________

people ______________

rectangle ______________

round ______________

to solve ______________

ruins ______________

ton ______________

triangle ______________

to trace, to draw ______________

Fold In ←

Capítulo 7   Fecha 5/8/23

El presente y el presente perfecto del subjuntivo con expresiones de duda (p. 318)

- When you want to express doubt, uncertainty, or disbelief about actions in the present, you use the present subjunctive.

  Dudo que los arqueólogos tengan todos sus instrumentos.
  I doubt the archaeologists have all their instruments.

  Other verbs and expressions that indicate doubt, uncertainty, and disbelief include:

No creer	**Es improbable**	**Es dudoso**
Es probable	**Es imposible**	

- In contrast, expressions of belief, knowledge, or certainty are usually followed by the indicative.

  Es verdad que los arqueólogos trabajan mucho.
  It's true that the archaeologists work a lot.

  Other verbs and expressions of belief, knowledge, or certainty include:

Creer	**No dudar**	**Es cierto**
Estar seguro/a de	**Saber**	**Es evidente**

A. Circle the verb in each of the following sentence endings. Then, choose the appropriate sentence starter. If the verb you circled is in the subjunctive or present perfect subjunctive, check the column that says "**Dudamos.**" If the verb is in the indicative, check the column that says "**Estamos seguros de.**"

Modelo ... que los marcianos (vivan) en nuestro planeta.

☑ Dudamos ...   ☐ Estamos seguros de ...

1. ... que Chichén Itza (es) el sitio arqueológico más famoso del mundo.

   ☐ Dudamos ...   ☑ Estamos seguros de ...

2. ... que muchas ruinas mayas (están) en el Yucatán.

   ☐ Dudamos ...   ☑ Estamos seguros de ...

3. ... que (existan) evidencias de una nave espacial.

   ☐ Dudamos ...   ☑ Estamos seguros de ...

4. ... que los arqueólogos (resuelvan) todos los misterios de la civilización maya.

   ☑ Dudamos ...   ☐ Estamos seguros de ...

5. ... que el observatorio (está) en el centro de la ciudad.

   ☐ Dudamos ...   ☑ Estamos seguros de ...

B. Find the expression that indicates doubt (subjunctive) or certainty (indicative) in each sentence below. Write **S** for subjunctive and **I** for indicative. Then, complete the sentences with the correct form of the verb in parentheses. Follow the model.

Modelo __*I*__ Es cierto que nadie __*puede*__ explicar todo lo misterioso de nuestro universo. (**poder**)

1. __S__ Es dudoso que los arqueólogos _excaven_ hoy porque llueve. (**excavar**)

2. __S__ Creo que los diseños geométricos _tenían_ un diámetro de cinco metros. (**tener**)

3. __I__ Los arqueólogos saben que nosotros _querremos_ investigar ese sitio. (**querer**)

4. __I__ Es cierto que la arqueóloga _trazque_ una línea entre los dos edificios. (**trazar**)

5. __S__ Es posible que los estudiantes _veya_ unos fenómenos extraños durante su viaje a Perú. (**ver**)

- When you express doubt or uncertainty about actions that took place in the past, use the present perfect subjunctive.

  Es dudoso que los arqueólogos *hayan medido* todas las pirámides.
  It's doubtful that the archaeologists measured (have measured) all the pyramids.

- Use the present perfect indicative after expressions of belief, knowledge, or certainty.

  Es verdad que los arqueólogos *han encontrado* unos objetos de cerámica.
  It is true that the archaeologists found (have found) some ceramic objects.

C. First, underline the expression that indicates doubt or certainty in each sentence. Then, complete the sentences with the present perfect indicative or present perfect subjunctive. Follow the models.

Modelos (ver) <u>No creo</u> que ellos __*hayan*__ __*visto*__ una nave espacial.

(pesar) <u>Es evidente</u> que los científicos __*han*__ __*pesado*__ las piedras.

1. (estudiar) Es evidente que los mayas _____ _____ mucho la astronomía.

2. (ver) Dudamos que tú _____ _____ un extraterrestre.

3. (hacer) No es probable que ellos _____ _____ todos los viajes que planearon.

4. (ir) Estamos seguros que tú _____ _____ a un sitio muy famoso.

5. (comunicar) Los científicos no creen que los incas se _____ _____ con los extraterrestres.

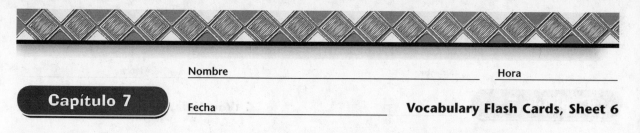
Write the Spanish vocabulary word below each picture. If there is a word or phrase, copy it in the space provided. Be sure to include the article for each noun.

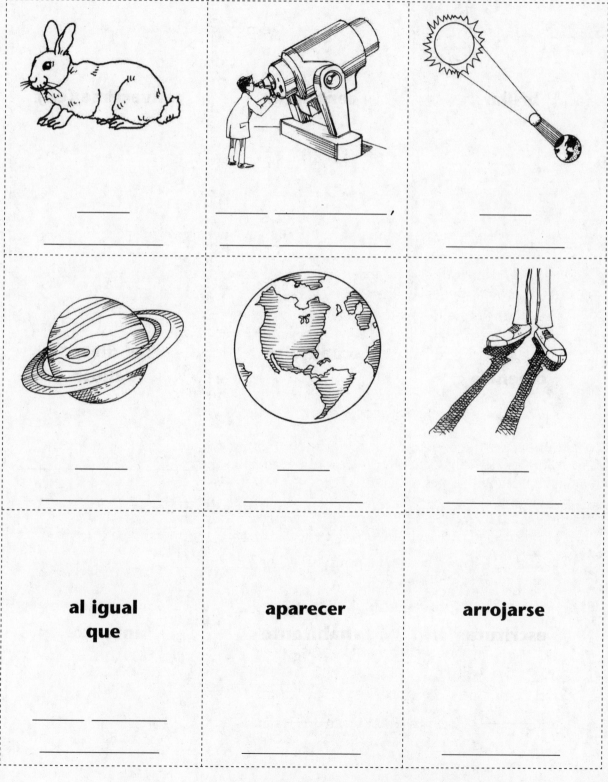

al igual que

aparecer

arrojarse

Copy the word or phrase in the space provided. Be sure to include the article for each noun.

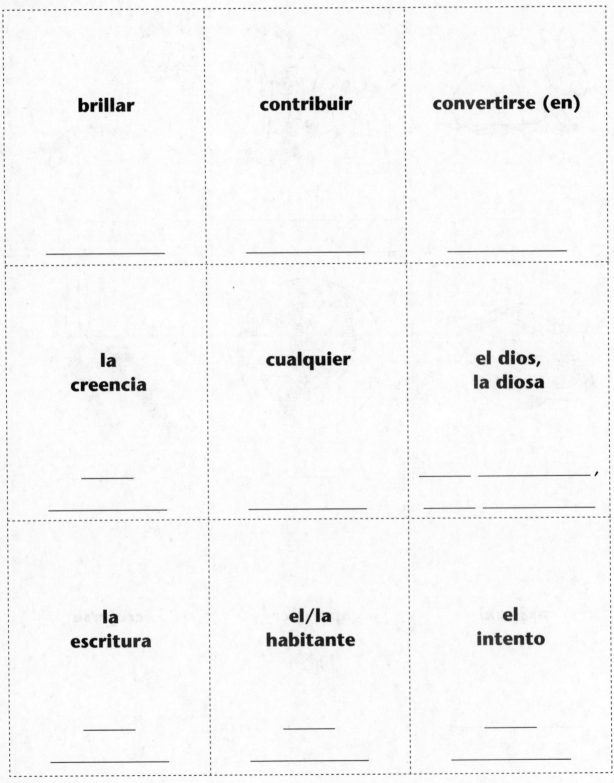

brillar

_____

contribuir

_____

convertirse (en)

_____

**la
creencia**

_____

_____

cualquier

_____

**el dios,
la diosa**

_____ _____,

_____

**la
escritura**

_____

_____

**el/la
habitante**

_____

**el
intento**

_____

_____

Copy the word or phrase in the space provided. Be sure to include the article for each noun.

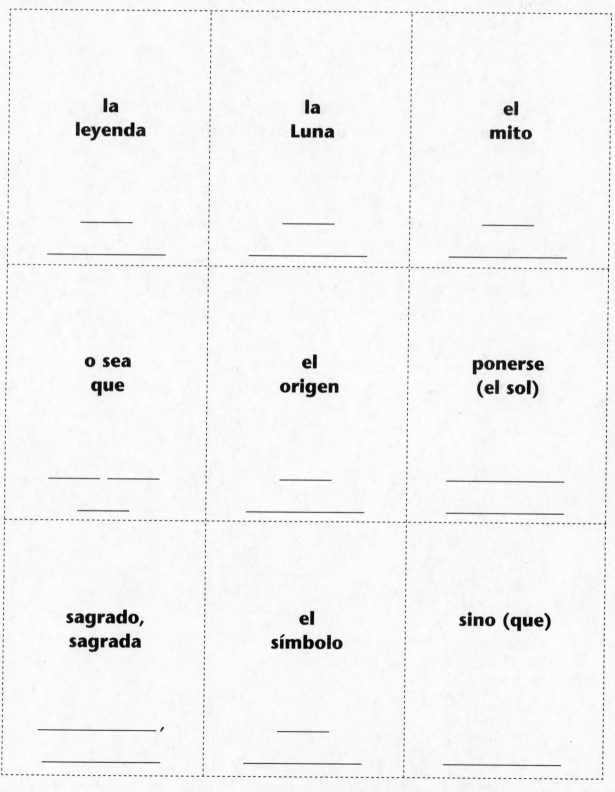

la leyenda	la Luna	el mito
o sea que	el origen	ponerse (el sol)
sagrado, sagrada	el símbolo	sino (que)

Copy the word or phrase in the space provided. Be sure to include the article for each noun. The blank cards can be used to write and practice other Spanish vocabulary for the chapter.

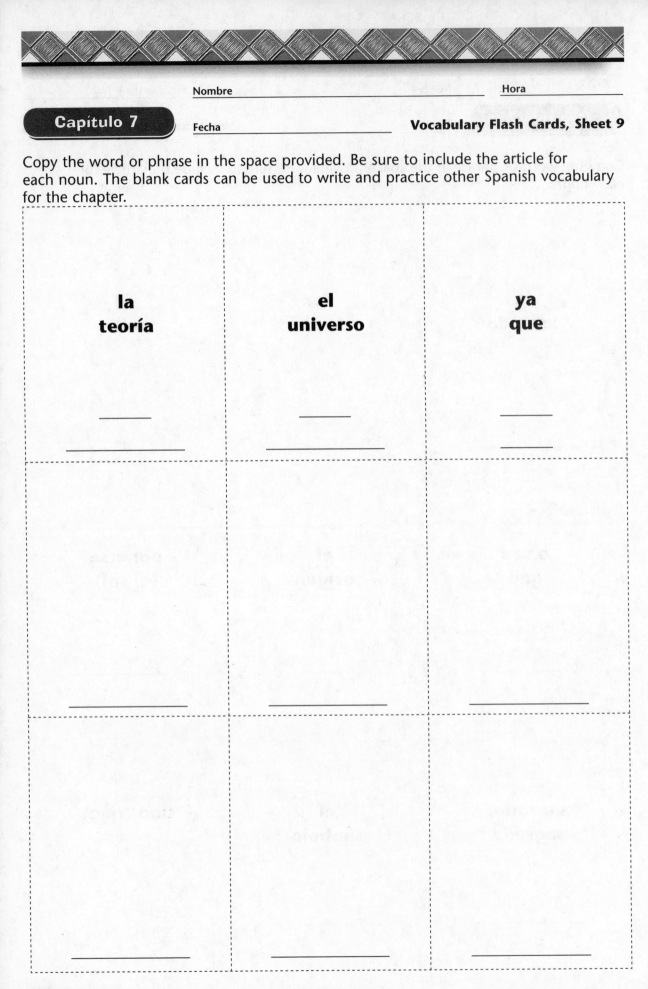

**la
teoría**

_____

_____

**el
universo**

_____

_____

**ya
que**

_____

_____

_____

_____

_____

_____

_____

_____

Tear out this page. Write the English words on the lines. Fold the paper along the dotted line to see the correct answers so you can check your work.

al igual que _____

aparecer (zc) _____

arrojar(se) _____

el astrónomo, la astrónoma _____

brillar _____

convertirse (en) _____
_____

contribuir (u➡y) _____

la creencia _____

cualquier, cualquiera _____

el dios, la diosa _____

la escritura _____

el eclipse _____

el/la habitante _____

el intento _____

Fold In

Tear out this page. Write the Spanish words on the lines. Fold the paper along the dotted line to see the correct answers so you can check your work.

as, like   _____

to appear   _____

to throw (oneself)   _____

astronomer   _____

                                   _____

to shine   _____

to turn (into);
to become   _____

to contribute   _____

belief   _____

any   _____

                                   _____

god, goddess   _____

writing   _____

eclipse   _____

inhabitant   _____

attempt   _____

Fold In ◄

Tear out this page. Write the English words on the lines. Fold the paper along the dotted line to see the correct answers so you can check your work.

la leyenda _____

la Luna _____

el mito _____

el origen _____

o sea que _____

el planeta _____

ponerse (el sol) _____

sagrado, sagrada _____

el símbolo _____

sino (que) _____

la sombra _____

la teoría _____

la Tierra _____

el universo _____

Fold In

Tear out this page. Write the Spanish words on the lines. Fold the paper along the dotted line to see the correct answers so you can check your work.

legend   _____

moon   _____

myth   _____

origin   _____

in other words _____

planet   _____

to set (sun)   _____

sacred   _____

symbol   _____

but; but instead _____

shadow   _____

theory   _____

Earth   _____

universe   _____

Fold In ←

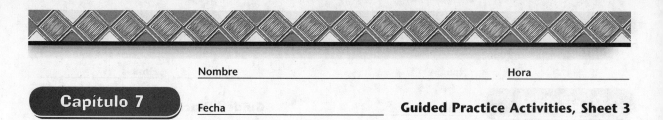

Pero y sino (p. 331)

- To say the word "but" in Spanish, you usually use the word **pero**.

   *Hoy hace mal tiempo, **pero** vamos a visitar las pirámides.*

   However, there is another word in Spanish, **sino**, that also means "but." **Sino** is used after a negative, in order to offer the idea of an alternative: "not this, but rather that."

   Los aztecas no tenían un sólo dios *sino* muchos dioses diferentes.
   The Aztecs did not have only one god, but (rather) many different gods.

A. Underline the verb in the first part of each sentence. If the verb is affirmative, circle **pero** as the correct completion. If the verb is negative, circle **sino** as the correct completion. Note: if the verb is negative, you will also need to underline "**no**" if it is present. Follow the models.

Modelos   Mi tío <u>no es</u> arquitecto ((sino) / **pero**) arqueólogo.

   Mi hermano <u>lee</u> libros sobre las civilizaciones antiguas (**sino** / (pero)) nunca ha visitado ninguna.

1. Esta escritura azteca me parece muy interesante (**sino** / **pero**) no la puedo leer.

2. Los mayas no estudiaban la arqueología (**sino** / **pero**) la astronomía.

3. Esta historia no es una autobiografía (**sino** / **pero**) una leyenda.

4. Los conejos son animales muy simpáticos (**sino** / **pero**) mi mamá no me permite tener uno en casa.

5. Va a haber un eclipse lunar este viernes (**sino** / **pero**) no podré verlo porque estaré dormido.

B. Choose either **pero** or **sino** to complete each of the following sentences.

Modelo   Ese mito es divertido ((pero) / **sino**) no creo que sea cierto.

1. Los mayas no eran bárbaros (**pero** / **sino**) muy intelectuales y poseían una cultura rica.

2. El alfabeto azteca no usaba letras (**pero** / **sino**) símbolos y dibujos.

3. Los mayas y los aztecas no vivían en España (**pero** / **sino**) en México.

4. Tengo que preparar un proyecto sobre los aztecas (**pero** / **sino**) no lo he terminado todavía.

5. Según los aztecas, uno de sus dioses se convirtió en el Sol (**pero** / **sino**) al principio no podía moverse.

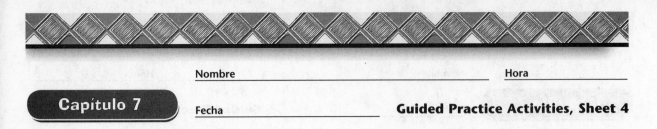
Pero y sino (continued)

- **Sino** is also used in the expression **no sólo... sino también...** , which means *not only... but also.*

    *Los mayas **no sólo** estudiaban las matemáticas **sino también** la astronomía.*

C. Finish each sentence with the "**no sólo... sino también**" pattern using the elements given. Follow the model.

Modelo   Al niño *no sólo le gusta el helado sino también las galletas* .
            (le gusta el helado / galletas)

1. Hoy _____. (**hace sol / calor**)

2. Esta profesora _____.
   (**es cómica / inteligente**)

3. Las leyendas _____.
   (**son interesantes / informativas**)

4. Mis amigos _____.
   (**son comprensivos / divertidos**)

5. La comida mexicana _____.
   (**es nutritiva / deliciosa**)

- When there is a conjugated verb in the second part of the sentence, you should use **sino que**.

    Ella no perdió sus libros *sino que* se los prestó a una amiga.

    She didn't lose her books but (rather) she lent them to a friend.

D. Choose either **sino** or **sino que** to complete each of the following sentences.

Modelo   Los aztecas no tenían miedo de los fenómenos naturales (sino /(sino que))
            trataban de explicarlos.

1. Los españoles no aceptaron a los aztecas (**sino / sino que**) destruyeron su imperio.

2. Según los aztecas, no se ve la cara de un hombre en la luna (**sino / sino que**) un conejo.

3. Los arqueólogos no vendieron los artefactos (**sino / sino que**) los preservaron en un museo.

4. Esta leyenda no trata de la creación de los hombres (**sino / sino que**) del origen del día y de la noche.

El subjuntivo en cláusulas adjetivas (p. 332)

- Sometimes you use an entire clause to describe a noun. This is called an adjective clause, because, like an adjective, it *describes*. When you are talking about a specific person or thing that definitely exists, you use the indicative.

  Tengo unas fotos *que muestran* **los templos mayas.**
  I have some photos that show the Mayan temples.

- If you are not talking about a specific person or thing, or if you are not sure whether the person or thing exists, you must use the subjunctive.

  Busco un libro *que tenga* **información sobre el calendario maya.**
  I am looking for a book that has information about the Mayan calendar.

  Sometimes **cualquier(a)** is used in these expressions.

  Podemos visitar *cualquier* **templo** *que nos interese.*
  We can visit whatever temple interests us.

A. Circle the adjective clause in each of the following sentences. Follow the model.

Modelo   Queremos leer un cuento (que sea más alegre)

1. Busco una leyenda que explique el origen del mundo.

2. Los arqueólogos tienen unos artefactos que son de cerámica.

3. Queremos tomar una clase que trate de las culturas indígenas mexicanas.

4. Conocemos a un profesor que pasa los veranos en México excavando en los sitios arqueológicos.

5. Los estudiantes necesitan unos artículos que les ayuden a entender la escritura azteca.

B. First, find the adjective clause in each statement and decide whether it describes something that exists or possibly does not exist. Place an **X** in the appropriate column. Then, circle the correct verb to complete the sentence. Follow the model.

	Existe	Posiblemente no existe
Modelo Busco un artículo que (**tiene** /(**tenga**)) información sobre los mayas.	____	**X**
1. Necesito el artículo que (**está** / **esté**) en esa carpeta.	____	____
2. Visitamos un museo que (**tiene** / **tenga**) una exhibición nueva.	____	____
3. Voy a llevar cualquier vestido que (**encuentro** / **encuentre**) en el armario.	____	____
4. En mi clase hay un chico que (**puede** / **pueda**) dibujar bien.	____	____
5. Queremos ver unas pirámides que (**son** / **sean**) más altas que éstas.	____	____

C. Complete each sentence using the present indicative or the present subjunctive mood of the verb in parentheses. Follow the model.

Modelo   (tener) Necesitamos usar una computadora que ___*tenga*___ más memoria.

1. **(ser)**   Tengo una clase de arqueología que _____ muy divertida.

2. **(poder)**   Buscamos una profesora que _____ ayudarnos con nuestro proyecto sobre los aztecas.

3. **(medir)**   En el museo de arte hay una estatua maya que _____ más de dos metros.

4. **(conocer)** Quiero un amigo que _____ todos los mitos indígenas.

5. **(querer)** La sociedad arqueológica busca dos estudiantes que _____ ir a México este verano.

- The subjunctive is also used in adjective clauses when they describe something that doesn't exist, using a negative word such as **nadie, nada,** or **ninguno(a)**.
    No hay *nadie* aquí *que pueda* interpretar el calendario maya.
    There is no one here who can interpret the Mayan calendar.

- When an adjective clause refers to something or someone unknown in the past, or something that does not exist or has not happened in the past, you can use the present perfect subjunctive.
    Quiero un profesor *que haya estudiado* el calendario maya.
    I want a professor who studied (has studied) the Mayan calendar.

D. First, read each sentence and determine if the adjective clause describes something that exists (affirmative) or something that may not exist (negative). Place a checkmark in either the "+" or "–" column to indicate your choice. Then, circle the correct verb for the sentence. Follow the model.

		+	–
Modelo	Aquí tengo un libro que ((da)/ **dé**) información interesante sobre los mayas.	✓	____

1. No hay nada en este museo que (**es** / **sea**) de los mayas.   ____ ____

2. En México, D.F. hay unos murales que (**ilustran** / **ilustren**) la vida de los indígenas.   ____ ____

3. Yo encontré un artefacto que (**tiene** / **tenga**) un significado religioso.   ____ ____

4. En mi familia no hay nadie que (**sabe** / **sepa**) más que yo sobre las civilizaciones mesoamericanas.   ____ ____

5. Buscamos a alguien en la escuela que (**ha visitado** / **haya visitado**) Chichén Itzá.   ____ ____

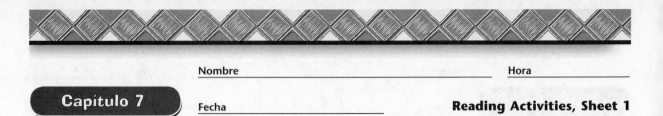

Puente a la cultura (pp. 336–337)

A. Look at the photo of the Moai statues on page 336 and the Olmec head on page 337 in your textbook. Below are some ideas for what each photo might represent. Choose which you think is the best explanation for each artifact and explain why you chose it.

Polynesian people	Kings	Spanish conquistadors	
extraterrestrials	Gods	athletic champions	political figureheads

1. estatua moai _____

2. cabeza olmeca _____

B. Read the following excerpt and check off the sentence that best represents the main point.

> ... *Allí se encuentran los moai, unas estatuas enormes de piedra que representan enormes cabezas con orejas largas y torsos pequeños. Se encuentran en toda la isla y miran hacia el cielo como esperando a algo o alguien. Pero la pregunta es ¿cómo las construyeron y las movieron los habitantes indígenas a la isla? Se sabe que no conocían ni el metal ni la rueda.*

a. ____ Las estatuas tienen orejas largas y torsos pequeños.

b. ____ Nadie sabe cómo las estatuas llegaron allí.

c. ____ Las estatuas miran hacia el cielo.

d. ____ Los indígenas no conocían ni el metal ni la rueda.

C. After reading about the Olmecs and the Nazca lines, complete the following by writing an **O** next to the statement if it corresponds to the creations of the **olmecas** and an **N** if it refers to the **líneas de Nazca**.

1. ____ Vivieron en México.

2. ____ Sólo es posible verlas completamente desde un avión.

3. ____ Construyeron cabezas gigantescas.

4. ____ La primera gran civilización de Mesoamérica.

5. ____ Representan figuras y animales.

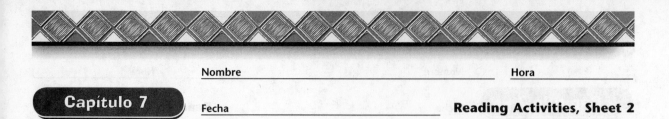

Lectura (pp. 342–344)

A. The excerpt you are about to read is from a well-known piece of literature about a man who *thinks* he is a knight. Think about what other depictions of knights you have seen in literature and/or movies.

1. What are knights usually like?

_____

2. Are the portrayals you have seen usually serious, comical, or both?

_____

B. Look at the excerpt below from page 343 of your textbook and answer the questions that follow.

> —Así es —dijo Sancho.
>
> —Pues —dijo su amo [master]—, aquí puedo hacer mi tarea: deshacer
>   fuerzas y ayudar a los miserables.

1. To whom is Sancho speaking?

_____

2. What does Sancho's master say is his duty?

_____

3. Does this duty sound like something a knight would do?

_____

4. What kind of person or profession would do this duty in today's society?

_____

C. Read the following sentences about the reading in your textbook. Write **C** (for **cierto**) if they are true and **F** (for **falso**) if they are false.

_____ **1.** Cuando Don Quijote ve a los hombres, él sabe que son prisioneros.

_____ **2.** El primer prisionero con quien habla Don Quijote le dice que va a la prisión por amor.

_____ **3.** El segundo prisionero con quien habla Don Quijote le dice que va a la prisión por robar una casa.

_____ **4.** El tercer prisionero lleva más cadenas porque tiene más crímenes que todos.

_____ **5.** A Don Quijote le parece injusto el tratamiento de los prisioneros.

_____ **6.** Don Quijote y Sancho liberan a los prisioneros.

_____ **7.** Don Quijote quiere que los prisioneros le den dinero.

_____ **8.** Los prisioneros le tiran piedras a Don Quijote.

D. Read the following excerpt from the reading in your textbook and answer the questions that follow.

> Don Quijote llamó entonces a los prisioneros y así les dijo:
>
> —De gente bien educada es agradecer (to thank) los beneficios que reciben. Les pido que vayan a la ciudad del Toboso, y allí os presentéis ante la señora Dulcinea del Toboso y le digáis que su caballero, el de la Triste Figura, ha tenido esta famosa aventura.

1. First, find the following cognates in the passage above and circle them. Then write their meanings on the spaces below.

a. aventura _____   **c.** educada _____

b. beneficios _____   **d.** prisioneros _____

2. In this excerpt, Don Quijote uses the **vosotros** command form when addressing the prisoners. First, underline the following two commands in the passage above. Then choose the correct meaning for each.

os presentéis   **le digáis**

☐ present yourselves   ☐ give her

☐ provide yourselves   ☐ tell her

Las palabras interrogativas (p. 353)

- Interrogative words are words used to ask questions. In Spanish, all interrogative words have a written accent mark. Look at the list of important interrogative words below.

¿cuándo? = *when?*	**¿para qué?** = *for what reason/purpose?*
¿dónde? = *where?*	**¿qué?** = *what?*
¿adónde? = *to where?*	**¿por qué?** = *why?*
¿cómo? = *how?*	

A. Circle the correct interrogative word in each short dialogue below. Follow the model.

Modelo —¿(Por qué /(Cuándo)) es el partido?

   —Mañana a las cuatro.

1. —¿(**Dónde / Cuál**) está José?

   —En el museo.

2. —¿(**Cómo / Cuándo**) se llama ese hombre viejo?

   —Sr. Beltrán.

3. —¿(**Qué / Por qué**) vas al teatro?

   —Necesito hablar con el director.

4. —¿(**Cuánto / Qué**) haces mañana?

   —Voy a la plaza a ver unos monumentos.

- Some interrogative words must agree with the nouns they modify.

   ¿cuál?/¿cuáles?   **¿quién?/¿quiénes?**
   ¿cuánto?/¿cuánta?   **¿cuántos?/¿cuántas?**

- Note that **¿quién(es)?** and **¿cuál(es)?** must agree in number with the nouns they modify.

   ¿Quiénes son los actores?   *¿Cuál es el teatro nuevo?*

- Note that **¿cuánto(s)?** and **¿cuánta(s)?** must agree in number *and* gender with the nouns they modify.

   ¿Cuánto tiempo?   *¿Cúantas sinagogas hay?*

B. In each question below, underline the noun that is modified by the interrogative word. Then, circle the interrogative word that agrees with the noun you underlined.

Modelo ¿(Cuál /(Cuáles)) son los <u>monumentos</u> más antiguos?

1. ¿(**Cuánto / Cuánta**) gente hay en la sinagoga?

2. ¿(**Cuál / Cuáles**) es la fecha de hoy?

3. ¿(**Quién / Quiénes**) es el presidente de México?

4. ¿(**Cuánto / Cuánta**) tarea tienes esta noche?

5. ¿(**Cuál / Cuáles**) son las calles que llevan al puente?

- When you need to use a preposition with an interrogative word, you must always place it ahead of the interrogative word.

  ¿Con quién vas a la mezquita?   *With whom are you going to the mosque?*

  ¿De dónde es Marta?   *Where is Marta from?*

- Note that with the word **Adónde**, the preposition, **a**, is attached to the interrogative word. In all other cases, however, the preposition is a separate word.

C. Circle the correct interrogative phrase to complete each dialogue below. Look at the responses given to each question to help you make your choice. Follow the model.

Modelo   —¿((De dónde)/ **Adónde**) es tu profesora de español?

—Ella es de Madrid.

1. —¿(**De quién / Con quién**) es la mochila?

—Es de mi amiga Josefina.

2. —¿(**Para quién / De quién**) es ese regalo?

—Es para mi hermano Roberto. Hoy es su cumpleaños.

3. —¿(**Adónde / De dónde**) vas?

—Voy al edificio histórico para estudiar la arquitectura.

4. —¿(**Por qué / Para qué**) se usa un puente?

—Se usa para cruzar un río.

- When interrogative words are used in indirect questions, or statements that imply a question, they also have a written accent.

  *No sé **dónde** está el palacio.*

D. Choose the interrogative word from the word bank that best completes each sentence and write it in the space provided. Follow the model.

~~cuál~~	cuántas	dónde	quién	por qué

Modelo   Necesito saber ____*cuál*____ de estos estudiantes es Juan.

1. Quiero saber _____ está la iglesia.

2. Tenemos que saber _____ causó ese accidente horrible.

3. Mi profesor me preguntó _____ no había asistido a clase.

4. Voy a averiguar _____ bebidas necesitamos comprar.

Verbos con cambios en el pretérito (p. 355)

- Remember that some verbs have a spelling change in the preterite. The verb **oír** and verbs that end in **-uir, -eer, -aer** have a "**y**" in the **Ud./él/ella** and **Uds./ellos/ellas** forms. The verb **leer** is conjugated below as an example.

leer	
leí	leímos
leíste	leísteis
leyó	**leyeron**

A. Complete each sentence with the correct preterite form of the verb in parentheses.

Modelo   (oír) Los cajeros ___*oyeron*___ una explosión en el mercado.

1. (**incluir**)   Yo _____ unas piedras preciosas en el collar que hice en la clase de arte.

2. (**destruir**) El dueño se puso enojado cuando un criminal _____ su tienda.

3. (**creer**)   Los policías no _____ las mentiras del ladrón.

4. (**caerse**)   Nosotros ____ _____ cuando corríamos porque teníamos mucho miedo del oso.

5. (**leer**)   Jorge _____ un artículo sobre cómo regatear en los mercados mexicanos.

- Remember that **-ar** and **-er** verbs have no stem changes in the preterite. Stem-changing **-ir** verbs have changes in the **Ud./él/ella** and **Uds./ellos/ellas** forms of the preterite.
- In verbs like **dormir** and **morir** (**o→ue**), the stem changes from **o** to **u** in these forms. In verbs like **sentir** and **preferir** (**e→ie**), or **pedir** and **seguir** (**e→i**), the stem changes from **e** to **i** in these forms.

B. Give the correct form of each of the following verbs in the preterite. Be careful not to make any stem changes where you don't need them!

Modelo   (él) **morir** ____*murió*____

1. (nosotros) **almorzar** _____

2. (los profesores) **servir** _____

3. (yo) **repetir** _____

4. (nosotros) **perder** _____

5. (tú) **contar** _____

6. (Uds.) **dormir** _____

7. (él) **mentir** _____

8. (tú) **pedir** _____

- There are several irregular verbs in the preterite. Remember that some verbs such as **decir, traer,** and **traducir** have irregular stems in the preterite, but they share the same endings.

  decir: **dij-**
  traer: **traj-** } **Endings:** -e, -iste, -o, -imos, -isteis, -eron
  traducir: **traduj-**

C. Complete each sentence with the appropriate form of the verb in the preterite tense.

Modelo (**decir**) (Yo) Le _____*dije*_____ a mi mamá: «Estoy asustado».

1. (**traducir**) El traductor _____ las instrucciones para el producto nuevo del español al inglés.

2. (**traer**) Nosotros _____ algunos aretes de oro al mercado para venderlos.

3. (**decir**) Tú _____ cosas terribles durante la pelea con tu novia.

4. (**traer**) Los dos estudiantes _____ su parte del proyecto y colaboraron para terminarlo.

5. (**traducir**) Mis profesores de español _____ unos documentos y la compañía les pagó muy bien.

- Another set of irregular verb stems share a slightly different set of endings.

andar	estar	tener	poder	poner	saber	venir
anduv-	**estuv-**	**tuv-**	**pud-**	**pus-**	**sup-**	**vin-**

Endings: -e, -iste, -o, -imos, -isteis, -ieron.

- The verb **hacer** is also irregular in the preterite:

  hice, hiciste, hizo, hicimos, hicisteis, hicieron

Notice that these verbs do not have written accent marks in the preterite.

D. Complete each sentence with the correct preterite form of the verb in parentheses.

Modelo (**venir**) Cuando estudiaba en España, mis padres _____*vinieron*_____ a visitarme.

1. (**estar**) La policía capturó al ladrón y éste _____ en la cárcel 20 años.

2. (**poder**) Nosotros no _____ refugiarnos en la cueva porque había un oso allí.

3. (**hacer**) Ellos _____ todo lo posible por resolver el conflicto.

4. (**andar**) ¿Tú _____ solo por el bosque? ¿No tenías miedo?

5. (**tener**) Ayer yo _____ que salvar a mi hermanito porque se cayó en un río.

Capítulo 8

Fecha _____   **Vocabulary Flash Cards, Sheet 1**

Write the Spanish vocabulary word below each picture. If there is a word or phrase, copy it in the space provided. Be sure to include the article for each noun.

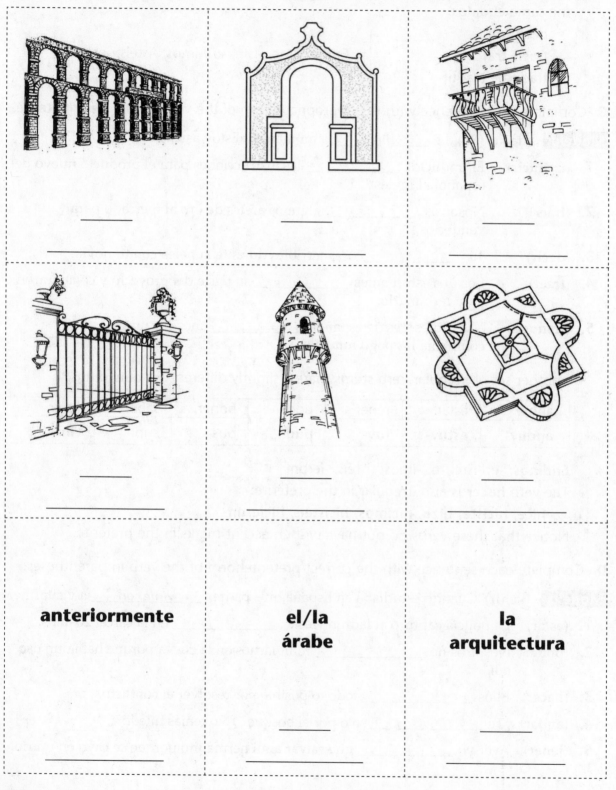

anteriormente

el/la árabe

la arquitectura

Copy the word or phrase in the space provided. Be sure to include the article for each noun.

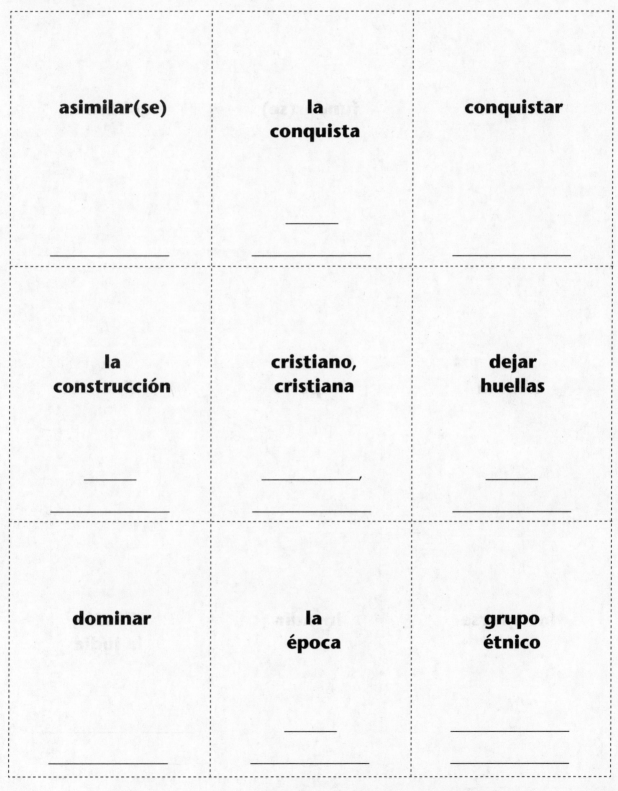

asimilar(se)

_____

la conquista

_____

_____

conquistar

_____

la construcción

_____

_____

cristiano, cristiana

_____,

_____

dejar huellas

_____

_____

dominar

_____

la época

_____

_____

grupo étnico

_____

_____

Copy the word or phrase in the space provided. Be sure to include the article for each noun.

expulsar	fundar(se)	gobernar
_____	_____	_____
el idioma	el imperio	la influencia
_____	_____	_____
integrarse	invadir	el judío, la judía
_____	_____	_____ ,

Copy the word or phrase in the space provided. Be sure to include the article for each noun.

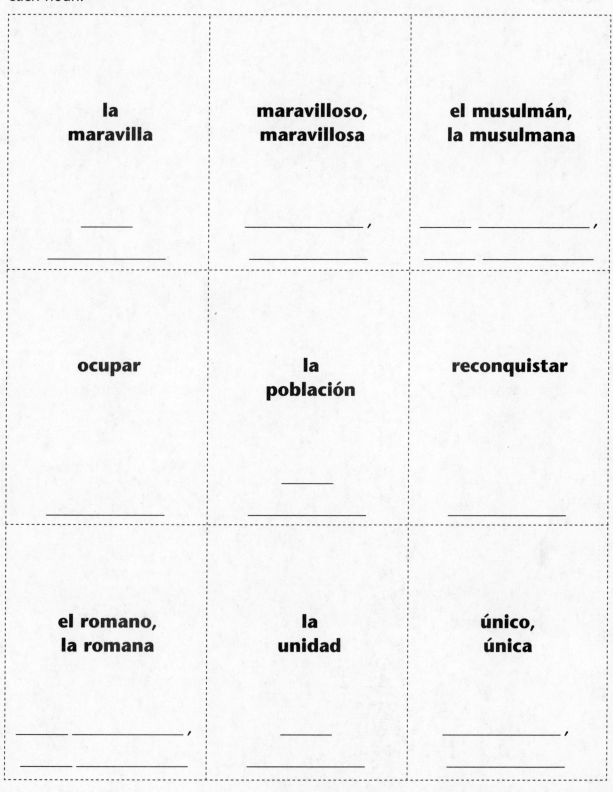

la maravilla	maravilloso, maravillosa	el musulmán, la musulmana
_____ _____	_____, _____	____ _____, ____ _____
ocupar _____	la población _____ _____	reconquistar _____
el romano, la romana _____ _____, _____	la unidad ____ _____	único, única _____, _____

Nombre _____ Hora _____

Capítulo 8

Fecha _____ **Vocabulary Flash Cards, Sheet 5**

These blank cards can be used to write and practice other Spanish vocabulary for the chapter.

Tear out this page. Write the English words on the lines. Fold the paper along the dotted line to see the correct answers so you can check your work.

el acueducto _____

anteriormente _____

el/la árabe _____

el arco _____

la arquitectura _____

asimilar(se) _____

el azulejo _____

el balcón,
(*pl. los balcones*) _____

la conquista _____

conquistar _____

la construcción _____

cristiano, cristiana _____

dejar huellas _____

dominar _____

la época _____

expulsar _____

fundarse _____

gobernar (ie) _____

Fold In →

Tear out this page. Write the Spanish words on the lines. Fold the paper along the dotted line to see the correct answers so you can check your work.

aqueduct _____

before _____

Arab _____

arch _____

architecture _____

to assimilate _____

tile _____

balcony _____

_____

conquest _____

to conquer _____

construction _____

Christian _____

to leave marks, traces _____

to dominate _____

time, era _____

to expel _____

to found _____

to rule, to govern _____

Fold In

Tear out this page. Write the English words on the lines. Fold the paper along the dotted line to see the correct answers so you can check your work.

el grupo étnico _____

el idioma _____

el imperio _____

integrarse _____

invadir _____

el judío, la judía _____

la maravilla _____

maravilloso, _____
maravillosa

el musulmán, _____
la musulmana

ocupar _____

la población _____

la reja _____

el romano, la romana _____

la torre _____

la unidad _____

único, única _____

Fold In

Tear out this page. Write the Spanish words on the lines. Fold the paper along the dotted line to see the correct answers so you can check your work.

ethnic group _____

language _____

empire _____

to integrate _____

to invade _____

Jewish _____

marvel, wonder _____

wonderful _____

_____

Muslim _____

_____

to occupy _____

population _____

railing, grille _____

Roman _____

tower _____

unity _____

only _____

Fold In ←

El condicional (p. 366)

- To talk about what you *would* do in a hypothetical situation or what things *would* be like, you use the conditional tense in Spanish. To form the conditional of regular verbs, you add the endings to the infinitive of the verb. Look at the examples below.

fundar		invadir	
fundaría	fundaríamos	invadiría	invadiríamos
fundarías	fundaríais	invadirías	invadiríais
fundaría	fundarían	invadiría	invadirían

- Note that the endings are the same for **-ar**, **-er**, and **-ir** verbs.

A. Alejandro is thinking about what his life would be like if he lived in Spain. Choose the correct form of the conditional tense to complete each sentence.

Modelo   (Yo) ((comería)/ comerías) tortilla española todos los días.

1. Mis amigos y yo ((hablarían)/ hablaríamos) español perfectamente.

2. Mi familia ((vivirí)a / vivirías) en una casa bonita con un jardín y muchas flores.

3. Mis hermanos ((estudiarían)/ estudiaríamos) en la universidad de Madrid.

4. Mis profesores me ((enseñarían)/ enseñaría) sobre los Reyes Católicos.

5. Mis compañeros de clase y yo ((prepararían)/ prepararíamos) un proyecto sobre la conquista de España por los árabes.

B. Some students were interviewed about what they would do if they were studying abroad in a Spanish-speaking country. Complete each sentence with correct form of the verb in the conditional tense.

Modelo   (escribir) Yo les ___*escribiría*___ cartas a mis abuelos todos los días.

1. (**visitar**)   Mi mejor amigo _visitaría_ todos los museos para aprender sobre las épocas pasadas.

2. (**conocer**)   Nosotros _conoceríamos_ a personas de varios grupos étnicos.

3. (**conversar**)   Todos los estudiantes _conversarían_ en español todo el día.

4. (**estudiar**)   ¿Tú _estudiarías_ la influencia de las diferentes culturas en el país?

5. (**sacar**)   Un estudiante _sacaría_ fotos de todos los lugares turísticos.

6. (**ir**)   Nosotros _iríamos_ a ver todos los sitios históricos del país.

- Some verbs have irregular stems in the conditional. These are the same irregular stems used to form the future tense. Look at the list below to review them.

hacer: **har-**	decir: **dir-**
poder: **podr-**	saber: **sabr-**
poner: **pondr-**	componer: **compondr-**
salir: **saldr-**	querer: **querr-**
tener: **tendr-**	contener: **contendr-**
venir: **vendr-**	haber: **habr-**

C. Fill in the correct stems of the irregular conditional verbs to complete the sentences about what people would do on a family trip to Spain. Follow the model.

Modelo   (querer) Mis padres y yo _____*querr*_____ íamos ver los azulejos.

1. (**salir**) Yo ____saldr____ ía a las discotecas a bailar.

2. (**poder**) Mis hermanos ____podr____ ían ver los acueductos.

3. (**tener**) Tú ____tendr____ ías que acostumbrarte al acento español.

4. (**decir**) Nosotros ____dir____ íamos muchas cosas buenas sobre el Alcázar Real.

5. (**hacer**) Yo ____har____ ía un viaje a Barcelona.

6. (**saber**) Toda la familia ____sabr____ ía mucho más sobre la cultura española.

D. Conjugate the verb given in the conditional to write complete sentences about what would happen if people won the lottery.

Modelo   Mis padres / no / tener / que trabajar más
          Mis padres no tendrían que trabajar más.

1. Yo / poder / comprar / un carro nuevo
   Yo podría comprar un carro nuevo

2. Mis amigos / venir / a cenar / a mi casa / todas las noches
   Mis amigos vendrían a cenar a mi casa todos las noches

3. Nosotros / querer / donar / dinero / a las personas pobres
   Nosotros querríamos donar dinero a las personas pobres

4. Haber / una fuente / en el pasillo / de mi casa
   Habría una fuente en el pasillo de mi casa

5. Mi mamá / poner / pinturas de artistas famosos / en las paredes
   Mi mamá pondría pinturas de artistas famosos en las paredes

Write the Spanish vocabulary word below each picture. If there is a word or phrase, copy it in the space provided. Be sure to include the article for each noun.

adoptar

africano, africana

_____ ,

Copy the word or phrase in the space provided. Be sure to include the article for each noun.

al llegar	los antepasados	la colonia
componerse de	la descendencia	desconocido, desconocida
el encuentro	enfrentar(se)	establecer(se)

Copy the word or phrase in the space provided. Be sure to include the article for each noun.

europeo, europea

_____ ,

_____

la guerra

_____

_____

la herencia

_____

_____

el/la indígena

_____

_____

el intercambio

_____

_____

la lengua

_____

_____

la mezcla

_____

_____

el poder

_____

_____

poderoso, poderosa

_____ ,

_____

Copy the word or phrase in the space provided. Be sure to include the article for each noun. The blank card can be used to write and practice another Spanish vocabulary word or phrase for the chapter.

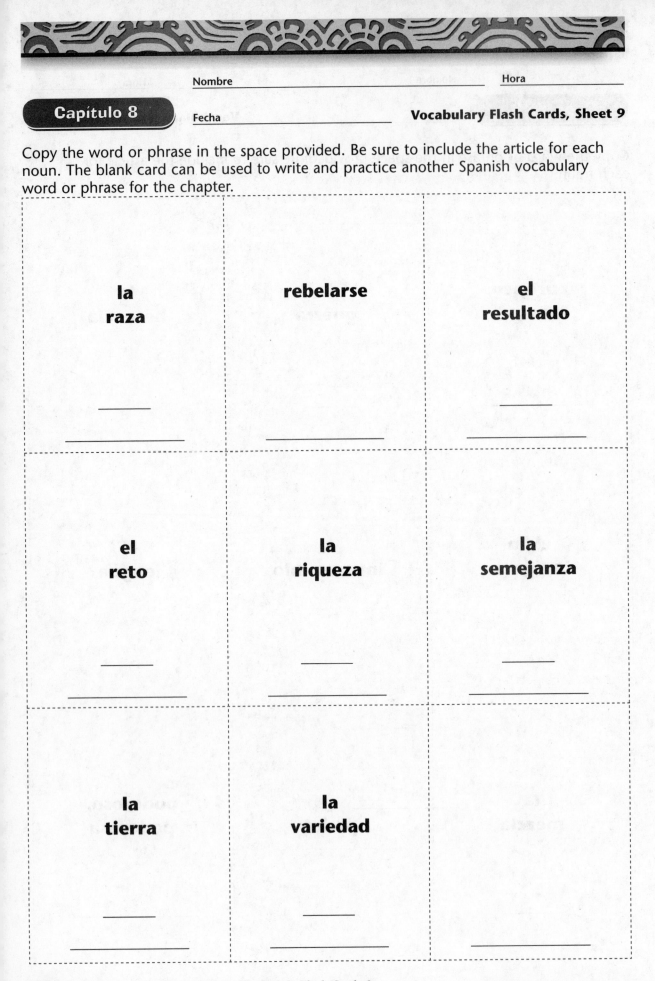

la
raza

_____

rebelarse

_____

el
resultado

_____

el
reto

_____

la
riqueza

_____

la
semejanza

_____

la
tierra

_____

la
variedad

_____

Tear out this page. Write the English words on the lines. Fold the paper along the dotted line to see the correct answers so you can check your work.

adoptar _____

africano, africana _____

el antepasado _____

el arma (*pl.* las armas) _____

la batalla _____

la colonia _____

componerse de _____

desconocido, desconocida _____

enfrentarse _____

el encuentro _____

establecer (zc) _____

europeo, europea _____

la guerra _____

la herencia _____

el/la indígena _____

el intercambio _____

Fold In →

Tear out this page. Write the Spanish words on the lines. Fold the paper along the dotted line to see the correct answers so you can check your work.

to adopt _____

African _____

ancestor _____

weapon _____

battle _____

colony _____

to be formed by _____

unknown _____

_____

to face, to confront _____

meeting _____

to establish _____

European _____

war _____

heritage _____

native _____

exchange _____

Fold In →

Tear out this page. Write the English words on the lines. Fold the paper along the dotted line to see the correct answers so you can check your work.

la lengua _____

luchar _____

la mercancía _____

la mezcla _____

la misión _____

el misionero,
la misionera _____

el poder _____

poderoso,
poderosa _____

la raza _____

rebelarse _____

el resultado _____

el reto _____

la riqueza _____

la semejanza _____

el/la soldado _____

la tierra _____

la variedad _____

Fold In →

Capítulo 8   Fecha _____   **Vocabulary Check, Sheet 8**

Tear out this page. Write the Spanish words on the lines. Fold the paper along the dotted line to see the correct answers so you can check your work.

language, tongue _____

to fight _____

merchandise _____

mix _____

mission _____

missionary _____

_____

power _____

powerful _____

_____

race _____

to rebel, to revolt _____

result, outcome _____

challenge _____

wealth _____

similarity _____

soldier _____

land _____

variety _____

Fold In ←

El imperfecto del subjuntivo (p. 378)

- You have already learned how to use the subjunctive to persuade someone else to do something, to express emotions about situations, and to express doubt and uncertainty. If the main verb is in the present tense, you use the present subjunctive.

  Nos alegramos de que la fiesta sea divertida.   *We are happy the party is fun.*

- If the main verb is in the preterite or imperfect, you must use the *imperfect subjunctive* in the second part of the sentence.

  Él se alegró de que *comieran* **buena comida.**   *He was happy they ate authentic food.*

- To form the imperfect subjunctive, first put a verb in the **ellos/ellas/Uds.** form of the preterite tense and remove the **-ron**. Then, add the imperfect subjunctive endings. Look at the two examples below.

luchar (ellos) = luch**aron** (pretérito)		**establecer** (ellas) = establec**ieron**	
luch~~aron~~		establec~~ieron~~	
luch**ara**	luch**áramos**	establec**iera**	establec**iéramos**
luch**aras**	luch**arais**	establec**ieras**	establec**ierais**
luch**ara**	luch**aran**	establec**iera**	establec**ieran**

- Note: The **nosotros** form of each verb has an accent at the end of the stem.

A. Circle the correct form of the imperfect subjunctive to complete the following sentences.

Modelo   La profesora recomendó que los estudiantes (estudiara / (estudiaran)) los aztecas.

1. A los conquistadores no les gustaba que los aztecas (**practicara / practicaran**) una religión diferente.

2. El rey español quería que Hernán Cortés (**enseñara / enseñaras**) su religión a los aztecas.

3. Fue excelente que nosotros (**miraran / miráramos**) una película sobre el imperio azteca.

4. Los españoles dudaban que el rey azteca (**se rebelaran / se rebelara**), pero eso fue lo que ocurrió.

- Any verbs that have stem changes, spelling changes, or irregular conjugation in the **ellos/ellas/Uds.** form of the preterite will also have these changes in the imperfect subjunctive. Look at a few examples of stems below.

leer-	leyeron-	**leye-**	ir-	fueron-	**fue-**
hacer-	hicieron-	**hicie-**	dormir-	durmieron-	**durmie-**

B. In the first space, write the **ellos/ellas/Uds.** preterite form of the verb. Then, conjugate the verb in the **él/ella/Ud.** form of the imperfect subjunctive. Follow the model.

Modelo (**construir**) __construyeron__ : el trabajador __construyera__

1. (**dar**) _____ : el rey _____

2. (**ir**) _____ : la reina _____

3. (**poder**) _____ : Papá _____

4. (**morir**) _____ : Ud. _____

5. (**sentir**) _____ : Juanita _____

6. (**andar**) _____ : Carlitos _____

C. In the following sentences, conjugate the first verb in the imperfect indicative and the second verb in the imperfect subjunctive to create complete sentences. Follow the model.

Modelo Yo / querer / que / mi profesor / mostrar / un video / sobre los aztecas
   Yo quería que mi profesor mostrara un video sobre los aztecas.

1. Ser / necesario / que / los aztecas / defender / su imperio

   _____

2. Los aztecas / dudar / que / Hernán Cortés / tener razón

   _____

3. Yo / alegrarse / de que / los estudiantes / estar / interesados / en la cultura azteca

   _____

4. Nosotros / no estar seguros / de que / los aztecas / poder / preservar todas sus tradiciones

   _____

5. Ser / malo / que / muchos aztecas / morirse / de enfermedades

   _____

El imperfecto del subjuntivo con *si* (p. 381)

- The two tenses you have learned in this chapter, the conditional and the imperfect subjunctive, are often combined in sentences where you talk about hypothetical, unlikely, or untrue events. These sentences include the word **si** ("if") followed by the imperfect subjunctive and a main clause with a verb in the conditional tense. Look at the following examples.

  > **Si viviera en España, podría ver la influencia árabe en la arquitectura.**
  > *If I lived in Spain, I would be able to see the arabic influence in the architecture.*

  > **Haríamos un viaje a México para ver las pirámides si tuviéramos tiempo.**
  > *We would take a trip to Mexico to see the pyramids if we had time.*

- Notice that the order of the phrase can vary, but the imperfect subjunctive must **always** be paired with the **si**.

A. Complete the sentences with the conditional of the verb in parentheses. Follow the model.

Modelo (**comprar**) Si tuviera un millón de dólares, yo _*compraría*_ un carro.

1. (**ir**) Si tuviera un avión, yo _____ a una isla privada.

2. (**ser**) Si pudiera tener cualquier trabajo, yo _____ embajador a España.

3. (**ver**) Si pudiera ver cualquier película esta noche, yo _____ una romántica.

4. (**sentirse**) Si tuviera que tomar cinco exámenes hoy, yo ____ _____ enfermo.

B. What would happen if you participated in an exchange program in Mexico? Read the following statements and decide which part of the sentence would use the imperfect subjunctive form of the verb and which part would use the conditional. Circle your choice in each part of the sentence. Follow the model.

Modelo Si ((comiera) / comería) en un restaurante mexicano, (pidiera / (pediría)) platos auténticos.

1. Si nuestros profesores (**fueran** / **serían**) más exigentes, nos (**dieran** / **darían**) exámenes todos los días.

2. Yo (**fuera** / **iría**) a las montañas si (**tuviera** / **tendría**) un caballo.

3. Si nosotros (**trabajáramos** / **trabajaríamos**) para el gobierno (**fuéramos** / **seríamos**) muy poderosos.

4. Si tú (**vendieras** / **venderías**) unas mercancías, (**ganaras** / **ganarías**) mucho dinero.

El imperfecto del subjuntivo con *si* (*continued*)

C. Conjugate the boldface verbs in the imperfect subjunctive and the underlined verbs in the conditional tense to form complete sentences. Follow the model.

Modelo Si / yo / **tener** / dinero / <u>comprar</u> / unas joyas preciosas

Si yo tuviera dinero, compraría unas joyas preciosas.
_____

1. Si / nosotros / **hablar** / con nuestros antepasados / <u>aprender</u> / cosas interesantes

_____

2. Si / tú / **ir** / a México / el 1 de noviembre / <u>celebrar</u> / el Día de los Muertos

_____

3. Si / yo / **tener** / un examen sobre los aztecas / <u>sacar</u> / una buena nota

_____

4. Si / mis amigos / **tocar** / instrumentos / <u>tener</u> / una banda

_____

5. Si / yo / **hacer** / un viaje a la Costa del Sol / <u>nadar</u> en el mar

_____

- After **como si** ("as if") you must **always** use the imperfect subjunctive. The other verb can be in either the present or the past tense.

  Martín habla como si *fuera* **un hombre poderoso.**
  Martin speaks as if he were a powerful man.

  La comida del restaurante era tan buena que él se sentía como si *estuviera* **en España.**
  The food at the restaurant was so good that he felt as if he were in Spain.

D. Complete each of the following sentences with the imperfect subjunctive form of the verb given. Follow the model.

Modelo (tener) Juan Pablo Fernández tiene 80 años, pero baila como si ___*tuviera*___ 20.

1. (**hacer**) Hace calor hoy, pero Pepita está vestida como si _____ frío.

2. (**querer**) Marta hablaba de México como si _____ vivir allí.

3. (**ser**) Rafael cocinaba como si _____ un chef profesional.

4. (**estar**) ¡Mi mamá habla como si _____ enojada conmigo!

5. (**tener**) Conchita gasta dinero como si _____ un millón de dólares.

Puente a la cultura (pp. 384–385)

A. You are about to read an article about missions established in California in the 18th century. Check off all of the items in the following list that you think would be found in these missions. You can use the pictures in your textbook to give you ideas.

soldier barracks _____   dance halls _____   a pool _____

eating areas _____   a church _____   rooms for priests _____

B. Look at the following excerpts from your reading and decide which is the best definition for each highlighted word. Circle your answer.

1. «...tenían la función de recibir y **alimentar** a las personas que viajaban a través del territorio desconocido»

   a. educar   **b.** aconsejar   **c.** dar comida

2. «Las misiones incluían una iglesia, cuartos para los sacerdotes, depósitos, casas para mujeres **solteras**...»

   a. tristes   **b.** no son casadas   **c.** con sombra

3. «Muchas personas **recorren** hoy el Camino Real...»

   a. viajar por   **b.** correr rápidamente   **c.** nadar

C. Read the following excerpt from the reading. List the three functions of the missions mentioned.

> *Las misiones fueron creadas no sólo para enseñar la religión cristiana a los indígenas sino también para enseñarles tareas que pudieran realizar en la nueva sociedad española. Asimismo (Likewise) tenían la función de recibir y alimentar a las personas que viajaban a través del territorio desconocido de California.*

1. _____

2. _____

3. _____

D. Look at the paragraph on page 385 of the reading and fill in the key pieces of information below.

1. El nombre del hombre que fundó las misiones: _____

2. El número de misiones que fundó: _____

3. El nombre de la ruta en la que se encuentran las misiones: _____

Lectura (pp. 390–392)

A. In this story, a modern-day teenager is transported into the world of the Aztecs just prior to the arrival of Hernán Cortés. What background information do you remember about the Aztecs from what you have learned in this chapter? List two elements in each category below.

1. religion: _____ ,

   _____

2. architecture: _____ ,

   _____

B. The first part of this story finds the protagonist, Daniel, in a very confusing situation. How does he figure out where he is? Check off all of the clues below that he uses to try to determine where, and when he is.

☐ está durmiendo en un *petate* y no en su cama

☐ lleva jeans y una camiseta

☐ el emperador Moctezuma está en su casa

☐ habla un idioma extraño

☐ su novia lo llama "Tozani" y "esposo"

C. Daniel determines the date by using his knowledge of the Aztec calendar and the Aztec dates his "wife" gives him. Read the excerpt and fill in the dates below in the Aztec and then the modern form.

> —Acatl. El año 1-Caña, el día de 2-Casas.
>   Trato de recordar el calendario azteca. Un escalofrío (chill) me invade el cuerpo cuando por fin descifro el significado de aquella fecha. Acatl, equivalente al año 1519 del calendario cristiano. El día 2-Casas, o sea, el 29, probablemente del mes de junio. Un mes antes de la entrada de Hernán Cortés en Tenochtitlán.

Azteca	**Moderna**
El año _____1-Caña_____	El año _____
El día _____	El día _____

D. According to this account, does it seem the "beings" look more like humans or animals? Give examples below from the excerpt.

> *Los mensajeros de Moctezuma que han visto a estos seres, cuentan que son grandes de estatura, que tienen la cara cubierta de cabello. Y algunos de ellos tienen cuatro patas enormes y dos cabezas, una de animal y otra de hombre.*

1. According to this passage, who has seen these "beings"? _____

2. What does it seem the "beings" look more like, man or animal, according to this account? Give examples.

    _____

    _____

3. These beings are described as tall and some as "two-headed." Why might Moctezuma think they were gods?

    _____

    _____

E. As you read the story, you have gone on a path of discovery with Daniel to find out who he is, where he is, and what he is supposed to do. By the end of the story, he has his situation figured out, but does not like the task he is given. Number the following statements in the order in which Daniel experiences them. Then, answer the question that follows.

_____ Daniel se da cuenta de que su misión es llevar regalos a los «dioses blancos» y guiarlos a la ciudad de Tenochtitlán.

_____ Daniel se da cuenta de que su nombre es «Tozani» y que tiene una esposa llamada «Chalchi».

_____ Daniel se da cuenta de que tiene que ir a un lago y luego al Templo Mayor.

When Daniel has realized who he is and what he has been told to do, what is his reaction? Why does he react this way? (*Hint:* does he know something others do not?)

_____

_____

Verbos como *gustar* (p. 401)

- Remember that you use the verb **gustar** to talk about likes and dislikes. When you use **gustar**, the subject of the sentence is the thing that is liked or disliked.

- If the thing liked or disliked is a singular object or a verb, use the singular form of **gustar**.

    *(A mí) me **gusta** el camión amarillo.*   *¿Te **gusta** conducir?*

- If the thing liked or disliked is a plural object, use the plural form of **gustar**.

    *Nos **gustan** los cuadernos con papel reciclado.*

A. First, underline the subject of each sentence. Then, circle the correct form of **gustar** to complete the sentence. **¡Recuerda!** The subject is the thing that is liked or disliked.

Modelo   A los padres de Juana les ((gusta) / gustan) <u>el parque</u>.

1. A nadie le (gusta / gustan) la contaminación.

2. A mí me (gusta / gustan) los ríos claros.

3. A nosotros nos (gusta / gustan) el barrio Norte.

4. A mi hermano le (gusta / gustan) los coches rojos.

- **Gustar** is used with an indirect object pronoun to indicate to whom something is pleasing. The indirect object pronouns appear below.

me	nos
te	os
le	les

- To clarify the person to whom the indirect object pronoun refers, use the personal *a* plus a noun or a subject pronoun. This is often used with the pronouns **le** and **les**.

    A ella le gustan los grupos que protegen el medio ambiente.

    A los voluntarios les gusta mejorar las condiciones para la gente.

    You can also use the personal **a** plus a pronoun for emphasis.

    A Marta le gusta pasear en barco pero a mí no me gusta porque no puedo nadar.

B. Match the beginning of each of the following sentences with the correct ending. The first one has been done for you.

<u>D</u> **1.** A los estudiantes...   **A.** ...nos gusta colaborar.

_____ **2.** A la gente...   **B.** ...le gusta la naturaleza.

_____ **3.** A mí...   **C.** ...te gusta hacer trabajo voluntario?

_____ **4.** ¿A ti...   ~~**D.** ...no les gusta el tráfico.~~

_____ **5.** A mis amigos y a mí...   **E.** ...me gusta pasar tiempo en el aire libre.

Nombre _____   Hora _____

Capítulo 9   Fecha _____   **AVSR, Sheet 2**

- There are several other Spanish verbs that often follow the same pattern as **gustar**. Look at the list below.

encantar	to love	doler	to ache, to be painful
molestar	to bother	faltar	to lack, to be missing
preocupar	to worry	quedar (bien/mal)	to fit (well / poorly)
importar	to matter	parecer	to seem
interesar	to interest		

C. Write the correct indirect object pronoun and circle the correct form of the verb to complete each sentence. Follow the model.

Modelo   A mis padres _____*les*_____ ((encantaba)/ encantaban) montar en bicicleta.

1. A mí _____ (**interesaba / interesaban**) los insectos.

2. A mis amigos _____ (**preocupaba / preocupaban**) la contaminación del lago que estaba cerca de su casa.

3. A nosotros _____ (**dolía / dolían**) la espalda después de subir árboles.

4. A mi mejor amiga _____ (**importaba / importaban**) reciclar papel.

5. A ti _____ (**quedaba / quedaban**) mal los zapatos de tu papá.

D. Use the elements below to write complete sentences. You will need to add the appropriate indirect object pronoun and conjugate the verb in the present tense.

Modelo   a mis padres / molestar / zonas de construcción.
    A mis padres les molestan las zonas de construcción.

1. a mí / doler / los pies / después de correr

   _____

2. a ti / faltar / dinero / para comprar el carro

   _____

3. a nosotras / preocupar / las causas de la contaminación

   _____

4. a la profesora / importar / las buenas notas en los exámenes

   _____

5. a mí / encantar / manejar el camión de mi abuelo

   _____

Usos del artículo definido (p. 403)

- In general, the definite article (**el, la, los, las**) is used in Spanish the same way it is in English, whenever you need the word "the." However, it is also sometimes used in Spanish when it is not needed in English, in the following ways:
- When you are referring to someone by a name and title, in front of the title (Note: This is not used when speaking directly to the person.)

    El doctor Fuentes no está aquí hoy.   Hola, profesora Martínez.
- With a street, avenue, park, or other proper name.

    La avenida Yacútoro es una calle muy larga.
- In front of a noun that represents an entire species, institution or generality.

    Los gatos duermen más que **los** perros.   **La felicidad** es fundamental.

A. Read the following sentences to determine the reason the underlined definite article is needed. Write **T** for title (such as profession), **P** for proper name, and **G** for generality.

| Modelo | _G_ | El chocolate es delicioso. |

1. _____ La profesora Corzano llega a las nueve.

2. _____ Las universidades son instituciones importantes.

3. _____ La Torre Eiffel está en Francia.

4. _____ El Parque Nacional de Yellowstone es impresionante.

5. _____ Los policías de nuestro barrio son valientes.

6. _____ Caminamos por la calle Córdoba.

B. Complete each sentence with the appropriate definite article. Follow the model.

| Modelo | Mi profesor de biología es _el_ Sr. Rivera. |

1. _____ hormigas son insectos que me molestan mucho.

2. Hay un semáforo en la esquina de _____ avenidas Santiago y Castillo.

3. _____ señora Ramos fue a las montañas para acampar.

4. Voy a ir a Guatemala con _____ doctor Jiménez para estudiar la selva tropical.

5. _____ respeto es una parte importante de las relaciones.

6. _____ terremotos destruyen muchas casas cada año.

- The definite articles are also used with certain time expressions that refer to age, days of the week, hours (time of day) and seasons. Look at the examples below.

  *Aprendí a manejar a **los 16 años.***   *Vamos a salir a **las 8** de la mañana.*

  *La cena para los honrados es **el viernes.***   ***El verano** es mi estación favorita.*

C. Circle the correct definite article to complete each sentence. Follow the model.

Modelo   Voy a graduarme de la escuela secundaria a (las /(los) 18 años.

1. Me gusta muchísimo (**el / la**) otoño porque hace fresco.

2. La tormenta empezó a (**los / las**) diez de la noche.

3. El viaje al bosque es (**el / los**) miércoles que viene.

4. A (**los / la**) 5 años, mi papá vio un oso feroz en el bosque.

- The definite article is also included when it is an inseparable part of the name of a country or city, such as **El Salvador, La Paz,** and **La Habana.**

- Remember that the combination **a** + **el** produces the contraction *al* and the combination **de** + **el** produces the contraction *del.*

  *Salimos **del** parque zoológico y después caminamos **al** parque nacional.*

- However, when **el** is part of a proper name, it does not combine with **a** or **de**.

  *Viajamos **a El** Paso, Texas.*   *Somos **de El** Salvador.*

D. Combine the first part of the sentence with the phrase in parentheses, creating **al** or **del** when necessary. Remember, this only occurs with the article **el**, but not with proper names. Follow the model.

Modelo   Vamos a ir a (el campo). Vamos a ir _____*al campo*_____.

1. Mis amigos salieron de (el desierto). Mis amigos salieron _____.

2. Dimos una caminata a (las montañas). Dimos una caminata _____.

3. Quiero viajar a (el desierto africano). Quiero viajar _____.

4. Nosotros venimos de (La Paz). Venimos _____.

5. Me gustaría viajar a (el fondo del mar). Me gustaría viajar _____.

6. Carlos viene de (El Cajón), California. Viene _____.

Write the Spanish vocabulary word below each picture. If there is a word or phrase, copy it in the space provided. Be sure to include the article for each noun.

agotar(se)

amenazar

castigar

Copy the word or phrase in the space provided. Be sure to include the article for each noun.

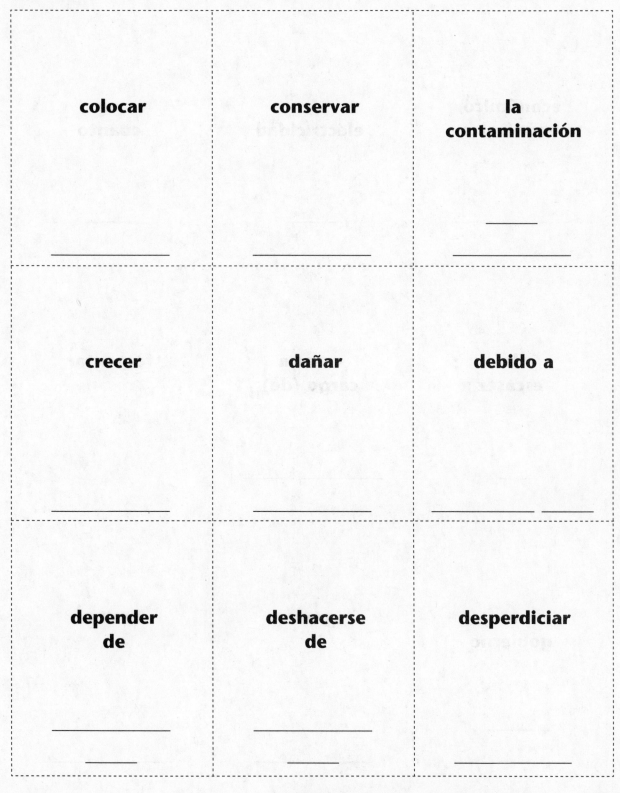

colocar	conservar	la contaminación
_____	_____	_____ _____
crecer	dañar	debido a
_____	_____	_____ _____
depender de	deshacerse de	desperdiciar
_____ _____	_____	_____

Copy the word or phrase in the space provided. Be sure to include the article for each noun.

económico, económica	la electricidad	en cuanto
_____, _____	_____	_____
la escasez	estar a cargo (de)	fomentar
_____	_____ _____	_____
el gobierno	grave	limitar
_____	_____	_____

Copy the word or phrase in the space provided. Be sure to include the article for each noun.

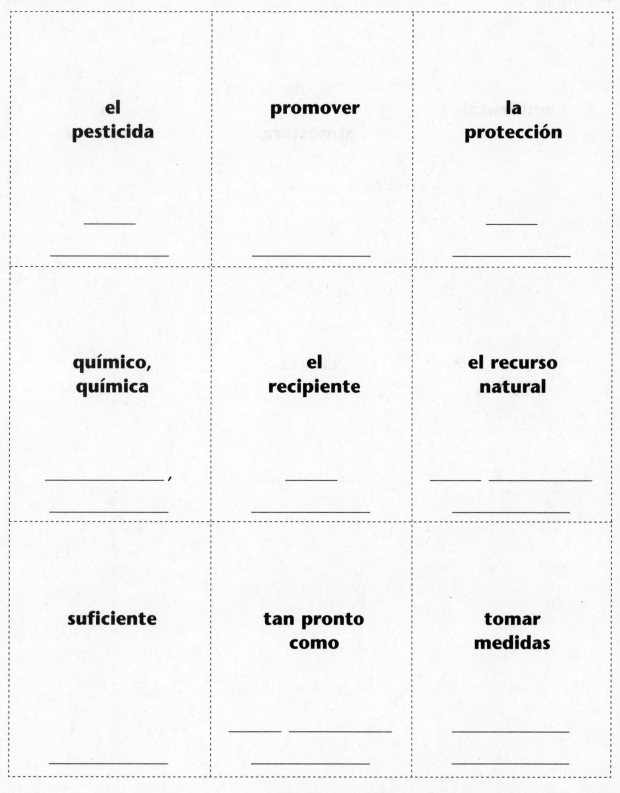

**el
pesticida**

_____

_____

promover

_____

**la
protección**

_____

_____

**químico,
química**

_____,

_____

**el
recipiente**

_____

_____

**el recurso
natural**

_____ _____

_____

suficiente

_____

**tan pronto
como**

_____ _____

_____

**tomar
medidas**

_____

_____

Copy the word or phrase in the space provided. Be sure to include the article for each noun. The blank cards can be used to write and practice other Spanish vocabulary for the chapter.

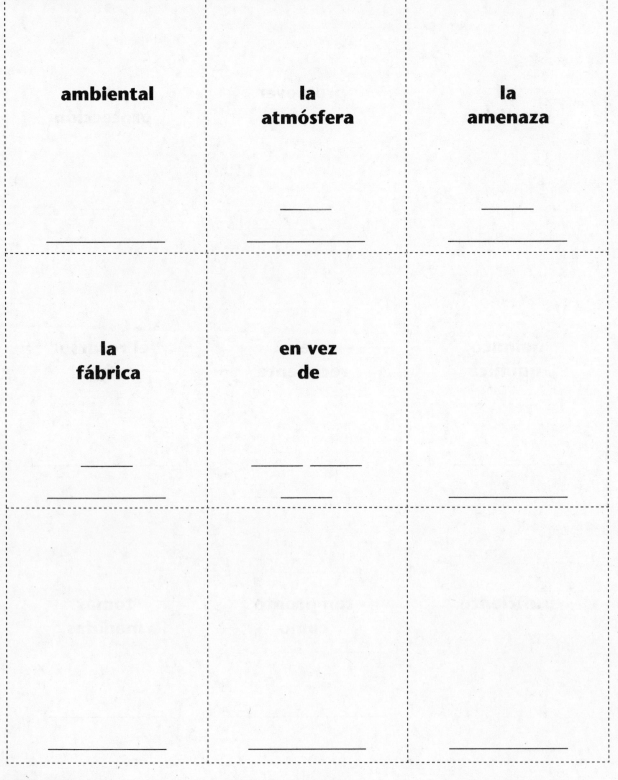

ambiental	la atmósfera	la amenaza
la fábrica	en vez de	

Tear out this page. Write the English words on the lines. Fold the paper along the dotted line to see the correct answers so you can check your work.

agotar(se) _____

la amenaza _____

amenazar _____

ambiental _____

castigar _____

colocar _____

conservar _____

la contaminación _____

contaminado,
contaminada _____

crecer _____

dañar _____

debido a _____

depender de _____

deshacerse de _____

desperdiciar _____

el desperdicio _____

Fold In →

Tear out this page. Write the Spanish words on the lines. Fold the paper along the dotted line to see the correct answers so you can check your work.

to exhaust, to run out   _____

threat   _____

to threaten   _____

environmental   _____

to punish   _____

to put, to place   _____

to preserve   _____

pollution   _____

polluted   _____
_____

to grow   _____

to damage   _____

due to   _____

to depend on   _____

to get rid of   _____

to waste   _____

waste   _____

Fold In ←

Tear out this page. Write the English words on the lines. Fold the paper along the dotted line to see the correct answers so you can check your work.

echar _____

la electricidad _____

la escasez _____

estar a cargo de _____

fomentar _____

el gobierno _____

grave _____

limitar _____

el pesticida _____

el petróleo _____

la pila _____

promover _____

químico, química _____

el recipiente _____

tomar medidas _____

el veneno _____

Fold In ←

Tear out this page. Write the Spanish words on the lines. Fold the paper along the dotted line to see the correct answers so you can check your work.

to throw (away)   _____

electricity   _____

shortage   _____

to be in charge of   _____

to encourage   _____

government   _____

serious   _____

to limit   _____

pesticide   _____

oil   _____

battery   _____

to promote   _____

chemical   _____

container   _____

to take steps (to)   _____

poison   _____

Fold In ←

Conjunciones que se usan con el subjuntivo y el indicativo (p. 414)

- Spanish has several conjunctions that refer to time.

  cuando: when   **en cuanto**: as soon as

  después (de) que: after   **mientras**: while, as long as

  tan pronto como: as soon as   **hasta que**: until

- These time conjunctions are followed by the subjunctive when they refer to actions that have not yet occurred.

  Vamos a usar coches eléctricos _tan pronto como_ se agote el petróleo.
  We are going to use electric cars as soon as oil runs out.

A. Complete each sentence with the correct form of the present subjunctive.

Modelo (sembrar) Habrá peligro de deforestación mientras nosotros no ___*sembremos*___ suficientes árboles.

1. (terminar) Reciclaré el periódico cuando yo _____ de leerlo.

2. (estar) Vamos a colocar estos recipientes en el depósito de reciclaje tan pronto como _____ vacíos.

3. (dejar) La contaminación no se eliminará hasta que la fábrica _____ de echar sustancias químicas al lago.

4. (beber) En cuanto _____ este refresco, voy a reciclar la botella.

- These time conjunctions are followed by the preterite when the action that follows has already taken place.

  Jorge recicló las latas _tan pronto como_ tuvo tiempo.
  Jorge recycled the cans as soon as he had time.

- If the action occurs regularly, the verb will be in the present indicative.

  Uso productos reciclados cuando _puedo_.   *I use recycled products when I can.*

B. Look at the underlined part of each sentence below and write **I** if it is in the indicative mood or **S** if it is in the subjunctive mood. Base your decision on whether the underlined part is something that has already happened or occurs regularly (indicative) or whether it has not yet happened (subjunctive). Follow the model.

Modelo ___*I*___ Los peces mueren cuando <u>el agua del lago se contamina</u>.

1. _____ El agricultor usó pesticidas hasta que <u>encontró productos orgánicos</u>.

2. _____ El medio ambiente sufrirá mientras <u>no conservemos los recursos naturales</u>.

3. _____ Dejaré de molestarte en cuanto <u>tú aprendas a reciclar</u>.

4. _____ Usan pesticidas mientras <u>los insectos se comen las verduras</u>.

C. Look at the first verb in each sentence to determine how to conjugate the second verb. If the verb is an action that happened, use the preterite; if the action has not yet taken place, use the present subjunctive; and if the first verb describes something that occurs regularly, use the present indicative. Follow the model.

Modelo (**beber**) **a.** Yo reciclo las botellas cuando __*bebo*__ jugo.

b. Yo reciclaré esta botella cuando __*beba*__ el jugo.

c. Yo reciclé la botella cuando __*bebí*__ jugo ayer.

1. (**lavar**) **a.** Yo cerraré la llave del agua tan pronto como _____ estos platos.

   b. Yo cerré la llave del agua tan pronto como _____ los platos ayer.

   c. Yo siempre cierro la llave del agua tan pronto como _____ los platos.

2. (**leer**) **a.** Los estudiantes trabajaron para resolver el problema después de que la profesora les _____ un artículo.

   b. Los estudiantes trabajarán para resolver el problema después de que la profesora les _____ un artículo.

   c. Los estudiantes generalmente trabajan para resolver problemas después de que la profesora les _____ artículos.

- You must always follow the conjunction **antes de que** with the subjunctive.

  *Voy a comprar un carro eléctrico antes de que este verano **termine**.*

- With the conjunctions **antes de, después de,** and **hasta**, conjugate the verbs only if there is a subject change. If there is no subject change, use the infinitive.

  Voy a comprar un carro eléctrico después de ahorrar mucho.

D. Circle the choice that correctly completes each sentence. If there is only one subject, choose the infinitive. If there are two subjects, choose the subjunctive.

Modelo Estaré a cargo del club estudiantil después de que la presidenta actual (**graduarse /** (**se gradúe**)).

1. Reciclaremos este papel después de (**escribir / escribamos**) el reportaje.

2. Los estudiantes empezarán a escribir antes de que la profesora (**llegar / llegue**).

3. Estudiarás hasta (**aprender / aprendas**) más sobre el medio ambiente.

4. Usaremos más energía solar después de que el petróleo (**agotarse / se agote**).

5. Limpiaremos el lago antes de que los peces (**morir / mueran**).

Los pronombres relativos *que, quien, y lo que* (p. 418)

- Relative pronouns are used to combine two sentences or to provide clarifying information. In Spanish, the most commonly used relative pronoun is **que**. It is used to refer either to people or to things, and can mean "that," "which," "who," or "whom."

    Se deshicieron del veneno *que* mató las hormigas.
    They got rid of the poison that killed the ants.

A. Your biology class is touring the community with an environmental expert. Match the beginnings of the tour guide's sentences with the most logical endings.

__*C*__ **1.** Estos son los contaminantes...

_____ **2.** Ésta es la fábrica...

_____ **3.** Éstos son los recipientes...

_____ **4.** La profesora Alcatrán es la persona...

_____ **5.** Ésas son las estudiantes...

A. ... que produce los contaminantes.

B. ... que hacen trabajo voluntario para educar a las personas sobre la contaminación.

~~**C.** ... que dañan el medio ambiente.~~

D. ... que dirige la organización *Protege la tierra*.

E. ... que contienen los productos químicos.

- When you use a preposition, such as **a**, **con**, or **en**, with a relative pronoun, **que** refers to things and **quien(es)** refers to people.

    El producto *con que* lavé el piso contiene algunos químicos.
    The product with which I washed the floor contains some chemicals.

    La mujer *de quien* hablo es una científica importante.
    The woman about whom I am speaking is an important scientist.

    Los jefes *para quienes* trabajo insisten en que reciclemos.
    The bosses for whom I work insist that we recycle.

- Notice that you use **quien** if the subject is singular and **quienes** if it is plural.

B. Read each sentence and determine whether the subject refers to a person or a thing. Then, circle the correct relative pronoun to complete the sentence.

Modelo   El profesor a (que /(quien)) le hicimos las preguntas es el Sr. Rodríguez.

1. La situación en (**que** / **quien**) me encuentro es divertida.

2. Los reporteros a (**quien** / **quienes**) pedí prestado el video ya salieron.

3. Los recursos con (**que** / **quienes**) trabajamos son escasos.

4. Los estudiantes con (**que** / **quienes**) hicimos los experimentos desaparecieron.

C. Fill in the sentences with **que, quien,** or **quienes**. Remember that **quien(es)** is only used after a preposition. When you refer to people without a preposition, use **que**.

> **Modelo**   El muchacho con _____*quien*_____ trabajé limpiando una sección del río se llama Manuel.

1. Nosotros vivimos en una comunidad _____ se preocupa mucho por conservar los recursos naturales.

2. Hay un autobús _____ va directamente al centro comercial. No es necesario ir en carro.

3. Los estudiantes de _____ hablo trabajan en una fábrica durante el verano.

4. El senador a _____ le escribí una carta me respondió la semana pasada.

- The relative phrase **lo que** is used to refer to situations, concepts, actions, or objects that have not yet been identified.

   > **Todos escuchamos con atención** *lo que* **el profesor dijo sobre la protección del planeta.**
   > *We all listened carefully to what the professor said about the protection of the planet.*
   > **Lo que necesitamos es más voluntarios.**
   > *What (The thing) we need is more volunteers.*

- As seen in the example above, **lo que** often occurs at the beginning of a sentence.

D. Complete each of the following sentences with **que** or **lo que**. Remember that you will use **que** to clarify a specific thing and **lo que** to refer to something abstract or not yet mentioned. Follow the model.

> **Modelo**   _____*Lo que*_____ me molesta más es el uso de los contaminantes.

1. La organización _____ escribió esos artículos hace muchas cosas buenas.

2. No podemos hacer todo _____ queremos para mejorar las condiciones.

3. Ayer hubo un accidente _____ afectó el medio ambiente.

4. _____ queremos hacer es crear un grupo para limpiar una sección de la carretera.

5. Hay muchos contaminantes en el aire, _____ no es bueno para la respiración.

6. El petróleo _____ usamos se va a agotar algún día.

Nombre _____   Hora _____

Capítulo 9   Fecha _____   **Vocabulary Flash Cards, Sheet 6**

Write the Spanish vocabulary word or phrase below each picture. Be sure to include the article for each noun.

Write the Spanish vocabulary word below each picture. If there is a word or phrase, copy it in the space provided. Be sure to include the article for each noun.

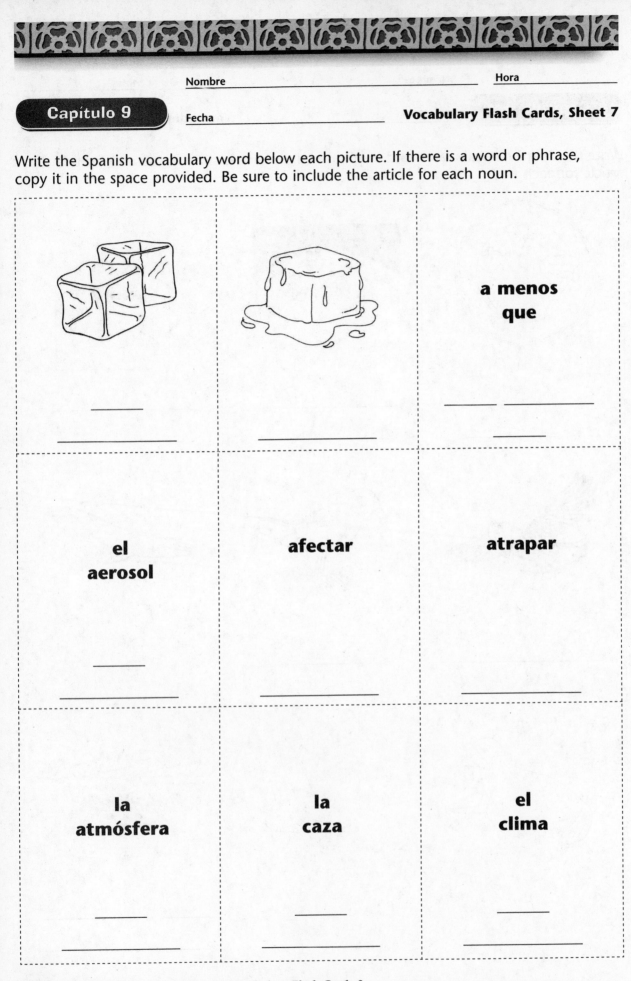

a menos que

_____ _____

el aerosol

afectar

atrapar

la atmósfera

la caza

el clima

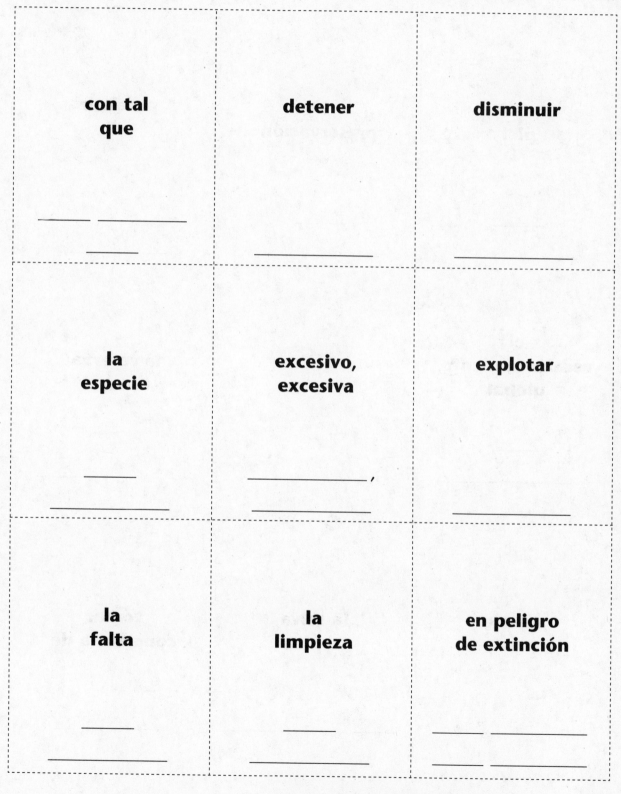

Copy the word or phrase in the space provided. Be sure to include the article for each noun.

con tal que	**detener**	**disminuir**
_____ _____ _____	_____	_____
la especie	**excesivo, excesiva**	**explotar**
_____ _____	_____ , _____	_____
la falta	**la limpieza**	**en peligro de extinción**
_____ _____	_____ _____	_____ _____

Nombre _____   Hora _____

Capítulo 9   Fecha _____   **Vocabulary Flash Cards, Sheet 9**

Copy the word or phrase in the space provided. Be sure to include the article for each noun.

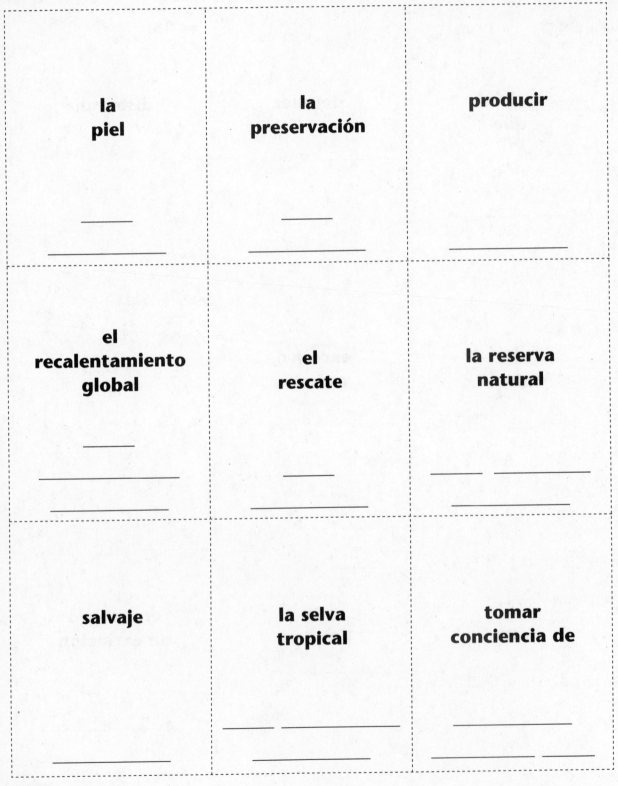

la piel	la preservación	producir
el recalentamiento global	el rescate	la reserva natural
salvaje	la selva tropical	tomar conciencia de

Tear out this page. Write the English words on the lines. Fold the paper along the dotted line to see the correct answers so you can check your work.

el aerosol _____

afectar _____

el agujero _____

el águila calva _____
(*pl. las águilas calvas*)

atrapar _____

el ave _____

la ballena _____

la caza _____

la capa de ozono _____

el clima _____

el derrame _____
de petróleo

derretir _____

detener _____

disminuir _____

el efecto _____
invernadero

Fold In

Tear out this page. Write the Spanish words on the lines. Fold the paper along the dotted line to see the correct answers so you can check your work.

aerosol   _____

to affect   _____

hole   _____

bald eagle   _____

                           _____

to catch, to trap   _____

bird   _____

whale   _____

hunting   _____

ozone layer   _____

weather   _____

oil spill   _____

                           _____

to melt   _____

to stop   _____

to decrease,   _____
to diminish

greenhouse effect   _____

                           _____

Fold In →

Nombre _____ Hora _____

Capítulo 9

Fecha _____ **Vocabulary Check, Sheet 7**

Tear out this page. Write the English words on the lines. Fold the paper along the dotted line to see the correct answers so you can check your work.

en peligro
de extinción   _____

la especie   _____

excesivo, excesiva _____

explotar   _____

la falta   _____

la foca   _____

el hielo   _____

la limpieza   _____

la piel   _____

la pluma   _____

la preservación   _____

el recalentamiento
global   _____

el rescate   _____

la reserva natural _____

salvaje   _____

la selva tropical   _____

tomar conciencia de _____

Fold In →

Tear out this page. Write the Spanish words on the lines. Fold the paper along the dotted line to see the correct answers so you can check your work.

(in) danger of
extinction, endangered

_____

species

_____

excessive

_____

to exploit,
to overwork

_____

lack

_____

seal

_____

ice

_____

cleaning

_____

skin

_____

feather

_____

conservation

_____

global warming

_____

_____

rescue

_____

nature preserve

_____

wild

_____

tropical forest

_____

to become aware of

_____

Fold In ←

Más conjunciones que se usan con el subjuntivo y el indicativo (p. 428)

- Earlier in this chapter, you learned some conjunctions that can be followed by the subjunctive or the indicative. Below is another list of conjunctions. These conjunctions are usually followed by the subjunctive to express the purpose or intention of an action.

  con tal (de) que: provided that

  a menos que: unless

  aunque: even if, even though, although

  para que: so that

  sin que: without

  Las águilas calvas desparecerán *a menos que* trabajemos para protegerlas.
  Bald eagles will disappear <u>unless</u> we work to protect them.

A. Circle the conjunction that most logically completes each sentence, according to the context. Follow the model.

Modelo   Van a la marcha ((para que) / a menos que) los animales estén protegidos.

1. No podemos usar aerosoles (**sin que / a menos que**) produzcan agujeros en la capa de ozono.

2. Las selvas tropicales serán bonitas (**a menos que / con tal de que**) no las explotemos.

3. El presidente va a crear una ley (**para que / sin que**) nadie pueda cazar las ballenas.

4. Tenemos que tomar conciencia de los problemas (**para que / aunque**) sea difícil hacerlo.

5. El grupo de voluntarios construirá una reserva natural (**sin que / a menos que**) no tenga suficiente dinero.

B. Complete the sentences with the correct present subjunctive form of the verbs in parentheses. Follow the model.

Modelo   (**usar**) Puedes protegerte de los rayos ultravioleta con tal de que
___*uses*___ anteojos de sol y loción protectora para sol.

1. (**proteger**)   Las especies en peligro de extinción no van a sobrevivir a menos que nosotros las _____.

2. (**hacer**)   La condición del planeta no puede mejorar sin que todas las personas _____ un esfuerzo.

3. (**tener**)   El gobierno va a crear varias reservas naturales para que los animales _____ un lugar protegido donde vivir.

4. (**poder**)   Es importante entender los peligros del efecto invernadero, aunque tú no _____ ver todos sus efectos personalmente.

- With the conjunctions **para** and **sin**, use the infinitive if the subject of the sentence does not change.

  Trabajo *para proteger* los animales.   *I work to protect animals.*

C. Complete each sentence below. If there is no subject change, choose **para** or **sin**. If there is a subject change, choose **para que** or **sin que**.

| Modelo | No debes comprar estos productos ((sin) / sin que) pensar.

1. La policía investigará el problema (sin / sin que) la compañía lo sepa.

2. Distribuiremos los artículos (para / para que) los lea el dueño.

3. Ellos se pondrán camisetas y anteojos (para / para que) protegerse la piel.

4. Los turistas deben disfrutar del parque (sin / sin que) dañarlo.

D. Circle the conjuction in each sentence. Then, complete each sentence with the infinitive or the present subjunctive of the verb in parentheses.

| Modelo | (rescatar) Nosotros hacemos un viaje (para) ___*rescatar*___ las ballenas.

1. **(conseguir)**   No podemos visitar la selva tropical sin _____ una guía.

2. **(poder)**   Debo salir de la cocina para que mamá _____ cocinar.

3. **(dar)**   Esa foca no va a sobrevivir sin que nosotros le _____ comida.

4. **(explicar)**   Un científico vino a la clase para _____ el efecto invernadero.

- The conjunction **aunque** is followed by the subjunctive when it expresses uncertainty. It is followed by the indicative when there is no uncertainty.

  Aunque la ballena esté muy enferma, vamos a cuidarla.
  Even though the whale may be very sick, we are going to take care of it.
  Aunque la ballena está muy enferma, vamos a cuidarla.
  Even though the whale is very sick, we are going to take care of it.

E. Select the best English translation for the underlined portion of each sentence.

1. Aunque no <u>haya mucha gente</u>, debemos continuar con la marcha.

   ☐ there aren't a lot of people   ☐ there may not be a lot of people

2. Aunque <u>son nuevos</u>, los viajes de ecoturismo son muy populares.

   ☐ they are new   ☐ they may be new

3. Aunque <u>no te guste</u>, es más importante protegerte del sol que estar bronceado.

   ☐ you don't like it   ☐ you may not like it

4. Aunque <u>el hielo se derrite</u>, no habrá una inundación en este lugar.

   ☐ the ice is melting   ☐ the ice may be melting

Puente a la cultura (pp. 432–433)

A. This reading contains several *cognates*, or words that look and sound like English words with the same meaning. See if you can determine what the following words mean:

1. volcánico: _____   **4.** velocidad: _____

2. piratas: _____   **5.** mamíferos: _____

3. tortugas: _____   **6.** flora y fauna: _____

B. Look at the statements below and match them with the century (**siglo**) in which they happened according to the reading. Use the topic sentences in the reading to help you.

    a. el siglo XX (1900s)   **c.** el siglo XVII (1600s)

    b. el siglo XVIII (1700s)   **d.** el siglo XIX (1800s)

1. _____ Los piratas ingleses llegaron a las islas.

2. _____ Los balleneros llegaron y cazaron muchas tortugas.

3. _____ Charles Darwin llegó a las islas e hizo un estudio para escribir su libro *El origen de las especies*.

4. _____ El gobierno ecuatoriano estableció una reserva natural.

C. The Galápagos Islands, once a perserved paradise, have suffered greatly in recent years. Look at the following list and cross out the one item that is *not* an issue that has affected the Galápagos Islands.

extinción de algunas especies	terremotos
exceso de población	faltas de recursos del gobierno ecuatoriano

D. In the Galápagos Islands, the government needed to get involved in order to save rare species of plants and animals. Can you think of other places where the government or environmental organizations have helped with preservation efforts? Think of the places you have studied or visited. Explain why outside involvement was needed to help save local wildlife.

_____

_____

_____

Lectura (pp. 438–440)

A. You are about to read an article about the monarch butterfly. Based on your previous knowledge or what you can determine from the pictures accompanying the text, write three characteristics that describe a monarch butterfly.

1. _____

2. _____

3. _____

B. Try to use context to help you detemine the meaning of the terms from the reading in your textbook which you may not know. Read the following selections and write the letter of the definition that best corresponds with the highlighted phrase.

    a. en la última parte de   **b.** aproximadamente   **c.** setenta y cinco por ciento

1. «*Tres cuartas partes* de los animales que viven en la tierra son insectos.» _____

2. «*Las mariposas, en general, viven **alrededor de** 24 días*» _____

3. «*Llegan **a fines de** octubre a la zona entre...*» _____

C. The introduction to the reading in your textbook includes several descriptions of the monarch butterfly. Read the first two paragraphs on page 438 and decide which of the following descriptions of the monarch butterfly are mentioned. Indicate with a check mark.

1. _____ hermosa

2. _____ más grande que la mayoría de las mariposas

3. _____ agente polinizador

4. _____ vive más tiempo que otras mariposas

5. _____ sólo vive en lugares tropicales

6. _____ resistente a las condiciones del clima

D. Look at each section title on pages 439 and 440 of the reading in your textbook. Based on the title given, decide which choice would most accurately represent what that section is about. Circle your choice.

1. **Llegada a México**

   a. los conquistadores españoles llegan a México
   b. el camino de la mariposa monarca

2. **Hibernación**

   a. cómo pasan el invierno   **b.** cómo pasan de un lugar al otro

3. **Migración**

   a. cómo sobreviven mudándose de un lugar al otro
   b. qué comen

4. **Refugios**

   a. dónde se reunen para pasar el invierno   **b.** sus colores

5. **Peligros**

   a. dónde viven   **b.** qué los amenaza

E. Now look more closely at each section. Use the following cues to help you look for a key piece of information in each section. Write in the most appropriate words to complete the statements from each section.

1. **Llegada a México**

   Las mariposas monarca vuelan de _____ a _____ antes de octubre, y regresan en abril.

2. **Hibernación**

   Las mariposas monarca pasan el invierno en _____, unas montañas que se encuentran entre Michoacán y el Estado de México.

3. **Migración**

   El número de mariposas monarca que llega a México para pasar el invierno todos los años está entre _____ y _____ millones.

4. **Refugios**

   Las mariposas monarca pasan el invierno en _____ al lado de las montañas.

5. **Peligros**

   Dos problemas que afectan a las mariposas monarca son la desaparición de su _____ y las variaciones extremas del _____.

Pretérito vs. imperfecto (p. 449)

- Remember that you must determine whether to use the preterite or the imperfect when speaking in Spanish about the past.

  Use the preterite:

  (gets interrupted)

  - to talk about past actions or a sequence of actions that are considered complete.

    *Mis padres **fueron** a la escuela y **hablaron** con mi profesor.*

  Use the imperfect:

  - to talk about repeated or habitual actions in the past

    *Yo siempre **hacía** mis tareas después de la escuela.*

  - to provide background information or physical and mental descriptions

    *Nacha, una chica que **tenía** diez años, **estaba** enojada.*

  - to convey two or more actions that were taking place simultaneously in the past.

    *Yo **leía** mientras mis padres **preparaban** la cena.*

A. Read the following sentences and decide if the action is a completed action (**C**), a habitual/repeated action (**H**), or background information (**B**). Follow the model.

Modelo   Los científicos **trabajaban** todos los días para proteger el medio ambiente.   C (H) B

1. El martes pasado el presidente **habló** sobre la injusticia.   (C) H B

2. Mi hermano mayor **tenía** 22 años.   C (H) B

3. Nuestro vecino nos **trajo** unos panfletos sobre la economía.   C H (B)

4. Los estudiantes siempre **luchaban** por leyes más justas.   C (H) B

5. Los miembros de la comunidad **estaban** muy entusiasmados.   C (H) B

B. Conjugate the verbs in parentheses in the preterite or imperfect to complete the sentences. Follow the model.

Modelo   El verano pasado nosotros _____*fuimos*_____ (ir) a un concierto en beneficio de los niños diabéticos.

1. Cuando mis padres __eran__ (**ser**) niños, ellos siempre _Obedecían_ (**obedecer**) las reglas de su escuela.

2. De niña, mi vecina _tenía_ (**tener**) pelo muy largo.

3. Yo _cump_ (**cumplir**) con todas mis responsabilidades hoy.

4. En sus conciertos de escuela, mi prima _____ (**cantar**) mientras mi primo _____ (**tocar**) el piano.

5. Todos los estudiantes _____ (**disfrutar**) de la fiesta del sábado pasado.

Nombre Christina Nguyen   Hora 6

Capítulo 10   Fecha 12/13/22   **AVSR, Sheet 2**

Pretérito vs. imperfecto (*continued*)

- You may use the preterite and imperfect together in one sentence when one action (preterite) interrupts another action that was already taking place (imperfect).

    *Nosotros **hacíamos** las tareas cuando nuestro vecino **llamó.***

C. Complete the following sentences with the preterite or imperfect of the verbs in parentheses. Remember to put the background action in the imperfect and the interrupting action in the preterite.

Modelo Los soldados __luchaban__ (**luchar**) cuando __empezó__ (**empezar**) a llover.

1. Mi hermana menor _____ (**estar**) en la clase de ciencias cuando _____ (**sonar**) la alarma contra incendios.

2. Nosotros _____ (**hablar**) de las obligaciones de la sociedad cuando mi amigo _____ (**salir**).

3. Constantino _____ (**caerse**) cuando _____ (**correr**) en el centro de la comunidad.

4. Yo _____ (**jugar**) al fútbol con mis amigos cuando José _____ (**meter**) un gol.

5. ¿Tú _____ (**ver**) el accidente cuando _____ (**caminar**) a la escuela?

D. Read the following paragraph about a surprising turn of events. Conjugate the verbs given in the preterite or imperfect, according to the context. The first one has been done for you.

Ayer después de clases, yo (1) _____salí_____ (**salir**) con mis padres. Yo (2)

_____ (**sentirse**) impaciente porque (3) _____ (**tener**) mucha

tarea y (4) _____ (**querer**) ver a mi novio. De repente, mi papá (5)

_____ (**parar**) el coche enfrente de mi restaurante favorito. Cuando nosotros

(6) _____ (**entrar**) al restaurante, (yo) (7) _____ (**ver**) que (8)

_____ (**estar**) todos mis amigos con un pastel grande en honor de mi

cumpleaños. ¡Qué sorpresa!

Nombre _____   Hora _____

Verbos con distinto sentido en el pretérito y en el imperfecto (p. 451)

- Remember that some verbs change meaning depending on whether they are used in the preterite or the imperfect tense. Look at the chart below for a reminder.

Verb	Preterite	Imperfect
conocer	met for the first time *Marta **conoció** a su mejor amiga en la escuela primaria.*	knew someone *El abogado y el juez **se conocían** muy bien.*
saber	found out, learned *El policía **supo** que el criminal se había escapado.*	knew a fact *Los ciudadanos **sabían** que tenían que obedecer la ley.*
poder	succeeded in doing *Después de mucho trabajo, la policía **pudo** arrestar al ladrón.*	was able to, could *El juez nos dijo que no **podíamos** hablar con nadie sobre el caso.*
querer	tried ***Quisimos** resolver el conflicto, pero fue imposible.*	wanted *El gobierno **quería** escuchar las opiniones de la gente.*
no querer	refused ***No quise** reunirme con el jefe. Salí temprano.*	didn't want *Nosotros **no queríamos** ir a la manifestación, pero fuimos.*

A. Match the conjugated forms of the following preterite and imperfect verbs with their English meanings. The first one has been done for you.

_*D*_ **1.** supe

_____ **2.** pude

_____ **3.** sabía

_____ **4.** quise

_____ **5.** conocí

_____ **6.** no quería

A. I met (somebody) for the first time

B. I didn't want to

C. I tried to

D. ~~I found out, learned~~

E. I knew

F. I managed to, succeeded in

B. Circle the preterite or the imperfect form of the verb, according to the context.

Modelo ((Conocí)/ Conocía) a mucha gente nueva en la manifestación.

1. (Conocí / Conocía) al hombre que la organizó. Era un amigo de mis padres.

2. No (supe / sabía) que la policía trabajaba con la organización.

3. Durante la manifestación, (**supe / sabía**) que un juez también luchaba contra el problema.

4. No (**supe / sabía**) mucho del problema antes de ir a la manifestación.

C. Circle the correct preterite or the imperfect form of the verb given, according to the context. The first one has been done for you.

No **1.**(**quise /** ~~queria~~) salir el viernes pasado porque tenía mucha tarea, pero fui al cine

con mi mejor amiga. Después ella me preguntó si nosotras **2.**(**pudimos / podíamos**) ir a

un restaurante. Yo le dije que sí y cuando llegamos, ella pidió los calamares. ¡Qué asco! Yo

3.(**no quise / no quería**) comerlos así que pedí una pizza. Cuando recibimos la cuenta,

nos dimos cuenta de que no teníamos dinero. No **4.**(**quisimos / queríamos**) llamar a

nuestros padres, pero no había otra opción. Mi padre nos trajo dinero y por fin

5.(**podíamos / pudimos**) pagar la cuenta.

D. Conjugate the verbs in the following sentences in the correct preterite or the imperfect form, depending on context. Follow the model.

Modelo   (querer) Mi madre no ____*quiso*____ comer en ese restaurante. Se quedó en casa.

1. (poder)   Después de hacer un gran esfuerzo, mis padres _____ resolver el problema.

2. (saber)   Yo siempre _____ que era muy importante decir la verdad.

3. (conocer) La semana pasada nosotros _____ al boxeador que ganó la pelea reciente.

4. (poder)   La policía le aseguró a la víctima que _____ garantizar su seguridad.

5. (querer) Paco no _____ respetar el límite de velocidad, pero la policía le dijo que tenía que hacerlo.

6. (conocer) El presidente y la senadora se _____ muy bien y se confiaban mucho.

Write the Spanish vocabulary word below each picture. If there is a word or phrase, copy it in the space provided. Be sure to include the article for each noun.

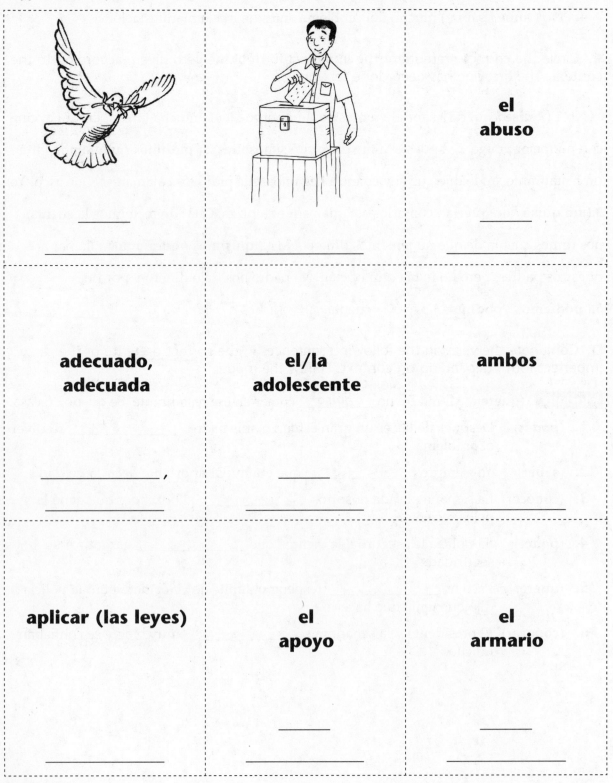

el
abuso

_____

adecuado,
adecuada

_____,
_____

el/la
adolescente

_____

ambos

_____

aplicar (las leyes)

_____

el
apoyo

_____

el
armario

_____

Copy the word or phrase in the space provided. Be sure to include the article for each noun.

el asunto	la autoridad	el código de vestimenta
de ese modo	el deber	discriminado, discriminada
discriminar	en cuanto a	la enseñanza

Copy the word or phrase in the space provided. Be sure to include the article for each noun.

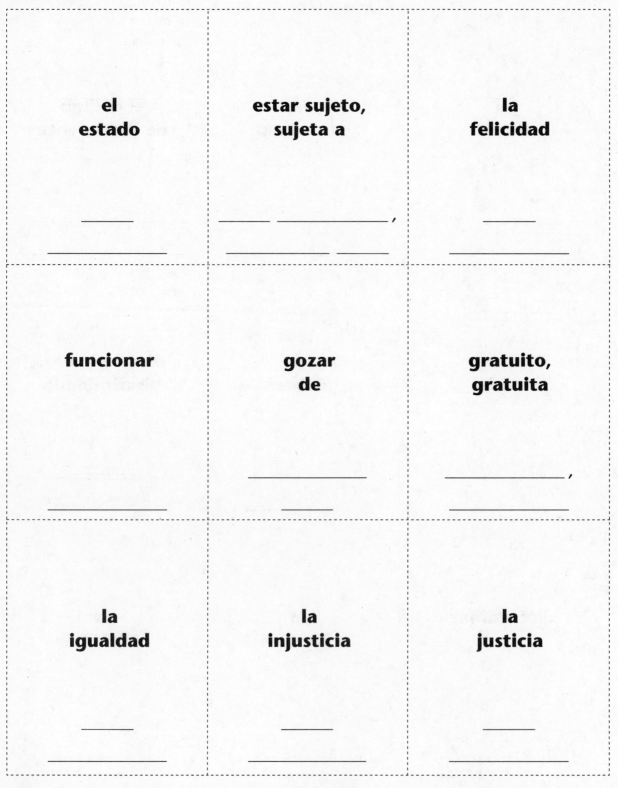

el estado	estar sujeto, sujeta a	la felicidad
_____ _____	_____ _____, _____ _____	_____ _____
funcionar	gozar de	gratuito, gratuita
_____	_____	_____, _____
la igualdad	la injusticia	la justicia
_____ _____	_____ _____	_____ _____

Copy the word or phrase in the space provided. Be sure to include the article for each noun.

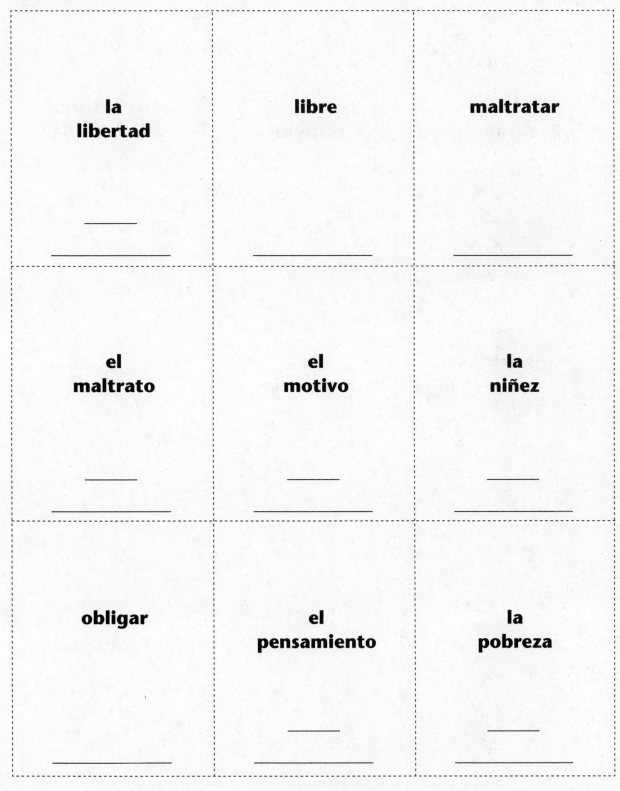

la libertad

_____

_____

libre

_____

maltratar

_____

el maltrato

_____

_____

el motivo

_____

_____

la niñez

_____

_____

obligar

_____

el pensamiento

_____

_____

la pobreza

_____

_____

Copy the word or phrase in the space provided. Be sure to include the article for each noun. The blank cards can be used to write and practice other Spanish vocabulary for the chapter.

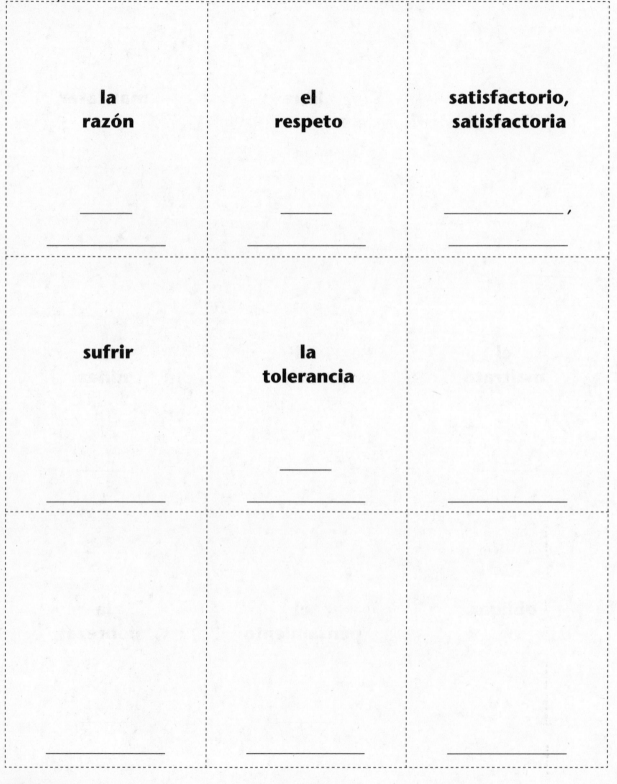

la
razón

_____

_____

el
respeto

_____

_____

satisfactorio,
satisfactoria

_____,

_____

sufrir

_____

la
tolerancia

_____

_____

_____

_____

_____

Tear out this page. Write the English words on the lines. Fold the paper along the dotted line to see the correct answers so you can check your work.

el abuso _____

adecuado, adecuada _____

ambos _____

aplicar (las leyes) _____

el apoyo _____

el armario _____

el asunto _____

la autoridad _____

el código de
vestimenta _____

el deber _____

discriminado,
discriminada _____

discriminar _____

la enseñanza _____

el estado _____

estar sujeto, sujeta a _____

la felicidad _____

funcionar _____

Fold In →

Tear out this page. Write the Spanish words on the lines. Fold the paper along the dotted line to see the correct answers so you can check your work.

abuse _____

adequate _____

both _____

to apply (the law) _____

support _____

locker _____

subject _____

authority _____

dress code _____

_____

duty _____

discriminated _____

_____

to discriminate _____

teaching _____

the state _____

to be subject to _____

happiness _____

to function _____

Fold In ←

Tear out this page. Write the English words on the lines. Fold the paper along the dotted line to see the correct answers so you can check your work.

gozar (de)   _____

la injusticia   _____

la libertad   _____

maltratar   _____

el maltrato   _____

el motivo   _____

la niñez   _____

obligar   _____

la paz   _____

el pensamiento   _____

la pobreza   _____

la razón   _____

el respeto   _____

satisfactorio,
satisfactoria   _____

sufrir   _____

la tolerancia   _____

votar   _____

Fold In

Tear out this page. Write the Spanish words on the lines. Fold the paper along the dotted line to see the correct answers so you can check your work.

to enjoy _____

injustice _____

liberty _____

to mistreat _____

mistreatment _____

cause _____

childhood _____

to force _____

peace _____

thought _____

poverty _____

reason _____

respect _____

satisfactory _____

_____

to suffer _____

tolerance _____

to vote _____

Fold In ←

La voz pasiva: *ser* + participio pasado (p. 462)

- In a sentence written in the *active voice*, the subject performs the action.

    El gobierno estudiantil *organizó* el evento.
    The student government organized the event.

- In a sentence written in the *passive voice*, the subject does not *perform* the action, but rather has the action "done to it" or receives the action.

    El evento *fue organizado por* el gobierno estudiantil.
    The event was organized by the student government.

- The passive voice is formed by using the verb **ser** + the past participle of another verb. Note how the past participle functions as an adjective, modifying the subject of the verb **ser**. As an adjective, it must agree in number and gender with the subject.

    Las clases son planeadas por la maestra.
    The classes are planned by the teacher.

    El texto fue leído por todos los estudiantes.
    The article was read by all the students.

A. Read each of the following statements and decide if it is active voice or passive voice. Write an **A** in the space for **voz *activa*** or a **P** for **voz *pasiva***. Follow the model.

Modelo ___P___ El pastel fue decorado por el cocinero.

1. _____ El director registró los armarios.

2. _____ Los derechos fueron respetados por todos los estudiantes.

3. _____ Las leyes fueron aplicadas de una manera justa.

4. _____ La estudiante pidió permiso para usar el carro.

5. _____ La lista de derechos fue creada por los adolescentes.

B. Circle the correct form of **ser** (**fue** or **fueron**) in the sentences below. Then, write the correct ending of the past participle (**o, a, os,** or **as**) in the blank. Make sure the subject and participle of each sentence agree in number and gender. Follow the model.

Modelo La celebración ((**fue**/ **fueron**) organizad*a*___ por el club de español.

1. Las leyes (**fue / fueron**) establecid____ por los líderes del país.

2. El presidente estudiantil (**fue / fueron**) elegid____ por los estudiantes.

3. Los abusos (**fue / fueron**) criticad____ por toda la gente justa.

4. La injusticia (**fue / fueron**) sufrid____ por los padres de la adolescente.

5. La lista (**fue / fueron**) hech____ por mamá.

La voz pasiva: *ser* + participio pasado (*continued*)

C. Underline the subject of each sentence. Then, write the correct preterite form of **ser** and the correct form of the past participle of the verb in parentheses. Follow the model. Remember to check number and gender agreement.

Modelo   (aceptar) <u>Las reglas</u> ___*fueron*___ ___*aceptadas*___ por todas las personas en la reunión.

1. (**resolver**)   Los conflictos _____ _____ por todos los miembros de la familia.

2. (**establecer**) El horario _____ _____ por los padres.

3. (**eliminar**)   La discriminación _____ _____ en la escuela.

4. (**tomar**)   Las decisiones _____ _____ por los miembros de la administración.

5. (**escribir**)   Los documentos _____ _____ por los consejeros.

6. (**cancelar**)   La reunión _____ _____ por el director porque nevaba.

• The passive voice can also be expressed by using the *impersonal se.* You often use the *impersonal se* when the person or thing who does the action is unknown. In these types of sentences, the verb usually comes before the subject. When the subject is an infinitive, the singular verb form is used.

   Se prohíbe la discriminación.   *Discrimination is prohibited*
   Se respetan los derechos.   *Rights are respected.*

D. Underline the subject of each sentence. Use the verb in parentheses to complete the sentence using the passive voice. Include the pronoun **se** with the correct third person form of the verb.

Modelo   (necesitar) ___*Se*___ ___*necesita*___ <u>una discusión</u> para resolver los conflictos.

1. (**registrar**) _____ _____ los armarios una vez por mes.

2. (**querer**) _____ _____ igualdad entre todos los estudiantes.

3. (**poder**) _____ _____ votar en las elecciones.

4. (**respetar**) _____ _____ la autoridad de los maestros.

5. (**deber**) _____ _____ seguir el código de vestimenta.

6. (**aplicar**) _____ _____ las leyes en esta situación.

El presente y el imperfecto del subjuntivo (p. 463)

- Use the *present subjunctive* or the *present perfect subjunctive* after **"que"** when the first verb is in the:

Present	*Espero que tú **hayas recibido** una educación gratuita.*
Command form	*Dígales que no **discriminen**.*
Present perfect	*Hemos exigido que ellos **sean** justos.*
Future	*Será excelente que nosotros **resolvamos** el conflicto.*

A. Circle the first verb of each sentence. On the line next to the sentence, write a **P** if that verb is in the present, **C** if it is a command, **PP** if it is in the present perfect and **F** if it is in the future. Then, underline the subjunctive verb.

Modelo ___P___ (Me alegro) de que todos <u>participen</u> en la vida de la escuela.

1. _____ Recomiéndenle que vaya a la reunión este viernes.

2. _____ Mis padres estarán felices con tal de que les diga adónde voy.

3. _____ Busco un horario que sea flexible.

4. _____ Hemos dudado que esa ley sea justa.

B. Circle the first verb in each sentence. Then, conjugate the verbs in the correct form of the present subjunctive to complete the sentences. Follow the model.

Modelo (venir) (Será) necesario que todos los estudiantes ____*vengan*____ a la reunión.

1. (participar) He esperado que Uds. _____ en la lucha por la igualdad.

2. (compartir) Dile al profesor que _____ esta información con sus estudiantes.

3. (apoyar) No hay nadie aquí que _____ los abusos del poder.

4. (haber) Este programa no funcionará bien a menos que _____ fondos adecuados.

El presente y el imperfecto del subjuntivo (*continued*)

- Use the *imperfect subjunctive* after **que** when the first verb is in the:

Verb Tense	Main Clause
Preterite	*Recomendé que ellos **siguieran** las reglas del club.*
Imperfect	*Dudábamos que él **gozara** de libertad de expresión.*
Pluperfect	*El profesor **había querido** que los estudiantes **se respetaran**.*
Conditional	*Sería fantástico que **se eliminara** por completo la discriminación.*

C. Underline the first verb in each sentence and determine whether the following verb will be present subjunctive or imperfect subjunctive. Circle your choice to complete each sentence. Follow the model.

Modelo   <u>Era</u> importante que los profesores siempre (respeten /(respetaran)) a los estudiantes.

1. No creo que (**sea / fuera**) justo discriminar por razones de raza, nacionalidad o sexo.

2. Buscaremos un trabajo que (**tenga / tuviera**) un ambiente de paz y tolerancia.

3. El profesor recomendó que nosotros (**pensemos / pensáramos**) libremente.

4. Yo dudaba que (**haya / hubiera**) una solución fácil al problema de la pobreza.

5. Fue terrible que tantas personas (**sufran / sufrieran**) maltratos y abusos por razones de su nacionalidad.

D. Conjugate the verbs in the appropriate form of the imperfect subjunctive.

Modelo   (**vivir**) Era triste que tantas personas ____*vivieran*____ en un estado de pobreza.

1. (**establecer**)   Nosotros habíamos sugerido que el comité _____ unas reglas nuevas.

2. (**ser**)   Me gustaría que la educación universitaria _____ gratuita.

3. (**respetar**)   El policía dudaba que el criminal _____ su autoridad.

4. (**ir**)   Me gustaría que nosotras _____ a la manifestación.

5. (**discriminar**)   Queríamos unas leyes que no _____.

Capítulo 10   Fecha _____ **Vocabulary Flash Cards, Sheet 6**

Write the Spanish vocabulary word below each picture. If there is a word or phrase, copy it in the space provided. Be sure to include the article for each noun.

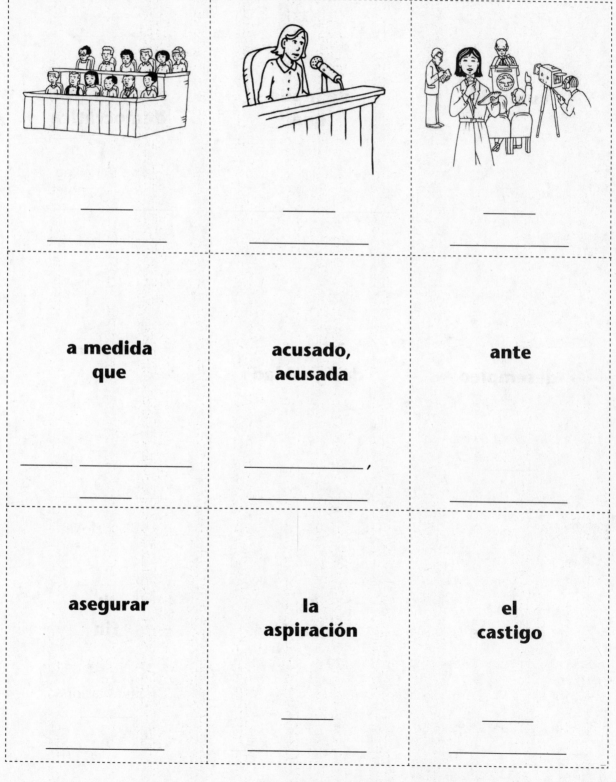

_____ _____	_____	_____
a medida que	**acusado, acusada**	**ante**
_____ _____ _____	_____ ,	_____
asegurar	**la aspiración**	**el castigo**
_____	_____ _____	_____ _____

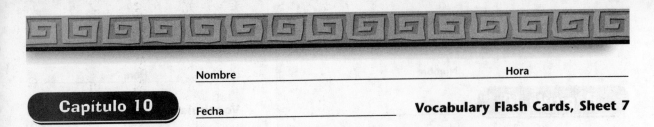

Copy the word or phrase in the space provided. Be sure to include the article for each noun.

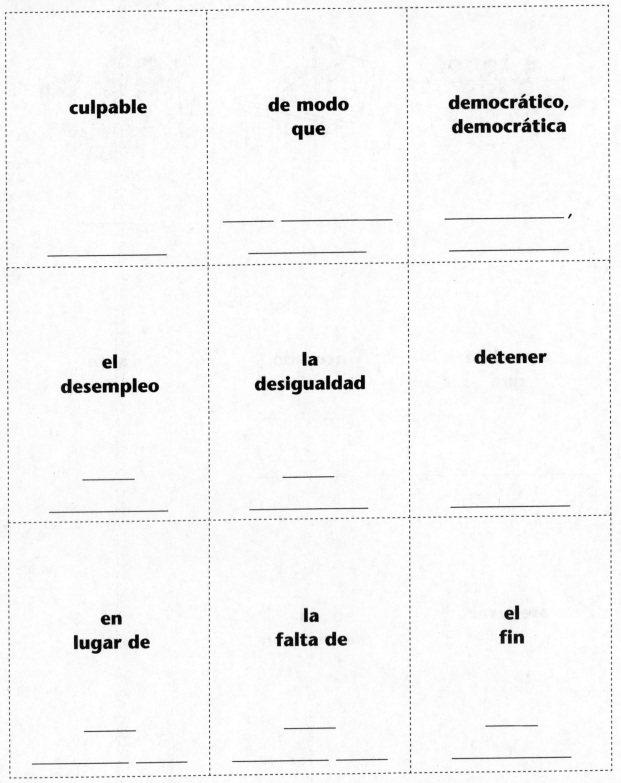

culpable

_____

de modo que

_____ _____

_____

democrático, democrática

_____ ,

_____

el desempleo

_____

la desigualdad

_____

detener

_____

en lugar de

_____ _____

la falta de

_____

el fin

_____

Copy the word or phrase in the space provided. Be sure to include the article for each noun.

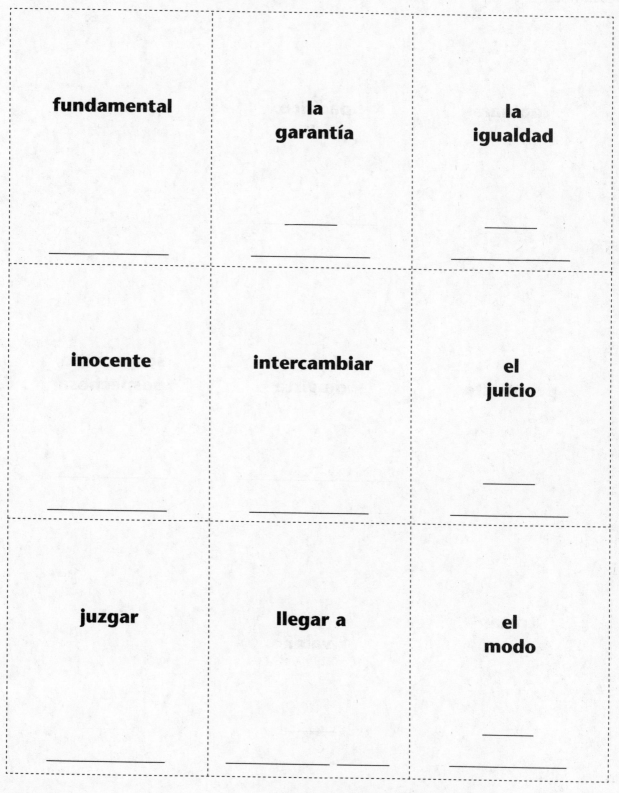

fundamental	**la garantía**	**la igualdad**
_____	_____	_____
inocente	**intercambiar**	**el juicio**
_____	_____	_____
juzgar	**llegar a**	**el modo**
_____	_____	_____

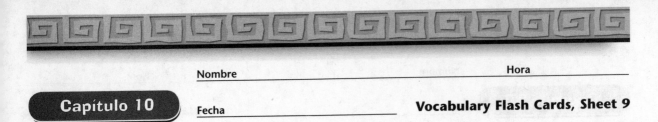

Copy the word or phrase in the space provided. Be sure to include the article for each noun.

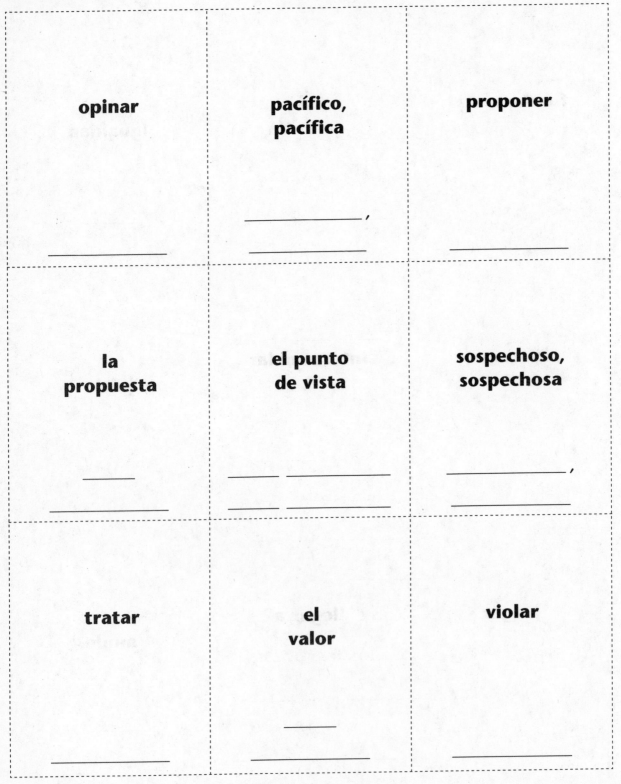

opinar	**pacífico, pacífica**	**proponer**
_____	_____ , _____	_____
la propuesta	**el punto de vista**	**sospechoso, sospechosa**
_____ _____	_____ _____	_____ , _____
tratar	**el valor**	**violar**
_____	_____ _____	_____

Tear out this page. Write the English words on the lines. Fold the paper along the dotted line to see the correct answers so you can check your work.

el acusado,
la acusada   _____

ante   _____

asegurar   _____

el castigo   _____

culpable   _____

la desigualdad   _____

el desempleo   _____

detener   _____

en lugar de   _____

la falta de   _____

el fin   _____

fundamental   _____

la garantía   _____

la igualdad   _____

inocente   _____

intercambiar   _____

el juicio   _____

Fold In ←

Tear out this page. Write the Spanish words on the lines. Fold the paper along the dotted line to see the correct answers so you can check your work.

accused, defendant _____
_____

before _____

to assure _____

punishment _____

guilty _____

inequality _____

unemployment _____

to detain _____

instead of _____

lack of _____

purpose _____

fundamental, vital _____

guarantee _____

equality _____

innocent _____

to exchange _____

judgement _____

Fold In

Tear out this page. Write the English words on the lines. Fold the paper along the dotted line to see the correct answers so you can check your work.

el jurado _____

la justicia _____

juzgar _____

llegar a _____

el modo _____

mundial _____

opinar _____

pacífico, pacífica _____

la prensa _____

proponer _____

la propuesta _____

el punto de vista _____

sospechoso, sospechosa _____

el/la testigo _____

tratar _____

el valor _____

violar _____

Fold In →

Tear out this page. Write the Spanish words on the lines. Fold the paper along the dotted line to see the correct answers so you can check your work.

jury   _____

justice   _____

to judge   _____

to reach, to get to   _____

the way   _____

worldwide   _____

to think   _____

peaceful   _____

                               _____

the press   _____

to propose, to suggest   _____

proposal   _____

point of view   _____

suspicious   _____

                               _____

witness   _____

to treat   _____

value   _____

to violate   _____

Fold In ←

El pluscuamperfecto del subjuntivo (p. 474)

- The *pluperfect subjunctive* is used when describing actions in the past, when one action takes place before the other. In the following sentences, note that the first verb is in the preterite or imperfect and the verb after **que** is in the pluperfect subjunctive.

   Yo me alegré de que el juicio *hubiera terminado*.
   I was happy the trial had ended.

   Nosotros esperábamos que los estudiantes *hubieran hecho* la propuesta.
   We hoped the students had made *the proposal*.

   To form the pluperfect subjunctive, use the imperfect subjunctive of **haber** plus the past participle of another verb. Here are the imperfect subjunctive forms of the verb **haber**:

   hubiera, hubieras, hubiera, hubiéramos, hubierais, hubieran

A. Underline the first verb in each sentence. Then, circle the correct form of the pluperfect subjunctive to complete the sentence.

> **Modelo**   <u>Fue</u> una lástima que el ladrón (**hubieras cometido** / (**hubiera cometido**)) el crimen.

1. El abogado dudaba que los testigos (**hubiera dicho / hubieran dicho**) la verdad.

2. Nosotros habíamos dudado que el acusado (**hubiera sido / hubieran sido**) un niño pacífico.

3. No había ningún testigo que (**hubiera participado / hubieras participado**) en un juicio antes.

4. ¿El juez no creía que tú (**hubiera conocido / hubieras conocido**) al acusado antes?

B. Complete each of the following sentences with the pluperfect subjunctive by using the correct form of **haber** with the past participle of the verb in parentheses.

> **Modelo**   (estudiar) La profesora dudaba que sus estudiantes ___*hubieran*___ ___*estudiado*___ durante el verano.

1. **(hablar)**   El presidente se alegró de que los líderes mundiales _____ _____ de los problemas internacionales.

2. **(ver)**   No había nadie que no _____ _____ la contaminación ambiental en la ciudad.

3. **(subir)**   Era una lástima que el nivel de desempleo _____ _____.

4. **(lograr)**   A tus padres no les sorprendió que tú _____ _____ tus aspiraciones.

- The *pluperfect subjunctive* can also be used when the first verb is in the conditional tense.

   Yo **me alegraría** de que ellos hubieran intercambiado sus ideas.

C. In each of the following sentences, underline the verb in the conditional tense and then complete the sentence with the pluperfect subjunctive of the verb in parentheses. Follow the model.

Modelo (experimentar) <u>Sería</u> una lástima que los jóvenes <u>hubieran experimentado</u> desigualdad social.

1. (tener) Me gustaría mucho que mis padres _____ _____ las mismas aspiraciones que yo.

2. (desaparecer) Sería terrible que las oportunidades _____ _____.

3. (violar) No creería que tú _____ _____ la ley.

4. (poder) Sería excelente que nosotros _____ _____ ver un juicio verdadero.

5. (ver) No habría nadie que no _____ _____ algo sospechoso.

- The expression **como si** (*as if*) always refers to something that is contrary to the truth, or unreal. In Chapter 8, you saw that **como si** can be followed by the imperfect subjunctive. It can also be followed by the *pluperfect subjunctive*.

   El ladrón hablaba del crimen como si no *hubiera hecho* nada serio.

   The robber talked about the crime as if he hadn't done anything serious.

D. Complete the following sentences using **como si** with the appropriate form of the pluperfect subjunctive. Follow the model.

Modelo (ocurrir) El juez recordaba el juicio como si <u>hubiera</u> <u>ocurrido</u> ayer.

1. (entender) La testigo habló como si no _____ _____ la pregunta del abogado.

2. (participar) El juicio fue tan duro que el juez sintió como si todos _____ _____ en una guerra.

3. (visitar) Jorge habló de México como si _____ _____ el país varias veces.

4. (ver) El hombre culpable corrió como si _____ _____ un fantasma.

5. (correr) Después de tanto trabajo, nosotros sentíamos como si _____ _____ en un maratón.

El condicional perfecto (p. 477)

- The conditional perfect is used to talk about what *would have happened* (but didn't) in the past.

  En esa situación, yo *habría dicho* la verdad.
  In that situation, I would have told the truth.

  Nosotros no *nos habríamos portado* así.   *We wouldn't have acted like that.*

  To form the conditional perfect, use the conditional form of the verb **haber** plus the past participle of another verb. Here are the conditional forms of the verb **haber:**

  habría, habrías, habría, habríamos, habríais, habrían

A. Pepe is making some statements about things he has done (present perfect) and some statements about things he would have done (conditional perfect), if he had studied abroad in Mexico. Mark the column labeled **Sí** if it is something he actually did, and **No** if it is something he didn't *actually* do, but would have done.

	Sí	No
Modelos He comido enchiladas en la cena.	X	___
Habría ido a la playa mucho.	___	___
1. Habría visitado el Zócalo.	___	___
2. He visto un partido del equipo de fútbol mexicano.	___	___
3. Mis amigos y yo hemos ido al mercado.	___	___
4. Habría ido a ver las pirámides aztecas.	___	___
5. Habría conocido al presidente de México.	___	___

B. Complete each of the following sentences about what you and others would have done if school had been canceled today with the correct forms of the conditional perfect.

Modelo   (nadar) Mis amigas Lola y Rafaela ___*habrían*___ ___*nadado*___ en la piscina de la comunidad.

1. (terminar)   Yo _____ _____ mi proyecto de filosofía.

2. (dormir)   Nosotros _____ _____ hasta las diez.

3. (leer)   La profesora _____ _____ un libro de Gabriel García Márquez.

4. (jugar)   Mis hermanos menores _____ _____ al fútbol.

5. (ver)   Yo _____ _____ un juicio en la tele.

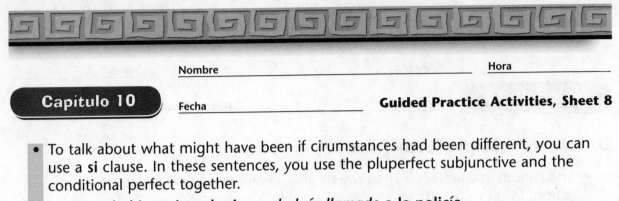

- To talk about what might have been if cirumstances had been different, you can use a **si** clause. In these sentences, you use the pluperfect subjunctive and the conditional perfect together.

    Si yo *hubiera visto* el crimen, *habría llamado* a la policía.
    If I had seen the crime, I would have called the police.

    Si nosotros no *hubiéramos hablado* del conflicto, no *habríamos encontrado* una solución.
    If we had not talked about the conflict, we would not have found a solution.

C. In each sentence below, underline the verb in the pluperfect subjunctive and complete the sentence with the conditional perfect of the verb in parentheses. Follow the model.

Modelo (decir) Si ellos no <u>hubieran estudiado</u> política, no ___*habrían*___ ___*entendido*___ lo que dijo el presidente.

1. **(agradecer)** Si yo hubiera conocido a Martin Luther King, Jr., le _____
   _____ su trabajo para eliminar la discriminación.

2. **(tener)** Si tú hubieras hecho un esfuerzo, _____ _____
   más oportunidades.

3. **(poder)** Si no hubiera nevado, los testigos _____ _____
   llegar a la corte a tiempo.

4. **(recibir)** Si el acusado hubiera dicho la verdad _____ _____
   una sentencia menos fuerte.

D. Form complete sentences by conjugating the infinitives in the pluperfect subjunctive and conditional perfect. Follow the model.

Modelo Si / yo / tomar / esa clase / aprender / mucho más

   <u>Si yo hubiera tomado esa clase, habría aprendido mucho más.</u>

1. Si / tú / venir / a la reunion / entender / el conflicto

   _____

2. Si / yo / experimentar discriminación / quejarse / al director

   _____

3. Si / ellas / tener más derechos / ser / más pacíficos

   _____

4. Si / tú / votar / en las últimas elecciones / cambiar / el resultado

   _____

Puente a la cultura (pp. 480–481)

A. The reading in your textbook is about heroes. Think about what being a hero means to you. Write three characteristics of a hero in spaces below.

1. _____

2. _____

3. _____

B. When you encounter unfamiliar words in a reading, a good strategy is to look at the context for clues. The word **o** ("or") is often used to introduce a definition to a new or difficult word.

Look at the following excerpts from the reading and circle the definitions for the highlighted words.

1. «*Este territorio tenía aproximadamente 17 millones de habitantes y estaba dividido en cuatro* **virreinatos**, *o unidades políticas.*»

2. « *Al sentir que la monarquía estaba débil, los* **criollos**, *o hijos de españoles nacidos en América, se rebelaron contra la Corona, iniciando así un movimiento de independencia...*»

C. In the reading, you learn about 3 different heroes. Write a **B** next to the following characteristics if they apply to Simón Bolivar, an **M** if they apply to José Martí, or an **H** if they apply to Miguel Hidalgo.

1. _____ Llamó al pueblo mexicano a luchar durante un sermón.

2. _____ Fue presidente de la República de la Gran Colombia.

3. _____ Era un gran poeta.

4. _____ Fue a prisión por lo que escribió contra las autoridades españolas.

5. _____ Quería crear una gran patria de países latinos.

6. _____ Motivó a la gente indígena a participar en la lucha por la independencia.

D. Which of the three countries mentioned in the reading actually gained independence from Spain first?

    a. México   **b.** Bolivia   **c.** Cuba

Lectura (pp. 486–488)

A. In this article, you will read about some of the responsibilities the narrator has outside of school. Take a minute to think about your responsibilities and obligations outside of school (to family, sports teams, etc.). Write two of your responsibilities on the lines below.

1. _____

2. _____

B. Look at the excerpt from the reading in your textbook. What word or words are synonyms for each of the highlighted words?

> «...nosotros teníamos una vivienda que consistía en **una pieza** pequeñita donde no teníamos patio y no teníamos dónde ni con quiénes dejar a **las wawas.** Entonces, consultamos al director de la escuela y él dio permiso para llevar a mis hermanitas conmigo.»

C. Read the following excerpt carefully and put an **X** next to the tasks for which the narrator was responsible.

> Salía de la escuela, tenía que cargarme la niñita, nos íbamos a la casa y tenía yo que cocinar, lavar, planchar, atender a las wawas. Me parecía muy difícil todo eso. ¡Yo deseaba tanto jugar! Y tantas otras cosas deseaba, como cualquier niña.

1. _____ trabajar en la mina

2. _____ llevar a sus hermanas a la escuela con ella

3. _____ dar de comer a los animales

4. _____ limpiar la casa

5. _____ preparar la comida

D. Use the following sentences to help you locate key information in the reading. The sentences are in order. Circle the choice that completes them with correct information about the story.

1. La narradora empezó a ir a la escuela sola porque (**sus hermanas tenían que trabajar / su profesora dijo que sus hermanas metían bulla**).

2. El papá de la hija quería que (**ella se graduara de la universidad / ella dejara de asistir a la escuela**).

3. Los problemas y la pobreza de la familia obligaron a los padres de la narradora a tener una actitud muy (**antipática / generosa**) hacia otras personas.

4. La narradora sufría castigos en la escuela porque (**no traía sus materiales a la escuela / no hacía su tarea**).

5. Cuando el profesor de la narradora le pidió que le contara lo que pasaba, ella (**le dijo la verdad / le mintió**).

6. La narradora tenía tantas responsabilidades porque (**su mamá había muerto / a su mamá no le gustaba trabajar**).

7. El padre de la narradora estaba (**muy enojado porque no tenía un hijo varón / muy orgulloso de sus hijas**).

E. Now look back at the opening line from the reading. Based on what you read after this, and using the excerpt below as a reference, answer the following questions.

‖ «Bueno, en el 54 me fue difícil regresar a la escuela después de las vacaciones...» ‖

1. Who is the narrator? Is this a fictional tale? Explain.

_____

_____

2. What is the tone of the reading? Is the author formal or informal? Explain.

_____

_____

3. How would you describe the main character of the book? Use adjectives and specific instances in the reading to support your answer.

_____

_____

Nombre _____ Hora _____

Fecha _____ **Vocabulary Flash Cards**

Notes

Notes

Notes

Notes

Notes

Notes